400
B26s

131487

DATE DUE			

SPEECH, WRITING,
AND SIGN

Advances in Semiotics
General Editor, Thomas A. Sebeok

SPEECH, WRITING, AND SIGN

A Functional View of
Linguistic Representation

NAOMI S. BARON

INDIANA UNIVERSITY PRESS · BLOOMINGTON

Portions of this book first appeared in *Journal of Creole Studies* 1 (1977); *Semiotica* 24 (1978), 26 (1979); and *Ars Semeiotica* 2 (1979).

Manufactured in the United States of America

Library of Congress Cataloging in Publication Data
Baron, Naomi S
    Speech, writing, and sign.
    Bibliography: p.
    Includes indexes.
    1. Language and languages. 2. Functionalism (Linguistics) I. Title
P106.B37   400   79-3626
ISBN 0-253-19373-7   1 2 3 4 5 85 84 83 82 81

For
Laura and Leslie
and
Lalita

Contents

Figures

Preface

THE ROOTS of this book are at once aesthetic, professional, and pedagogical. While much of the work presented here was not undertaken with the goal of integration into a functional analysis of linguistic representation, a chain of events over a period of three years made *Speech, Writing, and Sign* the logical outcome of my work on language.

While I was browsing in the Brown University bookstore several years back, a colleague pointed out the new Dover facsimile edition of the Codex Nuttall, a preconquest Mixtec manuscript which depicts the life of 8-Deer Tiger Claw, an eleventh-century military and political hero from central Mexico. To the untrained eye, the manuscript seems to be a series of pictures —hardly of professional interest to today's linguist. Yet further examination of the "pictures" (plus an assist from the introduction) reveals that what we are looking at is not art but written language. Western linguists have displayed little interest in written representation, viewing spoken language as the primary object from which writing is a theoretically uninteresting derivative. But then Western linguists have dealt almost exclusively with alphabetic writing schemes. Intuitively, I sensed that the fantastic figures depicted in the Codex Nuttall, when viewed with a linguist's eye, might help change the prevailing view that our understanding of human language can only be advanced by the study of speech. These intuitions, still inchoate, were strengthened when I had the privilege of viewing the original codex at the Museum of Mankind (the natural history branch of the British Museum).

Another visit, this time to the Rhode Island School for the Deaf, kindled a second intuitive fire. As I watched six- and seven-year-olds whose speech was unintelligible (or nonexistent) signing to one another, I again sensed that the linguistics profession had overlooked an important manifestation of human language. To paraphrase the comment of another member of the tour, "You see, you *don't* need phonemes to have language." The burgeoning field of sign language research has begun to make inroads into "oralist" linguistics, but belief in the primacy of the phoneme still dominates much of linguistic theory.

The more professionally familiar strands of this book can be traced back to 1967 when, at a Summer Institute of the Linguistic Society of America

held in Ann Arbor, I took my first course in historical linguistics. In inno-
cence (or better, naïveté), I persisted in asking *why* the changes which language undergoes occur. Teleology is always a sensitive subject at best, but
especially so in the intellectual milieu of the study of linguistics in the late
1960s. Nevertheless my interest in the *whys* of language persisted—initially
why language changes, and then later why it is learned at all (and learned
in the particular fashions that it is). This interest in language function,
which was sparked and nurtured by Nikhil Bhattacharya, has dominated my
thinking about language for the past seven years and forms the conceptual
backbone of this book.

The timeliness of a book which is a functional analysis of linguistic representation was enhanced by two concomitant developments which began outside of the formal study of grammar. The first of these was the emergence
of sociolinguistics and the second, the modern resurgence of semiotics. In
the first instance, the work of such seminal figures as Dell Hymes (and later,
within the bailiwick of linguistics, William Labov and Michael Halliday)
helped make the study of language in use linguistically respectable. In the
case of semiotics, despite Saussure's initial claims that spoken language is but
a branch of the broader study of semiotics, and Jakobson's sustained interest
in the linguistic sign, semiotics and linguistics have maintained separate
professional residences throughout much of the century. Only in recent years,
largely through the efforts of Thomas A. Sebeok, has a healthy working relationship between linguists and semioticians begun to flourish. One result has
been that linguists have begun rethinking the assumption that the only relevant code for the transmission of language is speech. Annual meetings of the
Semiotic Society of America and the international journal *Semiotica* have
provided professional meeting grounds for scholars who ordinarily perceive
themselves as semioticians *or* linguists.

In the last analysis, though, *Speech, Writing, and Sign* was written as a
textbook. Yet a textbook of a special sort, namely, one which poses hypotheses and presents evidence about relationships between spoken, written, and
signed languages. For three years I have taught a course at Brown entitled
"Modes of Linguistic Representation." It has been an introductory course in
linguistics, but one which begins with presuppositions about what human
language is and why its study is of interest. These presuppositions are different from those used in traditional introductory courses which present linguistics as the study of phonology, syntax, semantics, and diachrony. *Speech,
Writing, and Sign* was written as a text for an introductory course which
looks at language not only as an end in itself, but also, in Halliday's terms,
as "an instrument, a means of illuminating questions about . . . something
else" (1978:3). While my own approach focuses on language as a social
artifact, I would hope that more traditional courses studying language "in

and for itself" will find this book of use as well. As Halliday cautions, linguists will do well to consider language as an instrument "not simply out of a sense of social accountability of the discipline . . . , but also out of sheer self-interest—we shall better understand language as an object if we interpret it in the light of the findings and seekings of those for whom language is an instrument, a means towards inquiries of a quite different kind" (Halliday, 1978:3).

The term *text*, however, should not be misconstrued. The present book formulates and develops an *approach* to the study of human language, proceeding by argument and example. This book is not a textbook in the sense of presenting (and only presenting) a summary and synthesis of the work of others. It attempts to pose, and to provoke its readers to pose, as yet unanswered questions about human language.

My intellectual and personal debts are many and varied. Nikhil Bhattacharya taught me most of what I know about human language by insisting that I ask questions which go beyond the existing dogma of the day. In the writing of *Speech, Writing, and Sign,* he is directly responsible for introducing me to problems of linguistic function and representation, as well as for coaxing me to see the book through to publication. I can only hope that like wine and cheese, the manuscript has improved with age.

Thomas A. Sebeok has been an invaluable friend and colleague, encouraging me to work toward developing an interface between linguistics and semiotics. As a bibliographic gold mine, he has also brought to my attention many sources I would not have seen otherwise. I am deeply grateful for his help.

Another source of encouragement has been Merald Wrolstad, editor of *Visible Language.* Our discussions and correspondence have taught me a great deal about the "blinders effect" in academia—how an issue (here, the visual dimension of human language) can seem so obvious to one group of professionals, but anathema to another. The journal *Visible Language* has also proved a fountainhead of ideas.

Brown University has generously provided me with administrative support during the formative period in the preparation of my manuscript and financial assistance in preparing the illustrations. I am grateful for the released time I was allowed for preparing the course from which this book grew. My thanks also to students in "Modes of Linguistic Representation," who endured the setbacks along with accruing any advantages of working with a teacher who refuses to erect walls between university teaching and research.

The profusion of illustrations which appear in the book would not have been possible without the help of six people. I am grateful to Elizabeth

Carmichael of the Museum of Mankind for helping me obtain a slide from the Codex Nuttall, and to Liliane Pasquet of Tapisserie de Bayeux for sending a reproduction from the Bayeux Tapestry. The Gallic connection was greatly facilitated by Yvonne Morin, who graciously translated my inquiries and responses into French. E. Rozanne Elder of Cistercian Publications was especially kind in tracking down the original negatives for the examples of Cistercian sign language. My thanks to Brian Garvey, who prepared many of the other illustrations in the book. Susan Sharpton is responsible for handling the small mountain of correspondence necessary to keep track of all these illustrations. I thank John Braunstein and Karen Landahl for assistance in preparing the author and subject indexes.

I should also add a final note on writing style. In my spoken language, I consistently identify individuals whose sex is not specified as "he or she." In writing, I find the disjunction awkward. Therefore, I have fallen back on linguistic privilege by using the pronoun *he* throughout as the unmarked indicator of *he* or *she*. When English develops a common gender third person singular pronoun, I shall happily incorporate it into subsequent editions.

SPEECH, WRITING, AND SIGN

I

Introduction

> Your question also to receive beds for twins. For this I have great seeking made without O.K. As well from the Postmeister because the wife to this man give him many childs. This man admits no knowledge about beds for twins. Part of you may sleep in this place while your extras at the Postmeister go. It is only throwing a stone away.[1]

GETTING LANGUAGE to say what we mean can be problematic. The German hotelier's attempt to answer a potential English vacationer's query about sleeping accommodations reinforces the old adage about "losing something in the translation." The meaning of *twin beds* seems self-evident—until we are forced to think about it. There is a tendency, even among linguists, to take language as a given. We assume it will be there when we need it. Having hypostatized this entity "language," we then feel free to analyze it, to poke and jab at it with our analytic tools, be they drawn from descriptive linguistics, transformational grammar, stratificational grammar, or generative semantics. It is only when something goes wrong in our use of language—a translation fails, a schizophrenic is not understood, or our conversation degenerates into generalities or platitudes—that we recognize how delicate the communicative balance that we call human language actually is.

There is, though, another side to the coin. If language can be seen as a means of creating problems of communication, it can also be seen as solving them. That is, we can think about human language as a system of elements and constructs which exist for a purpose. We may be unable to explain the function of all—or even most—of the particular pieces of language we encounter. No one knows why the First Germanic Consonant Shift took place, leaving us with *father* rather than *pater*, or why English has around thirty phonemes (depending upon how we count them) rather than fifteen or fifty-five. We

3

can, however, ask why Eskimos have so many words for "snow," or why trade jargons seem to have no grammar, or why "sign language" is not universal. As we will see, these are questions about language use (or better yet, about people using language) more than questions of structure alone. The study of human language enables us, among other things, to explore how people put language to work for them, and what different kinds of language emerge as a result of different problems.

THE PROBLEM OF LANGUAGE

We have suggested that human language is both a source and a cure of communication problems between people. To understand this thesis, it will help first to establish some common terms of discussion.

Schematically, we can look upon human linguistic communication as the product of the interaction of four variables (see figure 1.1).

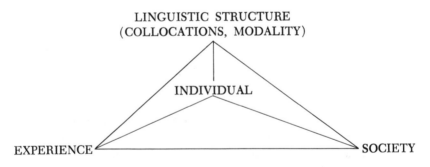

Fig. 1.1 Variables in Human Linguistic Communication

Linguists and semioticians have sliced up the communicative pie in a variety of ways, but for our purposes we can speak of the *individual* and his relationship to the world of *experience*, to language (*linguistic structure*), and to other people (*society*). Which of the four variables we place in the middle of the diagram may be indicative of which issue we see as most important in the use of language. The psychologist (or psycholinguist) might be happiest placing the individual in the center; the linguist, linguistic structure; the philosopher, experience;

and the sociologist (or sociolinguist), society. At this point, however, it is unnecessary to take sides with one group of specialists or another, since, regardless of how we arrange the variables, it is clear that each variable may interact with every other.

The scheme itself is straightforward. In communicating with one another, individuals use language which refers to their experiences. Language is a collocation of elements (be they sounds or letters, words or hand signs) which are encoded in a particular representational modality (speech, writing, or sign). Individuals use language as a way of representing their experiences, although the culture or social group of which those individuals (and their languages) are a part may influence which aspects of experience are represented linguistically and which specific structural manifestation these representations take.

But problems arise as soon as we try to put the scheme into practice; not problems with the scheme, but with the linguistic communication the scheme is designed to encode. We might group these problems into three categories for simplicity of discussion, although breakdowns in all three areas are interdependent.

What Do Users of a "Common Language" Hold in Common?

No matter what brand of linguistic analysis one subscribes to, be it Ferdinand de Saussure's *langue* (1959), Noam Chomsky's competence (1965), or Dell Hymes's communicative competence (1972), a necessary assumption is that users of a language hold something in common. Our question is, How much language actually is held in common in the best of circumstances, and what happens when conditions are less than ideal?

Signs and Sentences

Consider first the backbone of semiotic theory (and of much of linguistics as well): the linguistic sign. Both semiotics and linguistics assume the existence of an entity called a sign such that an expression (e.g., sound) and a meaning component can be identified (Saussure's [1959] *signifiant* and *signifié*, respectively) and that the pairing of that particular expression and meaning is shared by a community of users. But herein lies a paradox. Because no two individuals share the same histories, no two individuals share precisely the same pairings of sound and meaning. And if we do not have corresponding linguistic signs—and, worse yet, are *unaware* of the linguistic mismatch—then our language fails us at the most basic level of social interaction.

Is it an exaggeration to say that language users do *not* have shared linguistic signs? As soon as one goes outside the realm of contemporary linguistic discourse, one finds arguments which seriously question the existence of linguistic Platonic forms (either as meanings or as grammatical rules) which all native language users will "know." Perhaps the most forceful of these arguments has been put forth by Wittgenstein (1953, 1958), who denied the existence of unitary meanings for words.[2] At best, he argued, we can speak of "family resemblances" of words, in which each member of the family shares some property with some other member of the family, but there do not necessarily exist any specific properties which all members share:

> [Wittgenstein] illustrated this problem by the example of the word "game" with regard to which he said both (1) that if there is something common to all games, it doesn't follow that this is what we mean by calling a particular game a "game," and (2) that the reason why we call so many different activities "games" need not be that there is anything common to them all, but only that there is a "gradual transition" from one use to another, although there may be nothing in common between the two ends of the series. [Moore, 1959:312–313]

The philosophical literature is filled with critiques of the Platonic approach to meaning (e.g., Black, 1949; Cohen, 1962). However, with some isolated exceptions (e.g., Weinreich, 1966; Lakoff, 1970a, 1972; Lehrer, 1970; Kooij, 1971; Labov, 1973), the question of whether linguistic signs have definable boundaries is rarely raised among linguists.

The question of what is shared across language users becomes more problematical when we switch from the lexical to the grammatical level. Is every human language actually reducible to a delineable set of rules which all native users of the language "know"? Almost twenty years of investigation has gone into specifying the syntactic "knowledge" of native speakers of English. Unfortunately, as any student of transformational grammar knows, there remain hundreds of sentences—or sentence types—which we still do not know how to analyze.

A vivid backdrop against which to consider this question of the pervasiveness of grammatical knowledge is English composition. The contemporary literature on higher education is filled with the problem of why otherwise intelligent college students do not seem able to write grammatical English.

It is commonly assumed that such students speak perfectly well (slipups being accounted for by Chomskian performance factors), but something happens when they take pen in hand. If we take the Chomskian model of competence seriously, we are faced with a problem. If we assume that native language users "know the grammar" of their language, we would predict that their writing would be *more* grammatical than their speaking, since, paradigmatically, writing allows for more reflection than does normal speaking. There are, to my knowledge, no available data which accurately compare levels of grammaticality of writing and speaking in the populations we are talking about. What teachers of English composition are painfully aware of, though, is that many native speakers—and native writers— are unable to produce grammatical written prose, no matter how much time they are given to ponder their work. A linguistic theory which assumes universal "knowledge of grammar" will need to come to grips with this problem.

Once we have questioned the traditional assumption of the universality of grammatical competence, we can approach the issue of the commonality of signs among language users from two interconnected perspectives. We can ask whether, given normal physical and mental capacities, every human individual will become equally competent (i.e., fluent plus grammatical) as a user of the language of his native community. And, in those instances in which we have no overt reason to question fluency, we can examine what evidence might be necessary to show that, nonetheless, meanings of signs are not constant across language users.

Take, first, the issue of language-user fluency. Here are two sentences which I have heard uttered over the past few years:

I take an ecelectic approach to the study of cognitive development.

I'm sorry our paths crossed on Thursday evening, and I didn't see you.

One might wish to argue that what we are witnessing are slips of the tongue, garden-variety mistakes which the speaker would recognize upon reflection. Unfortunately, the argument holds no water, since these same mistakes were uttered on several occasions by the same individuals. Alternatively, one might contend that the speakers had not gone to school. Again, the hypothesis fails. The individual who believed the word *eclectic* was actually *ecelectic* held a Ph.D. and taught at a major American university, and the one who failed to realize the meaning of the phrase *paths crossed* has a college education.

As long as one assumes the existence of the ideal speaker-hearer within us, these sentences are difficult to explain. However, if we are willing to consider grammaticality as a variable rather than as an absolute property of language, we find that sentences such as those above can be encompassed within the broader question of whether language users indeed share signs, regardless of the surface grammaticality of their sentences.

To explore this question, let us begin by considering a third sentence:

Let's not get bogged down in a philosophical argument.

The comment is one I frequently hear from colleagues in all branches of academia; that is, in all but philosophy departments. Outside the discipline of philosophy, there seems to be a common—and incorrect—assumption that *philosophical argument* means just so much hand-waving. In fact, as those with any training in philosophy know, the phrase has precisely the opposite meaning. In the world of language use, this kind of problem arises repeatedly. We build up associations between words and objects, events, emotions, and the like. We then assume that when another person uses a word or phrase, his semantic intent is the same as ours.

But there is a paradox here. The only way in which speakers can determine what a word means is to build up public associations between that word and the concrete or conceptual domains to which it refers in the minds of other language users. In behavioral terms, we learn meanings by hearing them used in context. Or, in a less passive view of language learning, we conclude that we understand a word when its utterance brings results: the appearance of a slab of stone upon the utterance of the command "Slab!" The paradox is that we tend to jump to conclusions about mutual comprehension on the basis of very little evidence. Unless we are especially concerned to know precisely what a speaker means by a particular word, we tend to assume he means just the same thing that we do—"You know what I mean" "Yeah"—when the respondent merely knows what he *himself* means.

The phenomenon of assuming that we understand a speaker's signs when in fact we do not is often pointed up in literature. Hence the passage in Shakespeare's *Julius Caesar* in which Mark Antony reiterates his description of Brutus as an "honorable man." The irony of the statement does not become clear until well into the oration. It is precisely this embellishment of a conversation, this probing into one's meaning, that typically does not occur in everyday language. And for that reason, we are typically unaware of whether we actually share referents with our interlocutors.

Another reason why mismatches in meanings are frequently not perceived in casual conversation is that most of these individuations of meanings are found in the lexicon rather than in syntax. The lack of common syntax is far more easily perceived—and then brought into line—than the lack of common referents for signs. If I tell you that I'm sorry our paths crossed and therefore we didn't meet, you as interlocutor can immediately perceive the problem and question me until I learn what is wrong with my syntax. However, if you use a word or phrase (like *philosophical argument*), and I have no reason to suspect your meaning is not identical to mine, I have no simple way of perceiving the mismatch.

At this point in the argument, the devil's advocate might ask, "But what is so new about this observation that not all meanings are shared?" Jakobson, for example, in distinguishing between general and specific meanings of a word, argued that while every word has a general meaning, the specific meaning of a word can only be understood in context:

> The context indicates whether we speak about Napoleon in his infancy, at Austerlitz, in Moscow, in captivity, on his deathbed, or in posthumous legends, whereas his name in its general meaning encompasses all those stages of his life-span. [Jakobson, 1971:268]

The question, however, is, precisely what kind of entity is a general meaning? Is it a hypostatized entity whose only existence is in the world of lexicographers, linguists, and perhaps some rare individuals whose speech is largely made up of a limited number of rote phrases? If we actually tried the empirical task of selecting those meaning features which a community of language users have in common for a particular linguistic sign, it is not obvious that in their spontaneous (noncitation) use for that sign, speakers share enough features to construct a workable dictionary definition.[3]

A second question our devil's advocate might ask is whether we are
blowing the problem out of all proportion. What does it matter if
the meanings we attach to words are not precisely the same? We are
quite willing to admit exceptions to many of the defining features we
use to identify human languages in the first place. While maintaining
our belief in the arbitrariness of the linguistic sign (at least in spoken
language), we do not deny the existence of onomatopoeia, which we
tend to see almost as the exception that proves the rule. Yet is the issue
of the arbitrariness of the sign really comparable to the issue of whether
signs are shared between language users? Not at all. In the first instance, we might decide to abandon the notion of arbitrariness altogether as a design feature of human language without changing our
conception of language itself or of the fundamental ways in which
we analyze language. However, in the case of the sign, to acknowledge
that pairings of *signifié* and *signifiant* are not shared is to deny the
possibility of studying language as a social activity.

Individuals, Experience, and Society

The question of what users of a "common language" really hold in
common can be viewed from a nonlinguistic perspective as well. Since
structure, experience, and society are interdependent variables, many
of the same problems we have just been looking at in terms of linguistic constructs can be seen in terms of one's experience—individual
or social—which one uses language to encode. Thus, philosophers and,
say, chemists understand the phrase "philosophical argument" differently because of their differing experience with—and commitments to
—the use of philosophical arguments.

The literature is filled with graphic examples of the barriers which
experiential and social variables pose to mutual comprehension. Consider the case of a child in a Sunday school class who was asked "to
illustrate the story of the fall of Adam and Eve and their subsequent
punishment":

> The child drew a picture of a car and three persons in it, with the
> explanation that this was "God driving Adam and Eve out of the Garden
> of Eden." [Nida, 1954:231]

Or consider a story related by the children's poet Kornei Chukovsky.
A Russian child, when asked why she had not provided a knife and fork
for a dinner guest, replied, "Because I thought he didn't need them—

Daddy said he ate like a horse" (1965:13). Part of learning a language is learning to distinguish between literal and metaphoric meanings, which entails learning social conventions of language use. It may also entail, as in the first example, learning to place linguistic encodings in historical contexts (*Genesis* predates the Age of Henry Ford). In the second instance, language learning may include learning levels of social appropriateness—knowing what comments are permissible in which social settings.

TRANSLATION: A LOGICAL EXTENSION OF THE PROBLEM OF COMMONALITY

There are, as we have seen, inherent problems in communicating even between language users who purportedly use the same language. These problems intensify when we try to switch either language or modality of expression. The problems of translation between linguistic systems are similar to the language-internal problems we have just considered. In both, we confront language users who do not share structures, experience, or social conventions. The main difference is that in the first instance, incompatibility between languages is not recognized as easily as it is in the case of translation.

The most obvious examples are translations between languages. In poetry or literature—including the Bible—the problem arises repeatedly. Nida cites the difficulty of using a literal translation for "he beat his breast" (Luke 18:13):

> In the Chokwe language of Central Africa, this phrase actually means "to congratulate oneself" (the equivalent of our "pat himself on the back"). In such instances it is necessary to say "to club one's head." [1959:11–12]

Translation problems become more subtle—but no less real—when we must translate across representational modalities (e.g., sign vs. speech) as well as across languages which are expressed in the same modality (e.g., spoken English vs. spoken French). Court cases frequently involve deaf defendants who understand American Sign Language but not American English. Judges often insist that court translators (from speech to sign and vice versa) give the precise meaning of the questions addressed to the defendant and of the defendant's responses, without interjecting any of his (the translator's) own interpretation. However, since American Sign Language and American English are distinctly different languages formulated in markedly different modalities (see Chapter 7), such neutral translation is not always possible. How does one translate the subtleties of a leading question or an evasive answer?

Even closer to our own experience is the problem of how to translate paralanguage—those facial, gestural, and intonational nuances with which we accompany speech. In his metalogue "Why Do Frenchmen?" Bateson raises the question of "why . . . Frenchmen wave their arms about . . . when they talk" (1972:9). A father, in a hypothetical conversation with his daughter, observes,

> The point is that the messages which we exchange in gestures are really not the same as any translation of those gestures into words. . . . The point is that *no* mere words exist. There are *only* words with either gesture or tone of voice or something of the sort. [1972:12–13]

But his daughter persists in asking, "When they teach us French at school, why don't they teach us to wave our hands?" The father's honest reply is, "I don't know. I'm sure I don't know. That is probably one of the reasons why people find learning languages so difficult" (1972:13).

Do We Actually Try to Communicate at All?

Up to this point, I have been talking about problems of linguistic communication which arise because of incompatibilities between linguistic systems, experiences, and social conventions of individuals. I have been presupposing that the intent to communicate is present, but that for some reason the communicative system keeps breaking down.

But do we always work toward getting messages (feelings, impressions, or whatnot) across to an interlocutor? Or are there times—either personal or entrenched within an entire subculture—in which the individual is directly responsible for breaking the links in a potential communicative chain?

In most instances, the cues of communicative breakdown are difficult to pick up. Consider such a simple issue as whether people in contemporary American society communicate by talking with one another on a regular basis. Of course, you say. But do they? In the late 1960s, Ray Birdwhistell decided to find out. He studied one hundred couples who had been married fifteen years or more and were regarded as reasonably happy. The results showed the median amount of time spent in conversation with one another was twenty-seven and a half minutes per *week*. What is more, Birdwhistell notes that this figure is somewhat high because his subjects did a lot of visiting and "had to give each other driving instructions" (Sheehy, 1973:34). Birdwhistell points out that failure to *speak* does not necessarily mean failure to *communicate*, especially among people who have known each other for some time. And yet one cannot help but wonder how *much* communication is really going on among members of a society whose primary mode of communication is speech. Observers of the contemporary social scene such as Christopher Lasch (1979) or Peter Marin attribute the decline in speech to a rise in self-aggrandizement:

> In the worship of the self, life also gives way to an abstraction, in this case to an exaggeration of the will. The result in both cases is the same. What is lost is the immense middle ground of human communication. [Marin, 1975:48]

A similar breakdown has been observed in our use of the written word. While on the one hand the popular press has been critical of the decline of writing skills among the nation's youth, astute observers such as David Riesman and George Steiner have warned that the purposeful and private act of reading may be fading from the middle-class scene. (We will examine the status of reading and writing in contemporary America in some detail in Chapter 6). Regardless of where one wishes to heap the blame, it is now fairly clear that a significant portion of the "educated" population does not see writing as a means of making someone *else* understand what is on its mind. In the words of Donald Holden:

> The star of [a] book is not the writer, but the *reader*. Good scholarly writing, like good teaching, isn't an ego trip . . . but a service you perform for a stranger. [1979:E19]

These breakdowns in the desire to engage in social communication through the spoken and written word find their logical conclusion in pathology, in the language of the schizophrenic. The breakdown can be seen both in the generation of contradictory linguistic signals, which according to Bateson's double bind hypothesis (e.g., Bateson et al. 1956) can lead the receiver to schizophrenia, and in the language of the schizophrenic himself, who creates a code of which he is the only user. Just as the problems of commonality are greater between languages than across languages, so, too, schizophrenic language can be seen as the logical extension of a growing withdrawal from the use of speech and writing to foster social communication.

The book which follows is not a study of social problems. It is a study of the problems which language helps to solve. But in addition to its linguistic value, it has, we might hope, a derivative social value as well. By better understanding how and why language works in the ways it does, we may be in a better position to understand where and why it might fail us and what we can do about it.

THE OBJECT OF STUDY

I have said that this book is a study of human language. An introduction if you will. What it serves to introduce, though, distinguishes it from the classical (e.g., Sapir, 1921; Bloomfield, 1933) or modern (e.g., Bolinger, 1968; Langacker, 1973; Fromkin and Rodman, 1978) introductory works. Linguistics has evolved into a discipline whose primary purpose is to analyze the languages people speak (or have spoken) and to comment on the internal workings of the languages, i.e., on their structures. Whether such comments are intended to be descriptive or explanatory and whether the descriptions or explanations are taken to represent structure as potentially available to a speaker or structure as actually used in communicating with another person— all this depends on the theoretical interests (and biases) of the linguist doing the work.

These studies are useful, but are they enough? Is there anything else we wish to know about human language that turns out to be so fundamental that it lies at the very core of our subject? I suggest that there is. Some of the queries—and solutions—which we will raise here are not new. What *is* especially new is the suggestion that these problems constitute a coherent nexus which should be considered together, and that an examination of these problems is as fundamental to understanding human language as is an understanding of phonological and grammatical structures of human utterances. What is more, by locating these problems at the very core of a study of human language, we will derive not only a clearer understanding of human speech but also a more solid base than the one currently available for building linguistic theories.

The issues I propose moving to center stage stem from the same basic questions any linguist wishes to answer: What is a human language used for? How does it accomplish its ends? However, rather than accepting the stereotypic response that language is used to communicate, and does so by chaining together linguistic signs (forms paired with meanings) through identifiable patterns, we will be looking more deeply at *what* it is that is being communicated, *why* that information should be deemed important by the participants in the linguistic interchange, and *how* the interchange is accomplished. Our goal will be to figure out what influence the content (*what*), the reason (*why*), and the means (*how*) have upon these "identifiable patterns" (the grammatical forms and rules), which are being used for getting a message across.

To recast these questions somewhat, we will be considering three problems:

What is a linguistic representation?

What are the expressive or perceptive channels (or modalities) through which these representations can be made?

In what ways are the choices of linguistic representations (with respect to modality, lexical item, and grammatical patterning) derivable from the functional contexts in which the linguistic interchange occurs?

We shall see that the whole question of what a linguistic representation is and how that representation corresponds to the thing being represented has been neglected in the literature. We shall also find that the issue of modality has barely been raised, since it has been nearly universally assumed that speech is the only serious object of linguistic inquiry. Finally, we shall demonstrate that the functional orientation which is beginning to come into its own in the study of speech can productively be extended both to visual linguistic modalities (writing and sign language) and to studies of the composition of the linguistic sign itself.

NOVELTY AND TRADITION: CINDERELLA'S SLIPPER

The cross-modal perspective we will be assuming is at once a radical and conservative position from which to study human language. It is radical inasmuch as writing and sign language have not been objects of the typical linguistic text, but, as we shall see in this section, conservative in that twentieth-century linguistic theory was founded upon the premise that languages must be analyzed on their own terms.

The exclusion of written and sign languages from the mainstream of linguistic analysis is particularly ironic in the context of the American linguistic tradition. American linguistics, starting with the work of Franz Boas, Edward Sapir, and Leonard Bloomfield, developed in response to an ethnographic predicament. Confronted with a large number of American Indian languages which were unrelated to Indo-European tongues,[4] missionaries, and then government agents and anthropologists, had no firm grammatical guidelines for describing the languages they encountered in North America.

For the earlier explorers and missionaries, the most natural tendency was to interpret the languages either in light of their native tongue (typically French[5] or Spanish) or, particularly in the case of missionaries, in terms of Latin:

> The era of exploration brought a superficial knowledge of many languages. Travelers brought back vocabularies, and missionaries translated religious books into the tongues of the newly-discovered countries. Some even compiled grammars of exotic languages. . . . These works can be used only with caution, for the authors, untrained in the recognition of foreign speech sounds, could make no accurate record, and knowing only the terminology of Latin grammars, distorted their exposition by fitting it into this frame. [Bloomfield, 1933:7]

Missionaries' use of Latin as a linguistic standard is partially attributable to their training. The Jesuits, the most active missionary group concerned with North American Indian languages, uniformly "spent years of their early career teaching Latin and various subjects in Latin" before embarking on missionary work in America (Hanzeli, 1969:33). But the centrality of the Latin model in missionary linguistics was not entirely a function of prior linguistic exposure. Rather, deriving from the work of medieval speculative grammarians, Latin came to be recognized as the universal, essential language from which all other tongues derived (ibid.).

Armed with a Latin phonology and grammar, the missionary linguist set out to establish correspondences between Latin (or sometimes French or English, which were themselves grammatically formalized in Latinate terms) and the unknown American Indian tongue. Where constructions were—or at least appeared to be—comparable, the task of description proceeded smoothly. However, at points of divergence (i.e., where the new language lacked grammatical distinctions present in Latin or French, or presented distinctions not found in European tongues) the response was one of "plain bewilderment and the ensuing defensive assumption that the new language was 'imperfect' or 'lacked rules' " (Hanzeli, 1969:63). In the more linguistically enlightened treatises, the linguistic integrity of the newly discovered language was maintained by creating new categories of analysis as they became necessary. In other instances, however, the missionary's inability to puzzle out the grammatical rules of a language was taken as evidence that no such rules existed and that the inferred "primitive" nature of the language indicated a primitive mentality. If American Indian languages could not be fit into the Cinderella's slipper of Latinate grammar, then the strange languages must be inadequate.

Boas spent much of his professional life decrying this assumption of the cultural and linguistic inferiority of the American Indian. The Introduction to the *Handbook of American Indian Languages* (1911, reprinted 1966) contains his explicit attempts to argue for the independence of race, culture, and language, and to establish the need for a value-free method of linguistic description. This latter challenge was taken up by Bloomfield, who, in the second edition of *Language* (1933), laid the groundwork for American descriptive linguistics. Epitomized by Joos's dictum that "languages can differ from each other without limit and in unpredictable ways" (Joos, 1957:96), American linguistics of the 1930s, 40s, and 50s worked toward defining a procedure for deriving grammatical descriptions that acknowledged the linguistic integrity of "strange" languages and that were wholly unbiased by descriptions appropriate for other languages. Subsequent work in linguistics, most notably that of Chomsky and his students, has argued that earlier linguistic atomism made commonalities across languages difficult if not impossible to recognize. Interest in language universals has now swung the grammatical pendulum back toward the presupposition of a single "universal" grammar, although our experience with handling empirical data over the past six or seven decades should help us avoid the problems of apriorism to which our missionary predecessors often fell victim.

We have seen that American linguistic analysis grew out of the recognition that not all languages originate from the same linguistic mold, and therefore valid linguistic descriptions must be cast in terms of the actual language under investigation. What we have not noted so far, however, is that this insistence upon the integrity of the language under investigation was entirely restricted to spoken language. No comparable provisions were made in the American descriptivist tradition for considering the integrity of either written or sign languages as forms which needed to be recognized and analyzed in their own terms, with the results of these analyses being used to investigate the extent to which writing and sign were influenced by—or had influence on—spoken language. Instead, like the early missionaries attempting to reduce American Indian languages to Latin (and, where not possible, declaring the languages primitive or degenerate), American linguistics has reduced written language to the status of a "transcription" of what is spoken and has tended to regard sign language as a primitive or degenerate form of speech. Ironically, while American linguists were extolling the virtues of objective analysis for one set of languages, they systematically withheld objectivity from their dealings with another set. How did this irony come about?

In intellectual inquiry, one can never argue definitively why a phenomenon does not occur. Negative results may be the product of any one of a potentially infinite set of causes, the most unlikely of which may be the actual culprit. However, in the case of the failure of linguistics to make comparable attempts to understand written and sign languages as were made for speech, we can cite some relevant evidence for which any subsequent causal explanation would have to account.

> Writing is not language, but merely a way of recording language by means of visible marks. [Bloomfield, 1933:21]

Since the birth of nineteenth-century comparative philology, the position of writing in linguistic analysis has always been tenuous at best. Even in the work of the Neogrammarians, the languages being reconstructed were, presumably, spoken languages, although the only evidence available for reconstruction was written.[6] Saussure made the primacy of speech in linguistic analysis more overt, a move which was plausible (though not necessary) insofar as his concern was for contemporary speech. Nevertheless, he necessarily retained the duplicity inherent in the work of the Neogrammarians (i.e., he claimed to be analyzing speech, but used written records) to the extent that his concerns were diachronic.

From its modern European inception, the discipline of linguistics restricted its inquiry (at least in principle) to spoken language, introducing written materials only where necessary for diachronic study. In Europe, emphasis on spoken language derived, at least in part, from the growing interest in dialectal variation. Since in most cases nonstandard dialects were not written down,[7] written language was excluded from formal linguistic inquiry. The situation in the United States was actually quite similar. Since there was practically no indigenous writing in North America,[8] there was no question of studying written *or* spoken language. "Writing" entered the scene only as a way for the linguist to keep records of what his informants had said. Writing was, quite literally, "merely a way of recording language by means of visible marks."

Gesture languages are merely developments of ordinary gestures and . . . any and all complicated or not immediately intelligible gestures are based on the conventions of ordinary speech. [Bloomfield, 1933:39]

Sign language study in the American linguistic tradition has its own history of misunderstanding and neglect. At least two factors seem to have been significant here. The most important—and obvious— of these factors is that sign language was not the primary means of communication of any of the linguistic communities early American anthropologists were interested in studying. Sign language was in fact frequently used by American Plains Indians in the eighteenth and nineteenth centuries. However, use of sign had begun to subside by the turn of the twentieth century, and more significantly, sign had never been used by the Indians as their sole or even primary means of communication. Rather, it was used only in a circumscribed set of contexts (see Chapter 7). Despite a fair number of descriptions of American Indian sign (the most thorough being the work of Garrick Mallery), American Indian Sign Language was not given serious linguistic attention until La Mont West's studies (1960). Instead, sign was dismissed from the domain of linguistic inquiry as a poor approximation of spoken language in much the same way as trade jargons and pidgins were largely dismissed as bastardized forms of "real" languages before the work of Robert Hall (e.g., 1955—see Chapter 5).

A second factor concerns the status of sign language in deaf communities. Current observations of deaf individuals outside formal educational settings suggest that an elementary signing system typically develops when deaf individuals need to communicate with either deaf or hearing populations (e.g., Kuschel, 1974; Gleitman, Feldman, and Goldin-Meadow, 1978). In some instances, as in the case of late eighteenth-century France, the signs used by an indigenous deaf population are standardized and augmented, and taught to a broader deaf community. The Abbé de l'Épée was responsible for creating French Sign Language out of information gathered from native deaf signers, overlaid with some principles of French grammar. This system was brought to the United States by Thomas Gallaudet in 1816, and adopted (though also adapted) by the American deaf. While the signing system gained considerable currency in the United States in schools for the deaf which opened in the ensuing years, the use of sign in the classroom was offset by a strong move towards oralist education (see chapter 7). By the early part of the twentieth century, oralism had taken hold. Therefore, it is not surprising that interest in sign language in linguistic circles was all but nonexistent. Sign language was used only within the deaf community itself (not in view of the hearing community) both because of the educational dictum that the deaf must be taught to speak and because of the practical consideration that hearing people generally do not understand sign.

With very few (and mostly recent) exceptions, the educational level of the deaf in the U.S. has remained low, and until the 1970s there have been almost no fluent users of sign language—either deaf or hearing—who have been associated with the linguistics profession. Accordingly, there has, until recently, been no internal impetus for dispelling myths about the "degenerate" status of sign and its purported dependence on spoken language. Since the late 1960s and early 1970s, these assumptions have begun to change, largely because of the work spearheaded by Stokoe (1972, 1974, 1978) and Bellugi (Klima and Bellugi, 1979). However, while linguistic attention is currently being turned to sign language, there has been little effort to integrate the analysis of sign with that of the two other modalities of linguistic expression—speech and writing. Such an integration is one of the purposes of this book.

This integration is not its sole aim. Spoken, written, and sign languages are considered not simply as objects of linguistic analysis, through whose joint examination we can improve our understanding of the breadth of human language. Rather, they are seen as different linguistic means, or what we here call *modes*, of representing human experiences which people find reason to convey to one another. Interest in language as representation has been neglected nearly as much as have the visual modes of linguistic representation—writing and sign. Therefore, this discussion begins with representation as a linguistic problem.

OVERVIEW

The examination of representation in chapter 2 asks, What is a representation of any sort and what, more particularly, is a linguistic representation? Since linguistic representations are the basic fabric out of which human languages are woven, we are led to reexamine the fundamental question of what a human language is (chapter 3). This reexamination draws upon the discussion of representation and points forward to the issues of modality and purpose in language.

As we shall see, acontextual, structural attempts at definition break down when we try testing them against actual data. For this, as well as for additional reasons to be delineated, we turn to language use as a critical factor in defining what we mean by language (chapter 4). In the process, I shall elaborate upon the functional perspective which underlies one of our basic theses—that linguistic structure is, to a significant degree, a product of social, nonlinguistic factors.

This hypothesis is developed in some detail in chapters 5, 6, and 7, where it is argued that the choice of a particular modality, as well as development of subtypes within modalities (e.g., of different spoken languages, of varying forms of writing) can be analyzed functionally. In the course of the discussions of spoken, written, and sign languages, respectively, each means of linguistic expression is distinguished from related communicative but nonlinguistic representation. Once these elements are factored out, a comparison is made between structural and functional classifications of each mode of language. The relationships between structure and function are then illustrated for each modality.

II

Language and Representation

I HAVE SUGGESTED that human language can be studied as a social tool, one which both creates and cures difficulties in human communication. We have already seen some of the negative effects of language—translation failure, personal misunderstanding. These linguistic breakdowns occur at the level of syntactic collocation or cross-modal translation, but they also operate at the level of individual words. In fact, words themselves, the bricks of any linguistic construct, may lack a community of users.

To speak of a failure in commonality, however, implies the existence of a goal toward which words—or linguistic signs—are intended. That goal, as mentioned before, is to make a connection between something we wish to talk about and a physical means of saying it. If we are to understand linguistic signs—and their problems—we must first get a clearer sense of what we mean by "something we wish to talk about" and "a physical means of saying it." This task will become easier if we step back from our immediate focus on human language and see language as but one special response to a more general problem.

REFERENCE AND REPRESENTATION

Think of the following assortment of activities:

holding up a ball for a child to see

pointing to a monkey in a zoo

saying "What's that?"

imitating the walk of a Miss America contestant

drawing a picture of a cat

tying a string around your finger to remind yourself to mail a letter

saying "Bring me the chair that's in the corner."

saying "Last night I imagined I saw a ghost."

What do these activities have in common, and how do they differ?

Each activity points something out; it *refers*—that is, it separates part of one's environment or experience from its background. But here the similarity ends, for the activities we have listed exemplify different types of referring.

The most fundamental (though not always the most practical) means of referring is to point up or *present* the object or experience itself. I hold up a ball for a child or point to the monkey at the zoo. Presentation of objects themselves would seem an efficient and unambiguous way to single something out. The efficacy of such a scheme was appreciated by the savants in Jonathan Swift's Academy of Lagado, where Lemuel Gulliver encountered a unique linguistic experiment, a "Scheme for entirely abolishing all Words whatsoever" (1934: 182). Conversations were to be conducted not by using words, but by carrying about the objects one wished to signify:

> Since words are only names for *things,* it would be more convenient for all men to carry about them such things as necessary to express the particular business they are to discourse on. [ibid.]

Unfortunately, the seeming simplicity of communication through presentation collapses under the slightest scrutiny. To begin with, presentation is highly inefficient. As Gulliver discovered, the need to carry about one's referents is cumbersome at best:

> If a Man's Business be very great, and of various Kinds, he must be obliged in Proportion to carry a greater Bundle of *Things* upon his Back, unless he can afford one or two strong Servants to attend him. I have often beheld two of those Sages almost sinking under the Weight of their Packs, like Pedlars among us; who when they met in the Streets would lay down their Loads, open their Sacks, and hold Conversation for an Hour together; then put up their implements, help each other to resume their Burthens, and take their Leave. [ibid.]

In other cases, communication by presentation becomes impossible. How does one fit New York City or the Atlantic Ocean into one's sack? There are even some topics of reference for which no object corresponds, including movements (running), abstractions (happiness), and objects of our imagination (unicorns).

And the problem with presentation goes deeper. Mere presentation —holding the ball, pointing to the monkey, or even saying "What's that?" in the presence of an object of reference—may still yield extreme ambiguity. Nida reminds us that when a missionary trying to learn a native language points to a tree with his finger and says, 'What is that?', "the reply is more often than not, 'Your finger'" (1954:223). An example of such misunderstanding of intended referent involved Captain Cook:

> When he discovered Australia, Cook sent a sailor ashore to inquire of the natives the name of a strange animal they had brought to the ship from the land. The sailor reported that it was known as a *kangaroo*. Many years passed before it was learned that when the natives were asked the name of the animal, they replied "kangaroo" and were simply asking, "What did you say?" [Mueller, 1974:vi]

Tangible contact with the thing itself does not ensure transparency of semantic intent. As foreign travelers may learn, standing in a moving bus, tapping one's watch, and pointing backwards may not convey the intended question, "What time does this bus return to the city?" Physically extracting an item from its environment (e.g., holding up a ball) may still leave us with the problem of distinguishing between a class and an individual, since we do not know whether the thing being presented is to be understood as the thing itself or as an example of the class to which it belongs.

We avoid some of these problems in referring when we replace *presentation* with *representation*—that is, when we use something else to stand in place of that to which we wish to refer. We imitate the behaviors of others (Miss California's walk), we draw pictures of things (a cat), we tie strings around our fingers—and we use language.

Taken literally, a representation is a "re-presenting" or a "giving again." In actual use, though, that re-presenting cannot be of the thing itself. That which is represented "must be made present indirectly, through an intermediary; it must be made present in some sense, while nevertheless remaining literally absent (Pitkin, 1969:16). Picking up a stone when one wishes to refer to that particular stone is an act of presentation, but picking up the same stone and talking about it directly or using it to refer to the general class of stones or to the Rock of Gibraltar is an act of representation.

The advantages of representation over presentation are obvious. Representations enable us to refer to things (events, properties, objects) which are not present—either because they are somewhere else ("the conductor in the next train compartment"), do not now exist ("the first bicycle I ever owned"), or never did exist ("the ghost I imagined"). Of course, representations can be used in the presence of the things they represent. I can hold a photograph of my dog next to his head to compare the likeness, and I can ask you to "bring me the chair that's in the corner," using language to save myself the trouble of getting up and pointing to the object physically (presentation). Language used in the presence of its referent I shall call *direct reference*, while language used to refer to that which is absent I shall call *indirect reference*. The use of language for indirect reference (what Charles Hockett calls *displacement*—see chapter 3) has long been recognized as one of the properties distinguishing human speech from nearly all other communication schemes in animals. We have tended to overlook the fact that the entire modality of written language is predicated upon the use of language to refer indirectly (see chapter 6).

LEVELS AND FORMS OF REPRESENTATION: A MODEL

However one wishes to characterize the essential properties of human beings (e.g., man the speaker, man the tool maker, man the thinker), a fundamental part of being human is the ability to represent one's environment, be it real or imagined.[1] Therefore our primary "something" to be represented will be human experience. The next question is, of course, How is experience to be represented? Which pieces of it are to be singled out and through which medium? The answers are potentially infinite, but I shall consider only five illustrative domains of representation: language, science, cartography, art, and politics.[2]

The domains of experience represented in these five areas are neither coterminous nor predetermined. Language has, in principle, the entire range of experience as its domain, although, as anthropological linguists have shown, not all societies choose to encode the same distinctions of experience (the standard example here being the Eskimos' many terms referring to snow). Similarly, science—itself a specialized linguistic representation of reality—has the whole physical universe as its potential domain but has only exploited restricted portions of it during different periods. At the other end of the spectrum, maps, which were originally used for charting physical contours and man-made constructs (e.g., roads and cities) on the earth, have been extended to represent the heavens, the structure of the human brain, and many other realms (Robinson and Petchenik, 1976).

The range of phenomena in these kinds of representations and the means chosen for making such renditions are determined by the function the representations are meant to serve. If, for example, I am in Athens and wish to get from Syntagma Square to the Parthenon (but understand no Greek), the most helpful service a friendly bystander can perform is to draw me a map (this assumes that I understand how to read a map). The map will not need to include landmarks I shall not be passing, although a limited degree of redundancy may be useful (e.g., indicating both street names and major business establishments along the route). Similar examples which predict mode and range of representation can be given for each of the other domains as well.

I shall refer to these direct representations of human experience (by whatever mode) as "first-order representations." Each of these first order representations can itself be represented by second-order representations. The second-order representations in these domains are: linguistic theories, models of scientific theories, theories of maps, theories of art, and theories of political representation (we shall come to the choice of terminology shortly). And again, through third-order representation, many—but significantly not all—of these second-order representations can themselves be represented, yielding models of linguistic theories, models of theories of maps, models of theories of art, and models of theories of political representation. As with first-order representation, the range of phenomena represented in second- and third-order representation is determined by the function of the representation of the higher order. Figure 2.1 summarizes the levels and forms of representation we have discussed so far.

The model illustrates that the process and products of representation are not restricted to languages and linguistics. Rather, the more general act of representing is something in which languages and linguistics participate. This not to say that the *kinds* of representation used in different domains (e.g., language and map making) or on different levels (e.g., theory making and model making) are wholly parallel. In fact, it has been argued that analogies between, for example, maps and

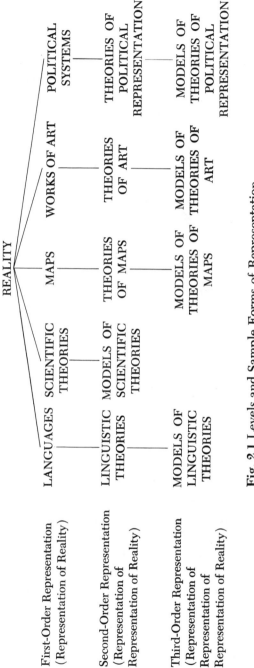

Fig. 2.1 Levels and Sample Forms of Representation

languages, or maps and scientific theories may be highly misleading (Robinson and Petchenik, 1976).

Moreover, the model itself generates a number of questions about items it contains. To begin with, I have used the terms *theory* and *model* without having defined them. Chao identifies thirty-nine different ways in which the term *model* has been used, "some of which have exactly opposite meanings" (1968:202). Similar counts can surely be made for the term *theory*. Both theories and models are representations, but how do they differ?

For purposes of discussion,[3] let us define a theory as a statement or set of statements that makes a generalization about a set of data such that all the current data are accounted for and future data can be predicted accurately. A critical feature of a theory is that it can be expressed verbally. Let us then define a model as a visual representation of a theory that encodes the significant generalizations made by the theory, but whose comprehension may depend on a prior understanding of the theory.[4]

In figure 2.1, I have encoded these definitions (of theories representing reality and models representing theories) by considering theories to be second-order representations and models to be third-order representations; and yet in a distinct sense the model itself is a representation either of the first order representation or of reality. For, if the theory has made an accurate representation of X, and the model is an accurate representation of the theory, then, by transitivity, the model should be an accurate representation—however abstract or distant—of X.

The one enigma in our otherwise symmetrical characterization of representation, however, is the status of scientific theories and models of scientific theories. In each of the other four examples, the first-order representation is a phenomenon in which ordinary members of a society might participate—a language, a map, a work of art, or a political system. In the case of science, however, the first-order representation is a theory—that is, a theoretical statement or statements used to talk about reality, but generally of interest to only a highly restricted portion of the population. The asymmetry continues in the second-order representation, which, in the case of science, is model making, while in the other instances, it is theory making. Finally, there is no third-order representation for science, while for the other four types of representation, models are the third-order of representation.

Is our characterization correct, and if so, does the asymmetry matter? Linguistic theorists, from the Neogrammarians (see Jankowsky, 1972), through the American structuralists (see Bloomfield, 1939), down to transformational grammarians (see Chomsky, 1968) have repeatedly stressed the parallels between physical science and linguistic science, and, especially in the case of Chomsky, the parallel ways in which theories and models are constructed and tested. If representation in language and linguistics is *not* comparable to representation in science, then the entire question of goals, methodology, and evaluation in linguistics will need to be rethought.

The crux of the problem is whether theories are actually direct representations of reality, or whether, as with language and maps, there is another first-order representation which mediates between reality and theory. One might argue, for example, that just as linguistic theory is a theory about language, scientific theories are dependent upon linguistic representation as a way of characterizing data. This observation is true—but it overlooks a critical distinction. While the task of linguistic theory is to characterize human language *as it exists*, the goal of scientific theory is to see *beyond* language to the phenomena themselves, and where necessary, to *change* language to suit its needs.[5] Except where new phenomena are introduced into their environments (lunar space probes, hula hoops), natural language users rarely need to alter their language to better characterize reality. Attempts are sometimes made by children and foreigners, but typically it is the neophyte who adapts to the existing language, rather than vice versa.[6]

Of what significance is this discrepancy in orders of representation between science on the one hand and language and linguistics on the other? The answer is not clear, given our very incomplete understanding of representation, theories, and models in a single modality. However, before we assume comparability of terminology across domains (e.g., *model* in science and *model* in linguistics), we should be aware that the terms may not be comparable at all.

PROBLEMS OF
LINGUISTIC REPRESENTATION

In constructing a representation, we use one thing to stand in place of another. In the case of human language, the type of representation most interesting to us, that place holder is typically a word (be it written, spoken, or signed). As stated in chapter 1, Saussure spoke of the representation as the *signifiant* (the "signifying"). That which was being represented was the *signifié* (the "signified"). Taken together, the *signifiant* and *signifié* form the *linguistic* sign.

Less clear, though, is what Saussure's *signifié* actually refers to. According to Saussure, the *signifié* belongs to the realm of ideas, not to the realm of the real world: "The linguistic sign unites, not a thing and a name, but a concept and a sound-image" (1959:66). This decision to make the referent an idea rather than a thing[7] has clear pragmatic advantage. Since much of what we use our language to talk about either never existed (unicorns, Martians) or would be impossible to identify in the objective world (dreams, constitutionality, or the prototype which the class term *chair* labels), we would not be able to use language to talk about intangibles if the referents of our linguistic signs were necessarily items of experience.

Yet the retreat from reality to ideation has its problems as well; we still have to figure out what our thoughts are representing. Unless we take all of our thoughts to be innate, we still must find a source for our mental referents in order to understand what we are talking about when we use language. The question is important to the linguist, but may also be vividly real to the average language user. R. W. Apple, Jr., described why the military in Iran, once loyal to the Shah and then to Prime Minister Shahpur Bakhtiar, switched their loyalty to the Ayatollah Khomeini: "most of the soldiers and many of their officers . . . ultimately refused to kill and be killed for abstractions called 'constitutionalism' and 'legitimacy'" (*New York Times*, 12 February 1979, p. A1).

In talking about what is being represented (or signified), I shall speak of experience rather than ideas—with full recognition that I shall have little to say about the referents of words such as *truth, lopsided,* or *confusion.* Placing the study of referents in the realm of ideas may not, however, help here. Besides, since thinking is grounded in experience, it seems sensible to get to the heart of the matter straightaway.

The Choice of a Signifié

We all know that societies differ in the ways they divide continuous phenomena in nature (and in their linguistic labels for these divisions). A favorite example here is the color spectrum. The Shona (in Rhodesia) do not distinguish linguistically between what speakers of English called *red, orange,* and *purple.* On the other hand, the Shona linguistically divide up the spectral band which English speakers generally call *green* (Krauss, 1968). The same kinds of discrepancies in labeling occur when naming parts of the human body. Old Norse *hond* can refer to the entire arm (from fingers to shoulder), while English *hand* refers only to the area from fingers to wrist.

The choice of which span of experience is to be represented by a linguistic sign may vary not only from language to language but also from modality to modality. In English, if I want to convey the message that I am looking at you, I need to say something like "I am looking at you"—a multiword utterance which distinctly specifies an agent, an activity, and an object. In visual representation systems, though, such individuated, linear representation may not be necessary. American Sign Language, for example, would encode the message with a single sign: a V hand shape (formed with the index and middle fingers) moving outward from the addresser's eyes to the individual being seen. Or consider the fact that some verbs incorporate locative markers within the verbs themselves, while others must be paired with lexically distinct prepositions (Old English *onwacnian* vs. Modern English *wake up*; Modern English *pare* vs. *file down*).

The American descriptivist tradition of linguistics has prepared linguists to expect stark variation among linguistic communities in the ways in which language will be used to label the world. Recall Joos's fabled pronouncement that "languages can differ from each other without limit and in unpredictable ways" (1957:96). There have, however, been contrary tendencies, especially in the semantic theories growing out of Chomsky's rationalist position (e.g., Katz and Fodor, 1963; Fillmore, 1968a; Schank, 1972), but also deriving from psycholinguistic studies (e.g., Rosch, 1973). The increasing reversion to an innatist stance with respect to the individual's classification of experience is strongly reminiscent of the universal language movements that flourished in the seventeenth and early eighteenth centuries. Universal language schemes and their implications for the study of linguistic representation will be examined in more detail later on in this chapter.

THE CHOICE OF A *SIGNIFIANT*: ARBITRARINESS AND ICONICITY

A different set of problems arises when we look at what kinds of linguistic "place holders" are available to represent our experience.

The central issue appears to be the existence of any recognizable like-ness between that which is being represented (the *signifié*) and that which is doing the representing (the *signifiant*). Although the ques-tion of the relationship between the *signifié* and the *signifiant* traces at least back to Plato's *Cratylus*, it was Saussure who enunciated the modern dictum that "the bond between the signifier and the signified is arbitrary":

> The idea of "sister" is not linked by any inner relationship to the suc-cession of sounds *s-ö-r* which serves as its signifier in French; that it could be represented equally by just any other sequence is proved by differences among languages and by the very existence of different lan-guages: the signified "ox" has as its signifier *b-ö-f* on one side of the border and *o-k-s* (ochs) on the other. [1959:67–68]

Saussure is careful to consider possible objections to his principle, namely, onomatopoeia and interjections. He concludes, however, that such words are few, that they often differ from language to language (dogs go *bow-wow* in English, but *ouaoua* in French), and that their symbolic origin is often in doubt (ibid., pp.69–70).

The dictum of the arbitrariness of the linguistic sign has so pervaded linguistic analysis that (by unwritten statute) any linguistic discussion must reaffirm this dictum whenever the data themselves are at all sug-gestive of iconic sources of signs (i.e., signs looking like that which they signify). The *reductio ad absurdum* of this position is a comment by John Waterman that Plato's discussion of the *physis* position in the *nomos* ("convention")/*physis* ("nature") controversy over the origin of language was "incredibly naïve":

> In fact, some scholars cannot believe [Plato] was serious; they feel he must have been joking. However professional philosophers are not noted for their published humor, and I rather suspect that Plato meant most of what he wrote about history and meaning of words. [1963:5–6]

Anyone who believes that Plato was lacking in humor, especially in the *Cratylus*, either has not read the text, or is already so committed to the principle of the arbitrariness of the linguistic sign that any attempt at counterargument is automatically interpreted as "naïve."

Less dramatic but equally strained are discussions of the linguistic bona fides of visual forms of communication. As shown in chapter 6, the insistence upon a phonetic base for writing leads to an arbitrary definition of language, which produces some undesirable consequences. Similarly, attempts to exaggerate the arbitrary pairings of signifier and signified in sign language leads to an incomplete understanding of ephemeral visual language (see chapter 7).

I have been considering problems which may arise in using language to represent our experiences. In chapter 1, in a different context ("What Do Users of a 'Common Language' Hold in Common?"), we observed that linguistic signs must be shared if we are to speak of a "language" or of a "linguistic community." Unfortunately, agreement between individuals is often lacking. Moreover, entire language communities may differ markedly in the ways they use language to divide their experience (consider Shona color terms). And yet there are those who maintain the extreme position that reality can be divided into a universal set of experiential—and linguistic—categories.

How might we hope to make sense out of these various perspectives? Recall the delineation, in chapter 1, of four variables of human linguistic communication: the individual, linguistic structure, experience, and society (Figure 1.1). By reorganizing and expanding our diagram, the relationship between experience and language can be viewed as potentially mediated by "filters" which regulate what portions of the objective world are linguistically encoded by the individual and the language community. Figure 2.2 summarizes the possible filters between language and experience.

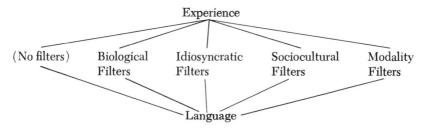

Fig. 2.2 Filters between Experience and Language

I shall examine each variable in turn, illustrating the effects each filter might have upon the formulation of a linguistic representation (either lexical or syntactic). In doing so, though, there is the risk of opening a Pandora's Box of problems which have troubled philosophers and psychologists for centuries. The limits of the present volume will not permit a thorough examination of the traditional arguments concerning the relationship between perception, cognition, and language. I can, however, indicate where the problem of linguistic representation intersects with inquiries made by students of perception and cognition.

No Filters

The simplest view of linguistic representation assumes that the human mind directly perceives what is "out there." This form of realism holds that sense data are received and processed with no interference from biological, cultural, or experiental presuppositions. Contemporary studies in the philosophy of science have rejected this position, arguing instead that any observation (be it the everyday occurrence of looking at a tree or an observation in a scientific experiment) is theory-laden. That is, it is impossible for a person to be objective about what he sees. Rather, our past history (both individual and social) shapes our perceptions, which, in turn, may condition our linguistic representations of those perceptions.

Norwood Russell Hanson has us

> Consider Johannes Kepler: imagine him on a hill watching the dawn. With him is Tycho Brahe. Kepler regarded the sun as fixed: it was the earth that moved. But Tycho followed Ptolemy and Aristotle in this much at least: the earth was fixed and all other celestial bodies moved around it. Do Kepler and Tycho see the same thing in the east at dawn? [1958:5]

In our own use of ordinary language, we reflect persisting dissonance between our common-sense perceptions and Keplerian beliefs. We are intellectually capable of referring to the earth revolving around the sun, yet in our everyday speech, we talk of the *sun* rising and setting.

Somewhat closer to home, we can ask whether humans must "learn" to order their perceptions, or whether our sensory apparatus is fully functioning at birth. If the former is the case, we must inquire further whether all humans develop their sensory abilities in the same way, regardless of individual or cultural differences (much as the human skull hardens and the vocal tract changes shape during the early months of life)—or, alternatively, whether environmental differences can produce differential perceptual abilities?

There is now a vast amount of data on human perceptual abilities, especially on the development of visual perception in young infants. Many of these studies suggest that people must "learn" to see, although how much is learned (and when) is still a matter of intense debate.[8] There are, nevertheless, clear examples which demonstrate the role of experience in directing—and selecting—what we are able to see.

One such case is described by R.L. Gregory (1966; Gregory and Wallace, 1963). A man (called S.B.) who was blind from birth regained his sight at the age of 52. Gregory wondered what effect the lack of visual experience would have on S.B.'s visual perceptual abilities. His study of S.B. indicates that experience (or lack thereof) played a significant role in S.B.'s perceptual judgments, as illustrated by the following three examples.

Just after regaining sight, S.B. could not make out the world of objects with the same degree of clarity that was later to develop:

> When the bandages were first removed from his eyes, so that he was no longer blind, he heard the voice of the surgeon. He turned to the voice, and saw nothing but a blur. He realized that this must be a face, because of the voice, but he could not see it. He did not suddenly see the world of objects as we do when we open our eyes. [1966:194]

S.B.'s initial problem is reminiscent of the reports of anthropologists that populations which are not accustomed to visual representations have difficulty recognizing objects—including themselves—in photographs (see Segall, Campbell, and Herskovits, 1966:32; Deregowski, 1973). Recent studies have shown that even when peoples not accustomed to visual representations are able to make out figures, the process may be laborious and tiresome. In a study of the Me'en, a remote Ethiopian tribe, Deregowski, Muldrow, and Muldrow (1973) note the following observation from a thirty-five-year-old man:

> EXPERIMENTER: Points to the picture: 'What do you see?'
> SUBJECT: 'I'm looking closely. That is a tail. That is a foot. That is a leg joint. These are horns.'
> E: 'What is the whole thing?'
> S: 'Wait. Slowly, I am still looking. Let me look and I will tell you. In my country this is a water buck.'
>
> [cited in Deregowski, 1973:168]

But, for S.B., experience did not bring the entire world of objects into focus. Particularly telling were S.B.'s attempts to draw a bus, which are illustrated in figure 2.3:

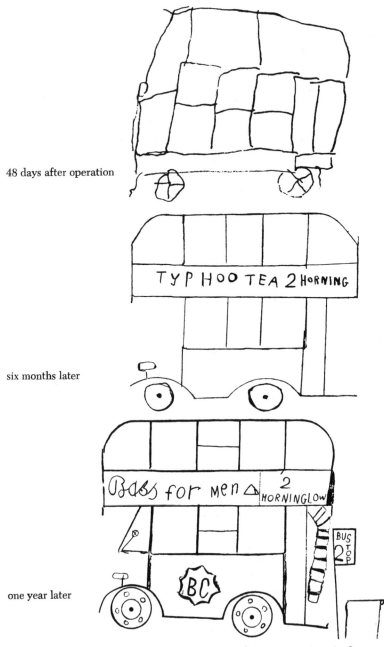

48 days after operation

six months later

one year later

Fig. 2.3 S.B.'s Drawings of a Bus after Regaining Sight at Age 52 (from Gregory, 1966:198–199)

> S.B.'s use of early touch experience comes out clearly in drawings. . . .
> The series of drawings of buses illustrates how he was unable to draw
> anything he did not already know by touch. In the first drawing the
> wheels have spokes, and spokes are a distinctive touch feature of wheels.
> The windows seem to be represented as he knew them by touch, from
> the inside. Most striking is the complete absence of the front of the bus,
> which he would not have been able to explore with his hands, and which
> he was still unable to draw six months or even a year later. [Gregory,
> 1966:197]

Similarly, although S.B. was able to recognize most objects at sight,
"On one real object he did show real surprise, and this was an object
he could not have known by touch—the moon" (ibid., p. 195).

A third example suggests that experience is a necessary ingredient
not only for perceiving specific items of our world, but also, more generally, for aiding us in discerning what kind of sensory input is significant for our purposes. William James's description of the infant's world
as "a blooming, buzzing confusion" seems to cast its shadow in a world
initially unordered by sight. Thus,

> before the operations, [S.B.] was undaunted by traffic. He would cross
> alone, holding his arm or his stick stubbornly before him, when the
> traffic would subside as the waters before Christ. But after the opera-
> tion, it took two of us on either side to force him across a road: he was
> terrified as never before in his life. [ibid.]

It would seem that S.B. had learned to determine which tactile (or
auditory) sensations were significant and which could be ignored, but
not so for visual stimuli; hence, the visual stimuli were overwhelming.

Biological Filters

By "biological filters" I mean genetic predispositions to perceive
one's environment in preestablished ways. Commonly known as innatism, this position maintains that our predispositions to certain sorts
of perception are part of what it means for us to be human. The linguistic concomitant to perceptual innatism is either that certain "ideas"
are innate and that language represents these ideas directly (like the
word *two* representing the number 2), or that the linguistic categories
themselves are innate.

The Cartesian theory of innate ideas presupposes that all humans
come to know the world through the same blueprint. Unlike the "no
filter" approach, innatists do admit that our perceptions are "filtered"

before being understood (or linguistically encoded), but they suggest that the blueprint is the same for all people.

The debate over innatism, from Plato's *Meno*, through Descartes and Locke, up to Chomsky's neo-Cartesianism, has a long and confused history.[9] It is not clear, for example, *how much* of human knowledge Plato believed to be innate, whether an ability that only manifests itself in the course of human development (rather than at birth) can be said to be innate, or precisely which aspects of language might be called innate. Further, there has been much discussion of the difference between "universals" and "innatism," a distinction that Hilary Putnam (1967) has argued for but that Chomsky has tended to minimize. In the domain of language proper, we do not really know what data for or against the linguistic hypothesis would look like. As long as we admit a distinction between surface and underlying levels of language analysis without placing any bounds on how abstract our underlying analysis may be, then it is possible to recode any apparent violations of language universals (read "innate ideas") into "underlying" commonalities with surface differences.

Perception is one domain in which it is possible to gather objective data on the issue of innate "filters." If humans are indeed "predisposed" to perceive their environments in the same way, then perceptual tests should yield similar results across culturally distinct populations. If we do not find such commonalities we have not disproved the notion of innatism in perception or language (properties other than the ones we have examined might still be innate), but we have at least cast doubt on the innatist enterprise.

One area for most clearly testing the innatism of perception is that of optical illusions. If perceptual abilities are innate, then we would expect all people (and all peoples) to make similar perceptual judgments on similar phenomena. Homogeneous responses in perception experiments would also support the "no filters" hypothesis—i.e., that the world is perceived (and labeled) directly as it really is.

In using optical illusions to test for homogeneity of perception, we make use of the fact that, by definition, more than one interpretation of the visual array is possible. In figure 2.4, we may "see" the single drawing as both an Eskimo and an Indian. In figure 2.5, our visual cues give us a different interpretation of the relative lengths of the two horizontal lines than would measurement. In the real world, the same object cannot be *both* an Eskimo and an Indian, and two lines cannot be both equal and unequal. We must therefore posit some mental

Fig. 2.4 Eskimo or Indian?—The Winson Figure (from Gombrich, 1973:239)

shaping (or filtering) of the data to account for these illusions. If we assume the ability to perceive optical illusions to be consistent among individuals (and across peoples), then we must also assume some common mental faculty which accounts for this ability.

Within the past two decades, an increasing amount of data has been gathered which suggests that the ability to perceive optical illusions is a product of sociocultural conditioning rather than biological programming. Rivers (1901, 1905) had observed in his early tests with optical illusions that "the non-Western peoples seem to be less subject to one illusion while more subject to another (cited in Segall et al. 1966:64). Gregory and Wallace, in their study of recovery from blindness, observed that "during the second postoperative month, the patient displayed either no illusion susceptibility at all or a degree of susceptibility considerably less marked than that typical of normal observers" (ibid., p.81). From this, the authors infer "that the patient may have lacked the opportunity to learn the perceptual habits that underlie the illusions" (ibid.).

Several contemporary studies have examined whether the ability to

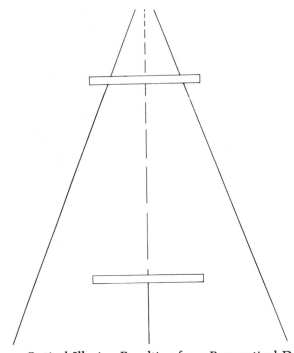

Fig. 2.5 Optical Illusion Resulting from Perspectival Drawing

perceive optical illusions is a product of biological predisposition or a case of cultural conditioning (see Segall et al. 1966; Deregowski, 1973). As one of their tests, Segall and his colleagues showed the Müller-Lyer illusion (figure 2.6) to large numbers of European and

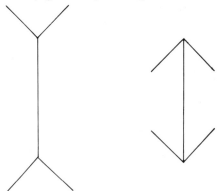

Fig. 2.6 The Müller-Lyer Illusion

non-European populations. Only the Europeans were highly susceptible to this illusion—they saw the vertical line to the left as being longer than the one to the right. One explanation for the Europeans' interpretation is "the carpentered world hypothesis":

> For people living in carpentered worlds, the tendency to interpret obtuse and acute angles in retinal images as deriving from rectangular objects is likely to be so pervasively reinforced that it becomes automatic and unconscious relatively early in life. For those living where man-made structures are a small portion of the visual environment and where such structures are constructed without benefit of carpenters' tools . . . straight lines and precise right angles are a rarity. As a result, the inference habit of interpreting acute and obtuse angles as right angles extended in space would not be learned, at least not as well. [Segall et al. 1966:84]

Idiosyncratic Filters

A third possible relationship between experience and our perception (and linguistic encoding) of it involves idiosyncratic filters that result from the unique histories of individuals. In some instances, our experiences become increasingly common (for example, as we become older, we read more of the same books and visit more of the same places). At other times, however, we persist in using similar language to encode very different sets of experience.

Let us consider metaphor and ambiguity as two prototypical examples of how our individual experiences—including both our interactions with our physical environment and our linguistic interactions with one another—can affect the links we make between language and experience. Take first the case of metaphor. If I tell you that my understanding of mathematics grows with time, neither of us conceives of a biological organism which increases in mass the way that a "growing" chicken or a "growing" petunia might. We understand the term *grow* to be used metaphorically, that is, sharing some but not all of the more literal (or more usual) senses of the verb *grow*. But metaphoric language must be learned. Werner Leopold illustrates the point in a study of how his daughter Hildegard learned to talk. When Hildegard was not quite two years old, Leopold was working on a picture frame and complained about the weather with the words *Es ist heiss* ("It is hot"). Leopold reports that Hildegard, who was raised to be bilingual in German and English, responded by feeling "different parts of the picture before me to see if they were hot. The range of the adjective was restricted to tangible objects" (1949:108–109).

As with metaphor, our experience helps determine how we interpret an ambiguous sentence. The two cases are not wholly analogous, though. While metaphor involves extending the meaning of words to new semantic domains—where the pairing needs to be learned (or created) by the language user—ambiguity is more akin to optical illusions in which we possess all the cultural information necessary to "see" both interpretations. At issue in the case of both ambiguity and optical illusions is whether there is one interpretation we are more likely to "see" first.

Transformational grammar has emphasized the fact that native speakers of a language have, as part of their linguistic skills, the ability to disambiguate sentences whose surface structures are ambiguous. Hence, presented with the sentence "He decided on the boat," speakers of English are able to derive two interpretations: "He chose the boat," or "He made a decision while physically located on the boat." And yet the likelihood of one interpretation coming to mind first is likely to be influenced by the context in which the sentence is uttered. Thus, in the sentence we have been using, the first interpretation ("He chose the boat") is more likely at a boat showroom, while the second is more likely when talking about a person who has weighed anchor.

Another important issue in linguistic ambiguity is whether speaker and hearer share the same experiential history or socio-cultural presuppositions. Sometimes people speak at cross-purposes—having different referents for the same linguistic symbols—without ever realizing their communicative failures. On one occasion I assumed I was commiserating with a colleague over a particularly boring business luncheon meeting we had recently attended. I commented, "Wasn't that business luncheon ghastly?" He concurred, and I was about to begin citing some of the prime examples of academic rhetoric to which we had both been subject for two grueling hours. Before I could speak, though, he continued, "Considering how much money we paid, you would have thought the hotel could have provided better food." Had the conversation ended with my initial comment and my colleague's assent, neither of us would have known that our individual tastes (I thought the food was tolerable and he found the meeting interesting) were leading us to provide radically different interpretations for the same linguistic expression.

Sometimes necessity makes us recognize how ambiguity arises from different presuppositions. A student of mine was studying language in blind children, comparing it with normal language development in their sighted counterparts. In her search of the literature, she encountered an article titled "Oral Problems of Blind Children." Only when a copy of the article arrived through the interlibrary loan office did she recognize that the subject of the article was not human language, but dentistry.

Sociocultural Filters

The discussions of the "no filters" and the "biological filters" positions have already illustrated the effect of social or cultural experience on what we perceive or what we encode in our language. We have seen that the ability to perceive a visual representation (a picture of a face or of a water buck) may be culturally conditioned, as may the ability to perceive certain optical illusions. An even more dramatic case of the influence of culture on perception and representation is that of traditional notions of navigation in the South Seas.

When we look at a map of Polynesia, Micronesia, and Melanesia (see figure 2.7), we are struck by the vast amount of water which separates comparatively minute bits of land. In Polynesia and Micronesia, for instance, there are roughly "two units of land for every thousand of water" (Lewis, 1972:15). Europeans were, for quite some time, puzzled as to how the population of these isolated islands could share such a high degree of uniformity in language and customs. Strong similarities in linguistic and cultural patterns presuppose regular contact between peoples. What has been unclear to western observers is how regular contact was possible in the South Seas without reasonably sophisticated navigational equipment or, at the very least, the aid of maps—and the indigenous populations had neither. Only careful study, typified by the work of Thomas Gladwin (1970) and David Lewis (1972), revealed a highly sophisticated system of indigenous navigational skills, including means of representing the relationship between sea, land, and sky which are unknown in the west.

The most vivid of these cases is probably the use of stick charting in the Marshall Islands,[10] or stone representations of waves reported by Gilbert Island navigators (such as figure 2.8).[11] These are not navigational charts in the western sense, but rather instructional and mnemonic devices concerned with swell patterns (Winkler, 1901:490).

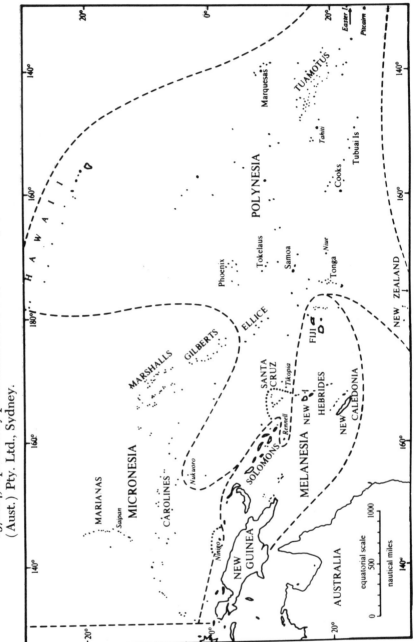

Fig. 2.7 Map of Polynesia, Micronesia, and Melanesia (from Lewis, 1972:14, reprinted by permission of Dr. David Lewis, c/o Curtis Brown (Aust.) Pty. Ltd., Sydney.

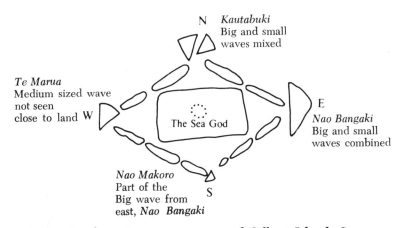

Fig. 2.8 Schematic Representation of Gilbert Islands Stone Chart (from Lewis, 1972:186, reprinted by permission of Dr. David Lewis, c/o Curtis Brown (Aust.) Pty. Ltd., Sydney.

Figure 2.8 is a schematic adaptation of a stone "chart" made by Temi Rewi, a Gilbert Islands navigator. The center stone can stand for either an island or a canoe, depending upon the pedagogical role of the "chart." Thus, for instance,

> when the model is being used to illustrate wave lore it is seen as an island, the triangular stones at the four corners representing by their size, shape, and angle the waves characteristic of each side of the island. [Lewis, 1972:185]

Novices being trained in the art of navigation learn to recognize islands not by their proximity to other islands (as they would in western navigation), but by the wave patterns characteristic of that island.

Somewhat harder to comprehend—but directly relevant to the issue of how cultural practices can mediate between experience and linguistic representation—is the concept of *etak* or "reference island" used in the Caroline Islands in Micronesia. Imagine yourself sitting in a moving train. You "know" as you "see the countryside flash by" that it is really you, not the countryside, that is moving. However, with some effort, you can make a gestalt shift and imagine the reverse to be true.[12]

The notion of *etak* not only makes this gestalt shift, but also creates a vocabulary which speaks of external reference points as actually moving. Instead of sitting in a train, one sits in a canoe, and rather than the scenery "moving," what "moves" is the islands one passes. Like distant mountains seen on a train ride, the stars one sees in voyaging appear to remain fixed.

Figure 2.9 illustrates how the concept of *etak* works for the sailor

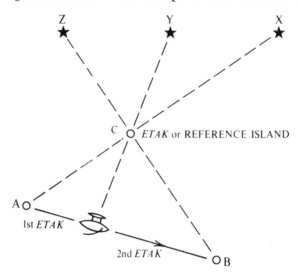

Fig. 2.9 The Concept of *Etak* or "Reference Island" in the Caroline Islands, Micronesia (from Lewis, 1972:133, reprinted by permission of Dr. David Lewis, c/o Curtis Brown (Aust.) Pty. Ltd., Sydney.

who is navigating between islands A and B. Points X, Y, and Z are stars which the navigator takes as the third point in a straight line of which his canoe is the first, and the *etak* point, the middle:

> Let us take the simplest case of a voyage that proceeds direct from island A to island B. A third island C is chosen as reference island [see figure 2.9]. Ideally it should be equidistant from the other two and located to one side of the line between them. In practice it is the exception to find one so conveniently sited.
>
> The navigator knows how the reference island bears from island A (and also from B, it having been part of his training to learn the direction of every known island from every other one). In Carolinian terms he has learnt 'under which star' C lies when visualised from A. In [figure 2.9] it lies under star X.
>
> When the voyage commences towards the objective B, the bearing of island C alters until, when the canoe has reached the position shown in the diagram, C has come to lie beneath star Y, the next point of the

sidereal compass. The canoe is then said to have travelled one *etak* and this is expressed by saying that the *etak* island C has 'moved' from one star point to the next, in this instance from 'under' star X to 'under' star Y.

This is the essence of the concept—that one *etak* along the course corresponds to the apparent 'movement' backwards by one star point of the reference island.

By the time the navigator arrives at his destination island B the reference island C will have 'moved' under the next star point Z. Since the voyage is only two *etak* long, very much shorter than a real one would be, he will be at his destination after covering only these two *etak*.

In other words, the canoe is conceived as stationary beneath the star points, whose position is also regarded as fixed. The sea flows past and the island astern recedes while the destination comes nearer and the reference island moves 'back' beneath the navigating stars until it comes abeam, and then moves on abaft the beam. (It can be appreciated from [figure 2.9] that if a voyage is undertaken in the opposite direction, the 'movement' of the *etak* island past the stars is simply reversed.) [Lewis, 1972:133–134]

The Carolinian concept of *etak* strongly resembles the contemporary western understanding of the relationship between the earth and the sun. We "know" that it is the earth, not the sun, which moves, although in ordinary language we continue to talk of the sun rising and setting. Similarly, "the Carolinians are perfectly well aware that the islands do *not* literally move," while at the same time, native navigators were "at very great pains" to make sure that Lewis "realized that all the islands concerned with a voyage 'moved' under the stars" (1972:134). In the case of the earth and the sun, our ordinary language has not kept pace with our theories, while among the Carolinians, the language of navigation is recognized as being at odds with empirical "knowledge." Yet in both instances, we cannot help wondering how much influence our linguistic patterns have upon our beliefs about what the physical world is actually like.

Modality Filters

So far, I have been talking about filters between experience and its representation which derive from individual or social factors. We can also consider whether the way in which the linguistic representation itself is formulated has any influence upon what sorts of linguistic representation are possible.

Until we have considered spoken, written, and signed languages with a comparative eye, we cannot assess the strengths or weaknesses each of the three modalities might have as a means of representing experience. The following are some of the beliefs that commonly circulate about the relative degree of representation possible in these three modalities and their implications for a study of linguistic representation:

Sign language is more "universal" than spoken or written language.

Implication: sign language is more "representative" physically of experience than is speech or writing.

Visual languages do not have the same expressive range as spoken languages—for example, visual languages cannot express abstractions, nor can they consistently distinguish between unique individuals and class terms.

Implication: visual linguistic schemes are either inferior to verbal schemas in an absolute sense or in ease of representation.

I shall consider hypotheses of this sort in chapters 5, 6, and 7.

UNIVERSAL LANGUAGES: UNWITTING LINGUISTIC THEORIES OF REPRESENTATION

During its modern history, linguistics has, as a discipline, paid reasonably little attention to the issue of representation. Instead, it has focused its attention on constructing good second order representations (linguistic theories) of languages (first order representations). The issues of what linguistic signs refer to (that is, the study of semantics) or of how one determines what those referents are (the problems of representation we have just been talking about) have been far less important than the enterprise of puzzling out how words and sentences are constructed out of smaller units.

There has been one important exception to this trend. It has counted relatively few professional linguists among its ranks (Otto Jespersen and Edward Sapir being major exceptions). Nonetheless, it has, perhaps unwittingly, laid the groundwork for the theory of semantics which was to become the theoretical companion of Chomsky's transformational model in syntax, namely the Katz-Fodor model of semantics (e.g., Katz and Fodor, 1963; Katz, 1966).

The exception to the prevailing linguistic tradition that has ignored problems of representation is the universal language movements. Because these movements have been largely ignored in the linguistic literature, we need to get some feeling for the contexts in which they arose if we are to understand why they have, so far, not succeeded. Some of these reasons are directly tied to their presuppositions about representation, while others are social or political. By highlighting the problems of representation in conscious universal language schemes, we can better understand the similarities between these problems and the ones confronted by contemporary semanticists who share some of their unacknowledged predecessors' presuppositions.

Interest in universal languages began to develop in western Europe in the early seventeenth century, becoming an issue of intense debate throughout the seventeenth and eighteenth centuries. The topic became less prominent during much of the nineteenth century, but reemerged in a somewhat different guise during the last decades of the 1800s and into the present century. We must investigate why the construction of a universal language was felt to be important, what kinds of languages have been proposed, and what success or failure they have met with—and why.

What is a universal language? Most simply, a universal language is a linguistic system that can potentially be used by speakers of all the world's languages. We need not restrict our definition to a particular mode of linguistic expression—spoken, written, or gestural. In reality, most proposed languages have entailed both a spoken and a written form, although in a few cases universal writing systems (without spoken counterparts) have been suggested, as have sign languages (for which durable visual representation is awkward).

Furthermore, we need not imply that a universal language would be the *sole* or even the primary language of speech communities throughout the world. In fact, in most nineteenth- and twentieth-century schemes, the originators explicitly speak of international *auxiliary* languages (rather than universal languages) to indicate their intention not to replace the native languages of various countries but rather to have speakers learn an *additional* language to be used only when needed to communicate with linguistic outsiders.

In a letter to Mersenne in 1629, René Descartes distinguished be-

tween two types of universal languages: a priori languages (later referred to as "philosophical languages") and a posteriori languages. A
priori languages, which were particularly popular in the seventeenth
and eighteenth centuries, were composed of "arbitrarily selected letters, syllables or words indicating an idea, or a group of ideas in
accordance with a determined classification and based in no way upon
natural languages" (Beaufront, 1919:vii). For the most part, the creation of these languages was motivated by the desire for a clarity of
thinking not possible with existing natural languages. The most famous of these schemes, which we shall discuss shortly, is Bishop Wilkins's "Real Character." A posteriori languages, on the other hand, have
been most prominent within the last hundred years. These languages
are "based on roots already existing in the natural languages with a
grammar reduced to its most simple expression and comprising neither
irregularity nor exception" (ibid., p. viii). A posteriori schemes have,
probably without exception, been devised primarily to foster international communication. In practice, though, they have often contained,
as an underlying current, the goal of philosophical languages: the creation of a language more logical than natural languages. Esperanto is
the best known of the a posteriori languages, although dozens of such
languages have been proposed over the last century.

MOTIVATIONS BEHIND THE CREATION OF UNIVERSAL LANGUAGES

Universal language schemes have been motivated by two different
classes of factors. The first, concerned with clarifying human thinking,
directly confronts the question of how language should represent experience. A second group of forces, dealing with increased cross-
national communication, is more social and economic in character. In
most instances, several individual factors have simultaneously made
the development of such languages desirable.

Universal Language as a Boon to Clear Thinking

The largest single impetus for developing a universal language, both
in the seventeenth and again in the twentieth century, was the development of empirical science. Seventeenth-century England experienced
a revolution in its philosophy and methodology of science. Francis
Bacon, declaring all knowledge to be his province, devised an elaborate
inductive procedure by which to know the world (his *Novum Orga-*

num was intended to replace Aristotle's Organon). According to Bacon, physicial nature is relatively easily comprehended, given the proper methodology. In *The Great Instauration,* he reveals his plans for a new empirical science, and many of his contemporaries and heirs shared his optimism. Typical of this enthusiasm was Thomas Sprat's declaration in his *History of the Royal Society* that "we may ghess that the absolute perfection of the True Philosophy is not farr off" (1667:29).

Richard Jones (esp. 1932, 1961) argues that this new scientific attitude towards man's relationship with nature was the primary motivation for seventeenth-century linguistic reform. Baconians became suspicious of ordinary language not only because of its association with the old science, which seemed to depend upon words more than upon nature, but also from a belief that current languages served to obscure rather than reflect reality:

> The vividness with which material reality was conceived filled the scientists with alarm lest that reality should be lost through a faulty medium of communication and lest the manner of expression should usurp an importance belonging to the thing described. [1932:327]

In the *Novum Organum,* Bacon assails the Idols of the Marketplace—vulgar communication—as the most troublesome of all false notions affecting human understanding. These idols

> have crept into the understanding through the alliances of words and names. For men believe that their reason governs words; but it is also true that words react on the understanding; and this it is that has rendered philosophy and the sciences sophistical and inactive. [Book I, Aphorism LIX]

In *Of the Advancement of Learning,* Bacon suggests that the first distemper of learning occurs "when men study words and not matter." He asks,

> And how is it possible but this should have an operation to discredit learning, even with vulgar capacities, when they see learned men's works like the first letter of a patent or limned book; which though it hath large flourishes, yet it is but a letter? [Book I, Bacon, 1863, vol. 6:120]

Matter, not form, must be the object of our attention. Otherwise, our capacity for expressing knowledge will be severely limited. For

whenever an understanding of greater acuteness or a more diligent
observation would alter those lines [of division which are most obvious
to the vulgar understanding] to suit the true divisions of nature, words
stand in the way and resist the change. [*Novum Organum*, Book I,
Aphorism LIX, Bacon, 1863, vol. 8:87]

Underlying Baconian science is the assumption that nature is
uniquely describable. While aware of observational contradictions, the
Baconian attributed such inconsistencies to insufficient observation or
a faulty linguistic system which obscured the true nature of the event.
Adherence to the uniqueness principle is a prerequisite for writing a
universal philosophical language. Wilkins clearly believed that a
unique analysis of nature was possible. In his *Essay* he writes, "As men
do generally agree in the same Principle of Reason, so do they likewise
agree in the same *Internal Notion* or *Apprehension of things*" (1668:
20).

Seventeenth-century arguments by Bacon and members of the
Royal Society that a new language was needed to clarify the findings
of scientific explorations were echoed more than two centuries later
in the work of early twentieth-century language reformers. In the
former case, the solutions proposed were largely a priori languages
(i.e., wholly artificial) and in the latter, a posteriori (i.e., based on
natural languages), but in both instances the goal was strikingly
similar.

The modern complaint has been that existing natural languages are
too imprecise and ambiguous to formulate the exact statements we
wish our scientific theories to make:

Science, philosophy, and technology are constantly waging a fierce
battle with existing languages. What they want is a language as simple
and clear as the fundamental laws of nature, as logical as the precision
of experiment, and as manysided as the complexity of the facts that it
has to describe. And so they are constantly working at the creation of
this language, all the words invented by science finding their way un-
ceasingly through the channels of technology into the general vocabulary. These words possess the special property of being international,
that is to say, understood by all civilised nations, including the Japanese. We do not wish, however, to stop at this stage of development;
we wish to be able to internationalise not only single ideas, but also the
whole train of thought. For this purpose it is impracticable to make use
of any of the national languages, since they are all so unsuitable, illogi-
cal, capricious, and complicated that the student must learn to steer

clear of thousands of difficulties before he is able to express himself fairly correctly. *It is possible to construct an artificial language with such a regular structure that it can be employed at once without making mistakes.* [Lorenz in Couturat et al. 1910:12–13]

Similarly, Ostwald has argued:

> We scientific men suffer a good deal from the fact that the same words are frequently employed for the vague ideas of daily life as well as for the perfectly definite concepts of science. This is indeed one of the most important reasons why new designations for scientific concepts should, as far as possible, be taken from the dead languages, such designations being thereby already international. It ought therefore to be a comparatively easy task to devise by means of this international material and the linguistic rules of the language of the Delegation a system of international names for the clearly defined concepts of the different sciences. [Ostwald in Couturat et al. 1910:63]

Sapir, one of the few linguists (along with Jespersen) to lend strong support to the international language movement, advocates more generally a logically structured international language:

> One of the most ambitious and important tasks that can be undertaken is the attempt to work out the relation between logic and usage in a number of national and constructed languages, in order that the eventual problem of adequately symbolizing thought may be seen as the problem it still is. [Sapir in Shenton et al. 1931:89]

Twentieth-century proponents of a universal language have, in fact, looked upon science as a prototype of modern thinking and as a model for a widespread move toward internationalism:

> Internationalisation of thought is the motto of the twentieth century, the device of the banner of progress. Science, the super-nation of the world, must lead the way in this as in all other things. [Couturat et al. 1910:vii]

Thus we might recognize the special plight of professional scientists, for whom the learning of a single universal language is advocated as an alternative to having to learn a number of already existing languages because

> expertness in the use of languages does not come so readily to the scientific investigator and the technologist, whose work lies in other directions, and so it is in these quarters that the movement for the introduc-

tion of an international auxiliary language receives the greatest support.
[Lorenz in Couturat et al. 1910:11–12]

Universal Language as a Means of Cross-National Understanding

Economics also contributed to universal language movements, the
focus here being on international understanding more than on improving the "match" between language and experience. In the seventeenth
century new trade routes were being charted and speakers of western
European languages were unable to make themselves understood in
the ports and crossroads where they wished to do business. A fairly well
established trading language known as Lingua Franca had developed
around the Mediterranean during the Crusades, which allowed for
some shared communication between merchants. But as the trade
routes extended to Africa and the Far East, where Lingua Franca was
not known, and the number of merchants increased, a common language was needed once more.

Because the expansion of trade in early modern Europe coincided
with interest in philosophical languages which aided clear thinking and
expression, it was not surprising that these same universal language
schemes should have been thought useful in facilitating international
trade. Historically, however, the linguistic solution which trading
groups adopted was not the imposition of a new language on both parties, but rather the gradual development of trade jargons.

Calls for an international language for trading purposes subsided
during much of the next two centuries. As trading relationships gave
way to empires, and individual Western powers began staking their
claims to different sectors of the non-European world, individual solutions to the linguistic problem were devised. In the case of a highly
civilized (though non-Western) country such as India, British officials
were required to learn Sanskrit before taking up residence in India.
In most instances, however, a pidgin language evolved which sufficed
for the amount of communication which was necessary between colo-
nizer and native (see chapter 5).

An impetus for universal language development was also provided
by religion, especially in the early modern era. To the extent that peoples of differing religious ideologies are also speakers of different languages (which is not always the case—as in the English Civil War),
a universal language is potentially useful in resolving ideological differences. Seventeenth-century language planners spoke of the religious

value of a universal language on two planes. The first bordered on the mystical, the second was wholly pragmatic.

Comenius, a Czech educational reformer who derived much of his ideology from the mystics Johann Valentin Andreae and Jakob Böhme, believed in a mystical harmony of nations which needed to be restored to its original balance. Andreae had hoped to organize a universal Christian intelligentsia which would pursue the knowledge needed to unite mankind. This wish is manifested in Comenius's envisioned philosophical college of Pansophia, which he charged with the task of fitting exact expressions in language to exact concepts.

A more mundane concern for religion was the conversion of the heathen. Concomitant with the rise of exploration and foreign trade in early modern Europe was the proliferation of Christian missionaries. Their problem was the same as that of merchants and later colonizers: how to communicate with those who do not speak the same language. The solutions, as it turned out, were also largely the same. Rather than appealing to theoretically useful but practically implausible language schemes, missionaries often forged pidgin languages out of their own languages and those of the indigenous populations. In many cases, missionaries learned the native languages of the people among whom they were proselytizing. In fact, missionaries have produced much of the grammatical information linguists now have on non-Indo-European languages.

BISHOP WILKINS'S *ESSAY TOWARDS A REAL CHARACTER, AND A PHILOSOPHICAL LANGUAGE*

What did these universal language schemes look like? Since there have been dozens—perhaps hundreds—of schemes proposed, it is not possible to characterize them all. Instead, let us consider the scheme which is perhaps best known, that of Bishop John Wilkins. Wilkins's scheme is instructive not only because it is more complete than any other but also because it provides striking parallels with linguistic proposals that emerged almost precisely three hundred years later.

Wilkins's *Essay* (1668) was written in response to a request by members of the Royal Society of London to create a language which clearly expressed the composition of the natural world and our place in it. The language was a priori in design, not relying upon any existing language for its model. It does seem likely, though, that the idea of creating a character that mirrored reality was influenced by growing knowledge of Chinese characters, which were seen as directly reflecting the world of experience.

In the *Essay*, Wilkins undertakes to divide all of nature into a series of genera (he calls them genuses and so shall I), predicaments, and species. Having thus divided nature, he then assigns both a phonetic representation and a written representation to each subdivision, so that it can be referred to in spoken and written language. He lists a total of forty genuses, grouped into predicaments (e.g., substance, quantity, quality). Each genus is then subdivided into differences, and each difference is divided into as many as nine species. Figure 2.10 shows Wilkins's forty genuses (grouped into predicaments), along with the phonological and written character used to express each genus.[13]

The next step is to break down each genus into between six and nine differences. Figure 2.11 shows the spoken and written indicators of each of these differences. The "sound" is placed on the right side of the genus symbol, while the written indicator for the difference is placed on the left. The same symbols are used in marking the subdivisions of each genus, although the referents being marked within the genus are obviously different. The final stage is to divide the differences into species, again using a standard set of sounds and characters to indicate all species differentiations (see figure 2.12). Both the phonological and written indicators of species are placed on the right hand of the difference marker.

Figure 2.13 presents a typical example of difference and species subdivisions of a genus. All items of experience are assumed to be identifiable by genus, difference, and species. To indicate any item linguistically, one strings together the sounds or written symbols for the appropriate genus, difference, and species. Thus if one wanted to refer to "sand," one would proceed as follows:

Sound	Division	Character
Di	stone (8th genus)	
Di + b	first difference under stone (vulgar)	
Di + b + yi	8th species under first difference under 8th genus	

Note that the availability of forty genuses, nine differences, and nine species only yields a potential 3,240 unique identifications. We know

	Sounds	Character
Forty Genuses, Grouped into Predicaments		
1. Transcendental General	Bœ	
2. Transcendental Relation Mixed	Ba	
3. Transcendental Relation of Action	Be	
4. Discourse	Bi	
5. God	Dœ	
6. World	Da	
Substance		
7. Element	De	
8. Stone	Di	
9. Metal	Do	
10. Leaf	Gœ	
11. Flower	Ga	
12. Seed-Vessel	Ge	
13. Shrub	Gi	
14. Tree	Go	
15. Exanguious	Zœ	
16. Fish	Za	
17. Bird	Ze	
18. Beast	Zi	
19. Peculiar parts	Pœ	
20. General parts	Pa	
Quantity		
21. Magnitude	Pe	
22. Space	Pi	
23. Measure	Po	
Quality		
24. Natural power	Tœ	
25. Habit	Ta	
26. Manners	Te	
27. Quality sensible	Ti	
28. Disease	To	
Action		
29. Spiritual	Cœ	
30. Corporeal	Ca	
31. Motion	Ce	
32. Operation	Ci	
Relation		
33. Oeconomical	Co	
34. Possessions	Cy	
35. Provisions	Sœ	
36. Civil	Sa	
37. Judicial	Se	
38. Military	Si	
39. Naval	So	
40. Ecclesiastical	Sy	

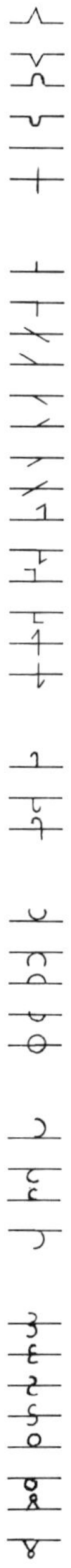

Fig. 2.10 Bishop Wilkins's Forty Genuses, Grouped into Predicaments

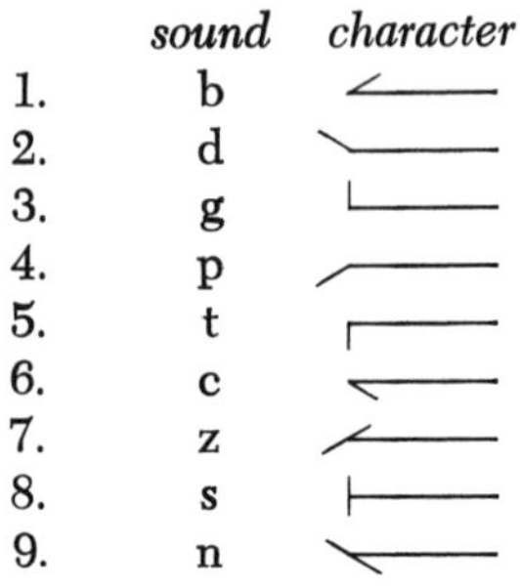

	sound	character
1.	b	
2.	d	
3.	g	
4.	p	
5.	t	
6.	c	
7.	z	
8.	s	
9.	n	

Fig. 2.11 Bishop Wilkins's Nine Indicators of Difference

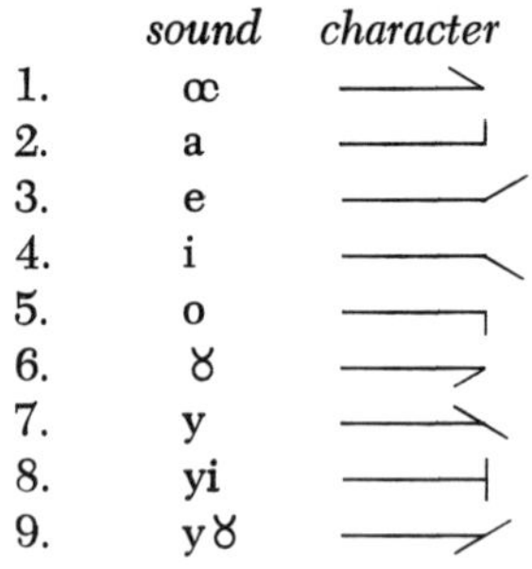

	sound	character
1.	œ	
2.	a	
3.	e	
4.	i	
5.	o	
6.	ʊ	
7.	y	
8.	yi	
9.	yʊ	

Fig. 2.12 Bishop Wilkins's Nine Indicators of Species

that there are far more than 3,240 items of experience to identify, and far more than that number of words in the English language. Wilkins obviously recognized the problem; he allowed for additional differences when necessary, and did not always distinguish between some related objects and words. In our example, both "sand" and "gravel" are given the same ontological and linguistic identification. Moreover, Wilkins created grammatical means for deriving adjectives and adverbs, as well as separate symbols for the copula, pronouns, interjections, prepositions, and conjunctions.[14]

PROBLEMS WITH UNIVERSAL LANGUAGE SCHEMES

In the 1920s, Sylvia Pankhurst envisioned a golden future for the idea of a universal language, a prototype of which she calls Interlanguage:

8.   Stone

Differences:
I.   vulgar and of no price
II.   middle-prized
III. precious, less transparent
IV.   precious, more transparent
V.   dissolvible
VI.   not dissolvible

Species under difference I (vulgar and of no price):
1.   free-stone, brick
2.   ragg
3.   flint, marchasite
4.   pibble
5.   slate, tile
6.   whet-stone, touch-stone
7.   pumice, emry
8.   sand, gravel

Fig. 2.13 Example of Difference and Species Subdivisions
of a Genus

The news will appear in the Interlanguage. Where thousands of people are to-day interested in reading of what others have done in art and science, millions will then delight in their actual pursuit. . . . By using the Interlanguage it will be possible to send all news to one world receiving-station, for retransmission everywhere. . . . Events of universal importance will be conveyed in concise words that will require no rewriting. . . . All scientific and technical books and journals will be written in the Interlanguage. . . . Scientists have such vital need of cooperation that they will gladly clothe their thoughts in the language that will be common to their international fraternity, just as they did of old in Latin. . . . Probably fifty (perhaps even thirty) years hence no one will be troubled by learning the Interlanguage. It will be acquired at the toddling age, side by side with the mother tongue. [1927:91–93]

Three hundred years earlier, Robert Boyle had expressed a similar sentiment:

If the design of the *Real Character* take effect, it will in good part make amends to mankind for what their pride lost them at the tower of Babel. And truly, since our arithmetical characters are understood by all the nations of *Europe* the same way . . . I conceive no impossibility, that opposes the doing that in words, that we see already done in numbers. [cited by Emery, 1948:175, from Thomas Birch's *Life of Robert Boyle*, London, 1744:73]

Today we are no closer to using an international language than we were in Boyle's time. Fifty years have passed since Pankhurst's prophecy, and we still lack a common language. What has gone wrong? We can identify two classes of problems: technical and theoretical. In many cases, the technical problems could be overcome, while the chances of solving the theoretical problems are far less certain.

Technical Problems

The first two technical problems apply largely (although not exclusively) to a priori languages. In creating a new language, one of the first problems is getting people to learn it. The more difficult the language, the less one's chance of success. Aware of this problem, language planners from the seventeenth century to the present have sometimes stressed the ease with which their schemes can be learned. Dalgarno, inventor of one early philosophical language,

> even reproduced in one of his broadsheets a certificate, dated May 1658, from Richard Love, then professor of divinity at Cambridge, to the effect that two young bachelors of arts, after spending two hours a day for a fortnight in the study of his character, had learnt to communicate with one another in that language and to translate anything into, or out of, it. [Cohen, 1954:61]

And Wilkins claimed at the end of his *Essay* (p. 453) that his new language was forty times easier to learn than Latin. In practice, however, the a priori schemes have proven difficult to learn and use, although one might argue that they have been insufficiently tested.

A second technical problem with a priori languages in particular is their zero level of redundancy; every sound (or every mark) has a distinct meaning which is represented nowhere else in the linguistic message. As Pankhurst observed,

> in a language of classification [i.e., an a priori language] a slight vocalic modification might produce, not a mere mispronunciation, but the transference of a word to another class. [1927:22]

In Wilkins's scheme, for example, *Za* denotes the class of fish, *Ze*, the class of birds, and *Zi* the class of beasts; a single mispronunciation might yield a totally unintended genus or species. We would expect a language with no redundancy to be very difficult to learn or to use.

There have been other problems as well. Most a posteriori languages that have actually been worked out have been demonstrably drawn from one of the European languages. Speakers of different European languages (or non-European tongues) have been loath to learn as an "international" language a scheme which is biased in this way. Moreover, no universal language system has received sufficient popular or governmental support to make the language's use widespread. The International Esperanto Society continues to meet, but neither boards of education nor university departments of modern languages actively support the teaching of Esperanto—or any of the other auxiliary languages. We cannot fairly judge the potential for success or failure of languages which have not been adequately tested.

Theoretical Problems

Even if the technical problems discussed above can be solved, a number of deeper problems concerning the whole conception of a universal language would seem to cast doubt upon the eventual success of the enterprise. All of these stem ultimately from the underlying assumption that a universal language—either a priori or a posteriori—is unchanging and eternally appropriate for all language users:

> At the present day the rapid development in every department of life has made us only too ready to regard everything around us as transient. We forget, however, that the rapidly accumulating inventions and discoveries which startle and surprise us always refer to new things. One must bear in mind that there also exist things which in their essential features can *only be invented once,* and that the international language in its final form is one of these. [Lorenz, in Couturat et al. 1910:20]

This belief in the eternal nature of a universal language has been manifested in many ways—and is susceptible to a large number of counterarguments. The most blatant of these assumptions about linguistic stasis was the belief that

> the human psyche has everywhere a common structure, which must find its expression in language and must be capable of a simpler and more uniform expression in a constructed language. [indirect quote from Otto Funke, paraphrased by Jespersen in Shenton et al. 1931:107]

Whatever one's views on the Sapir-Whorf hypothesis (which suggests that languages influence the way in which speakers think about and perceive the world), it is generally recognized that different historical and material conditions may make the linguistic expression of certain topics more critical to some peoples than others. Trobriand Islanders may not need a language which distinguishes types of stone used as permanent building materials (stones, Wilkins's eighth genus, are finely divided), while inhabitants of New York City may have no use for detailed distinctions of flora and fauna.

The failure of universal language schemes to recognize the lack of uniformity of linguistic needs is complemented by the presupposition made by language architects that their categories for describing "things themselves" are necessarily—and eternally—correct. The problem with this assumption is particularly clear in the case of a priori schemes which explicitly attempt to categorize all knowledge, although the problem is also seen with a posteriori languages to the extent that they claim to mirror reality directly. Pankhurst observes that a priori languages are necessarily doomed to failure as eternal systems since "ideas, and views as to their classification, are constantly changing" (1927:22). As an example, she points out that the Aristotelian classification of elements into earth, air, fire, and water, is no longer accepted. A near contemporary of Wilkins, the mathematician Thomas Baker, made a similar point:

> When Bishop Wilkins undertook this design *Substance* and *Accidents* [Substance being divided into inanimate and animate, and Accident being divided into Quantity, Quality, Action, and Relation] were a receiv'd Division and accordingly in ranking Things, and reducing them to Heads . . . he proceeds according to the Order they stand in, of *Substance* and *Accidents*, in the Scale of *Praedicaments*; but were he to begin now, and would suit his Design to the Philosophy in vogue, he must draw a new Scheme [*Reflections Upon Learning*, London, 1700; cited by DeMott, 1957:12–13]

The extent to which an a priori language could handle such changes in scientific theory and empirical knowledge would depend on the rigidity of the formulation of the scheme and on the extent of change in categorization implied by the new knowledge or theory. If, for example, one discovers (as zoologists did) that the whale is not a fish but a mammal, it would be rather simple to change the sound or symbol used to represent whales in the language. However, if the whole system of classification is challenged (as Baker suggested might be necessary in the case of Wilkins's scheme), then it is not clear what would remain of the original a priori language after the required changes. Moreover, by definition, it was assumed that the classifications made were correct, now and forever, since they were intended to reflect the *real* structure of things as directly perceived by all peoples.[15]

FROM ARISTOTLE TO (ANIMATE)

Since its inception, transformational grammar was intended as a theory of grammatical collocation, not as a theory of meaning. Chomsky explains in *Syntactic Structures* (1957: chap. 9) that he sees no obvious way in which semantic information is necessary or even useful for grammatical analysis. Largely as a result of this position, the study of semantics was ignored by most transformationalists into the 1960s.

One exception was the work of Jerrold Katz and Jerry Fodor. Their paper "The Structure of a Semantic Theory" (1963) laid the groundwork for the semantic component of grammar that would interpret the syntactic constructs generated by the syntactic component. The semantic theory was based on a set of semantic features which, in combination, were seen as specifying the meanings of all words and sentences in the language.

In the earlier version of the semantic theory, semantic features came in two varieties: *semantic markers* and *distinguishers*. Semantic markers (enclosed by parentheses in writing) were "intended to reflect whatever systematic semantic relations hold between that item and the rest of the vocabulary of the language" (Katz and Fodor, 1963:187). Distinguishers (enclosed by brackets) reflected "what is idiosyncratic" about the meaning of a word. Thus, the semantic reading of the word *colorful* would include the semantic marker (Color) and the distinguisher [Abounding in contrast of variety of bright colors] (ibid., p. 202). Later versions of the theory (Katz, 1966) eliminated the category of distinguisher, leaving only semantic markers.

Where do these features come from? How did Katz and Fodor select them? Are there any criteria for determining the right set? Before exploring these questions, it is only fair to point out that subsequent semantic theories (e.g., Chafe, 1970; Lakoff, 1970b; McCawley, 1968; Schank, 1972) have also proposed the equivalent of semantic features, though sometimes by other names. The question of how these subsequent theorists have selected their semantic primes is just as important —and its answer just as mysterious—as in the case of Katz and Fodor.

The Problem of Categorization

In his attempts to order or analyze his environment, man almost invariably begins to categorize. Our recorded heritage abounds with treatises on types of heavenly bodies, types of angels, type of angles, types of fish. Another favorite typology is that of language. How many parts of speech are there? How many declensions? How many types of sentences?

The precise relationship between ontological and linguistic categories has puzzled both philosophers and linguists. At one extreme we find linguistic relativists, according to whom a unique analysis of nature is impossible or else exceedingly difficult because of diverse human linguistic-perceptual patterns. At the opposite pole are universalists who, while recognizing a dependence between language and perception, imply that unique analyses in science are possible because of the uniformity of human thought and language. Between these extremes are linguists with no particular interest in nature—such as Katz and Fodor, and scientists with no particular interest in language—whom we may disregard here.

The best known of all categorizers is Aristotle; his biological treatises (e.g., *Historia Animalium, De Partibus Animalium, De Generatione Animalium*) directly confront the problem of classifying nature. One product of this endeavor is a "scale of nature" in which animals are grouped according to their mode of biological generation. Aristotle's *Categories* is, however, a troublesome book. To paraphrase Julius Moravcsik (1967), what is the list of ten categories a list of? Are the predicaments *substance, quantity, quality, relation, place, date, position, state, action,* and *passivity* meant to carve up language or nature? Aristotle's commentators have not been unanimous in their answer. One commentator observes that although most of these categories are mentioned in nearly all of Aristotle's works, "the doctrine is everywhere treated as something already established" (Ross, 1923:22). According to Antoine Arnauld, "The ten Aristotelian categories are the different classes into which Aristotle divided objects of thought (1662: 1964 edition, p.42). While the *Categories* is largely a linguistic treatise, it does not assume a one-to-one correspondence between the ten divisions and grammatical distinctions. Moravcsik resolves the dilemma through compromise:

> The theory of categories is partly a theory of language and partly a theory about reality. . . . Aristotle did not think of the structure of language as mirroring the structure of reality. But he did believe that there are specific items of language and reality the correlation of which forms the crucial link between the two. [1967:145]

Aristotle's stature throughout the Middle Ages is exemplified by one of the statutes of Oxford University under which

Bachelors and Masters who did not follow Aristotle faithfully were liable to a fine of five shillings for every point of divergence, and for every fault committed against the Logic of the Organon. [Jones, 1961:4, cited from J.L. McIntyre, *Giordano Bruno*, 1903:21]

The Baconian Renaissance, however, revolted against its scholastic heritage. Thomas Vaughan reflects the new empiricism when he urges Aristotelians not to let their

> thoughts feed . . . on the *Phlegmatic*, indigested Vomits of *Aristotle* [but to] look on the green, youthfull, and flowerie *Bosome* of the *Earth*. [*Magia Adamica*, 1650:86]

Wilkins himself explicitly rejected scholastic philosophy in his *Discourse Concerning a New Planet* (1640):

> Whatever the Schoolmen may talk, yet Aristotles Works are not necessarily true, and he himself hath by sufficient Arguments proved himself to be liable unto Error. [*Mathematical and Philosophical Works*, 1708: 271]

Nevertheless, Wilkins distinguished between Aristotle the philosopher and scientist, and Aristotle as interpreted by the Schoolmen. For the former, Wilkins had much respect. The Bishop's debt to Aristotle the classifier of nature is obvious. In his *Essay*, Wilkins defines forty genuses which are subclassified into differences, the difference-genus distinction stemming from Aristotle; and all five of the predicaments under which Wilkins distributes most of his genuses are Aristotelian in origin: *substance, quantity, quality, action,* and *relation.*

Katz and Categorization

Katz[16] approaches the language-nature duality in reverse. For Katz, the purpose of semantics is to

> [take] up the explanation of a speaker's ability to produce and understand infinitely many new sentences at the point where the models of the syntactic and phonological components leave off. [1966:152]

This explanation entails defining and distinguishing anomalous, unambiguous, ambiguous, and synonymous sentences. Nowhere does Katz explicitly relate his lexicon to the natural environment. A universalist in spirit, he implies adherence to some version of a Wilkinsian unique description of nature. Without claiming that all languages have identical subclassification systems, he suggests that at least the basic

categories of every language are identical. It takes but one more step
to identify this common core with a unique perception of nature. But,
unlike Wilkins, Katz never commits himself. In fact, references to scientific classification are entirely absent from his semantics.

Despite his indifference to natural description, Katz, like Wilkins,
returns to Aristotle's *Categories*. He is intensely aware of the severe
criticism the *Categories* has received in modern philosophy, summarizing the arguments as follows:

> Aristotle's system of categories does not itself, and is not embedded
> within a more general theory that might, provide us with an explanation
> as to why all natural languages utilize just these categories. . . .
>
> Aristotle's account is arbitrary because it does not answer the question
> of why these categories should be *the* categories of language and not
> others. . . .
>
> There is no theoretically satisfactory statement that explains what a
> category is. . . .
>
> Neither Aristotle nor Kant considers the relation of a theory of cate-
> gories to other theories having to do with the structure of language.
>
> [1966:226–227]

Three of these points assume that Aristotle's theory of categories is
strictly a theory of linguistic categories, an assumption Moravcsik
would deny.

Katz proceeds to offer linguistic cures for philosophical ills by em-
bedding Aristotelian categories within the now familiar framework of
Katzian semantics. Semantic categories are defined as "a subset of those
semantic markers which semantic theory specifies as substantive universals" (ibid, p.228). Semantic markers, in turn, are

> the conceptual elements into which a reading decomposes a sense. They
> thus provide the theoretical constructs needed to reconstruct the inter-
> relations holding between such conceptual elements in the structure of
> a sense. It is important to stress that, although the semantic markers are
> given in the orthography of a natural language, they cannot be identi-
> fied with the words or expressions of the language used to provide them
> with suggestive labels. Rather, they are to be regarded as constructs of
> a linguistic theory, just as terms such as 'force' are regarded as labels
> for constructs in natural science. [ibid., pp. 155–156]

But where does Katz derive his suggestions for labels? He implies
that semantic markers are basically formalizations of conventional
dictionary entries:

Semantic markers enable us to construct empirical generalizations about the meaning of linguistic constructions. For example, the English words 'bachelor,' 'man,' 'priest,' 'bull,' 'uncle,' 'boy,' etc., have a semantic feature in common which is not part of the meaning of any of the words 'child,' 'mole,' 'mother,' 'classmate,' 'nuts,' 'bolts,' 'cow,' etc. [ibid., p. 157]

Katz captures this empirical fact by including the semantic marker (Male) in the lexical readings for all words in the first group but not for those in the second. Our problem, however, still remains: How did he know to choose the marker (Male)?

While Katz does not allude to a source, there would seem to be several candidates: first, empirical knowledge of his natural environment and of the English language. As Narveson (1968) implies, (Male) is an "empirical generalization" only in that it suggests Katz's recognition that many words in the English language connote maleness. A second possible source is componential analysis. Although he never refers to componential analysis, it may be instructive to remember that the 1950s witnessed the growth of a theory of meaning which analyzed groups of words into shared parts. Most componential analyses have focused on kinship terms—where (Male) is a crucial category, though the technique is quite general (cf. Goodenough, 1968; J. Lyons, 1968). Note that some of Wilkins's discussion neatly dovetails with twentieth-century componential analysis. In a passage arguing against the suitability of Latin as a philosophical language, he observes:

There is a common word for the notion of *Parent*, abstracted from either sex, *Father* or *Mother*. And so for *Child, Liber*. But none for the relation of *Brother, Sister, Husband*, and *Wife, Uncle, Aunt, Nephew, Niece*, etc. And so for the names of several Plants, and Living Creatures of every kind, which no Dictionary doth sufficiently express. And though the Latin doth provide for some of those notions expressed by the Transcendental Particles, yet is not their number sufficient, there being several others (not provided for) which may as conveniently be in like manner exprest. [1668:443]

The third potential source is Aristotle himself. An analysis of commentaries on Aristotle reveals some striking precursors to the concept of semantic markers. Consider the introduction to Aristotle's *Categories* by the third-century A.D. commentator, Porphyry:

Substance indeed, is itself genus, under this is body, under body animated body, under which is animal, under animal rational animal, under which is man, under man Socrates, Plato, and men particularly.[17]

Porphyry's analysis persisted during the Middle Ages, as evidenced by the adaptation of a diagram found in Thomas Aquinas shown in figure 2.14.

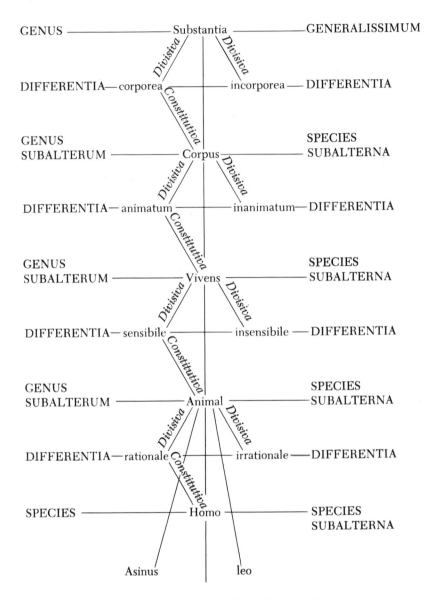

Fig. 2.14 Tree of Porphyry (from Thomas Aquinas, Opusculum XLIV, Tractatus II, Caput IV)

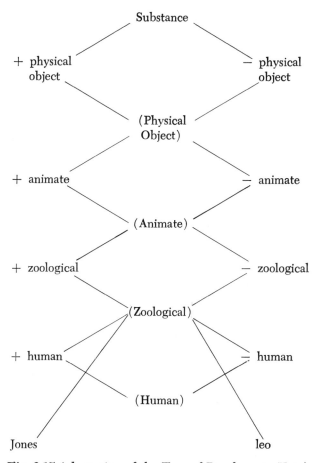

Fig. 2.15 Adaptation of the Tree of Porphyry to Katz's
Semantic Features

The tree is largely translatable into Katzian semantic markers. Divisions in the center correspond to the semantic markers themselves, while the branches on either side represent positive or negative values (figure 2.15). Aristotle's (Corpus) is interpreted by Katz as (Physical Object), and the next three categories—(Vivens), (Animal), (Homo) —have their direct counterparts in Katz's model. The most general Aristotelian category, (Substantia), however, has no equivalent in the Katzian scheme. One might argue that the category of substance is redundantly presupposed by Katz. Such redundancy is apparently intended in the *Categories*:

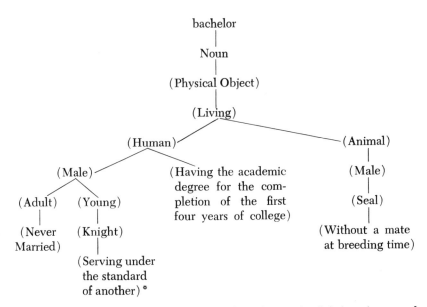

* Apparently, Katz has inadvertently omitted the feature (Male) from his second reading for *bachelor*. We have incorporated the correction here.

Fig. 2.16 Katz's Semantic Entry for *Bachelor* (from p. 155 of The Philosophy of Language by Jerrold J. Katz. Copyright © 1966 by Jerrold J. Katz. Reprinted by permission of Harper & Row, Publishers, Inc.)

Substance is the most generic, and that which alone is genus; but man is most specific, and that which alone is species; yet body is a species of substance, but a genus of animated body, also animated body is a species of body, but a genus of animal; again, animal is a species of animated body, but a genus of rational animal, and rational animal is a species of animal, but a genus of man, and man is a species of rational animal, but is no longer the genus of particular men, but is species only, and every thing prior to individuals being proximately predicated of them, will be species only, and no longer genus also. [Porphyry's Commentary on the *Categories*, Chapter II]

That (Substantia) is, in fact, the most general category on the tree is made explicit by the term (Generalissimum) in the upper right hand corner of Aquinas's diagram.

Having translated Porphyry's Tree into Katzian markers, it remains for us to translate Katz into Aristotelian terminology. Katz's citation for *bachelor* in his book *The Philosophy of Language* (1966) is shown in figure 2.16. Much of this lexical item is directly convertible into the Tree of Porphyry (figure 2.17).

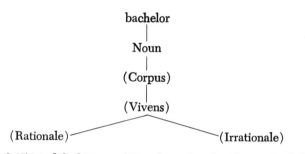

Fig. 2.17 Modified Tree of Porphyry for the Entry *Bachelor*

What do we learn from demonstrating a high degree of isomorphism between Katz's semantic categories on the one hand, and those of Aristotle (and, derivatively, Wilkins) on the other? If we believe that Aristotle's classification of nature is correct, we should have no objection to Katz's adoption of the scheme for contemporary linguistic analysis.

We do not know whether Katz intends to follow an Aristotelian scheme consistently, since he has not overtly identified his schematic model with Aristotle. Furthermore, there are many points on which contemporary science would disagree with Aristotle's classification. Finally, we have yet to establish that divisions made in nature are necessarily appropriate as linguistic categories. We may "know" that whales are mammals, but this academic knowledge does not prevent us from talking about the "gigantic fish" we saw in the aquarium.

III

What Is a Language?

I HAVE DISCUSSED linguistic representation in order to understand what it means to say that language represents human experience. But what do we mean when we say "human language"? What boundary conditions do we place on this phenomenon?

THREE PERSPECTIVES

Sapir defined language as

> a purely human and non-instinctive method of communicating ideas, emotions, and desires by means of a system of voluntarily produced symbols. [1921:7]

From this definition, we can identify three distinct definitional trends that have emerged in contemporary linguistic discussions.

HUMAN AND NON-HUMAN COMMUNICATION

From one perspective, the definition of language must distinguish between human and nonhuman means of communication (Sapir's "purely human and non-instinctive"). This position has been championed by Hockett (Hockett, 1960; Hockett and Ascher, 1964), who has characterized communicative behavior with respect to a set of "design features" (figure 3.1), of which only humans are reputed to exhibit all thirteen (figure 3.2). Others interested in differences or similarities between animal and human communication (notably Sebeok, e.g., 1968, 1977) have been less convinced of the ease with

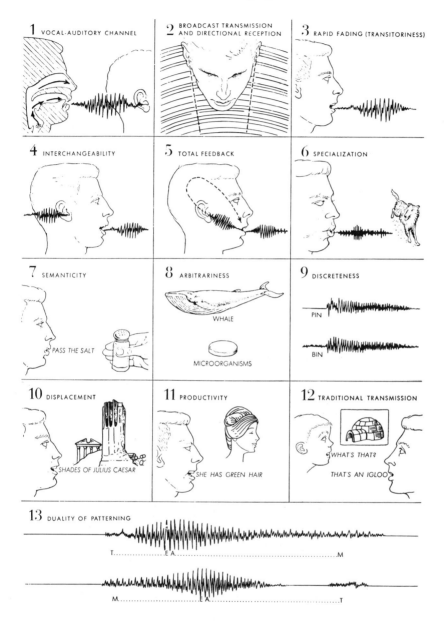

Fig. 3.1 Hockett's Thirteen Design Features of Animal Communication. From "The Origin of Speech" by Charles F. Hockett, p. 91. Copyright © 1960 by Scientific American, Inc. All rights reserved.

	A SOME GRYLLIDAE AND TETTIGONIIDAE	B BEE DANCING	C STICKLEBACK COURTSHIP	D WESTERN MEADOWLARK SONG	E GIBBON CALLS	F PARALINGUISTIC PHENOMENA	G LANGUAGE	H INSTRUMENTAL MUSIC
1 THE VOCAL-AUDITORY CHANNEL	Auditory, Not Vocal	No	No	Yes	Yes	Yes	Yes	Auditory, Not Vocal
2 BROADCAST TRANSMISSION AND DIRECTIONAL RECEPTION	Yes	Yes	Yes	Yes	Yes	Yes	Yes	Yes
3 RAPID FADING (TRANSITORINESS)	Yes, Repeated	?	?	Yes	Yes, Repeated	Yes	Yes	Yes
4 INTERCHANGEABILITY	Limited	Limited	No	?	Yes	Largely, Yes	Yes	?
5 TOTAL FEEDBACK	Yes	?	No	Yes	Yes	Yes	Yes	Yes
6 SPECIALIZATION	Yes?	?	In Part	Yes?	Yes	Yes?	Yes	Yes
7 SEMANTICITY	No?	Yes	No	In Part ?	Yes	Yes?	Yes	No (In General)
8 ARBITRARINESS	?	No		If Semantic, Yes	Yes	In Part	Yes	
9 DISCRETENESS	Yes?	No	?	?	Yes	Largely No	Yes	In Part
10 DISPLACEMENT		Yes, Always	No	?	No	In Part	Yes, Often	
11 PRODUCTIVITY	No	Yes	No	?	No	Yes	Yes	Yes
12 TRADITIONAL TRANSMISSION	No?	Probably Not	No?	?	?	Yes	Yes	Yes
13 DUALITY OF PATTERNING	? (Trivial)	No		?	No	No	Yes	

EIGHT SYSTEMS OF COMMUNICATION possess in varying degrees the 13 design-features of language. Column A refers to members of the cricket family. Column H concerns only Western music since the time of Bach. A question mark means that it is doubtful or not known if the system has the particular feature. A blank space indicates that feature cannot be determined because another feature is lacking or is indefinite.

Fig. 3.2 Distribution of Design Features among Eight Systems of Communication. From "The Origin of Speech" by Charles F. Hockett, pp. 94–95. Copyright © 1960 by Scientific American, Inc. All rights reserved.

which sharp lines of demarcation can be drawn between human and nonhuman species. The issue has become particularly volatile in the last decade with the growing number of experiments in which non-human primates have been taught an array of visual "languages." The most popular format, used by Beatrice and R. Allen Gardner (e.g., 1969), Roger Fouts (e.g., 1973), Herbert Terrace (e.g., Terrace and Bever, 1976), and Francine Patterson (e.g., 1978), has been a system based on American Sign Language,[1] although Premack and Premack (e.g., 1972) experimented with plastic chips, and Duane Rumbaugh (e.g., 1977) has used a computer panel. It is currently a matter of lively debate as to whether it is appropriate to call the communicative skills of these primates "language," or at least "language-like" (see Harnad, 1976; Rumbaugh, 1977; Terrace, 1979).

LANGUAGE AS SOCIAL EXCHANGE

A second definitional stance has focused on the idea of language as social exchange (in Sapir's words, a "method of communicating ideas, emotions, and desires"). How important is an understanding of the communicative function to the study of human language? Linguistics texts commonly remind us that "the purpose of language is to communicate," but the notion of communication presented is often no more precise than it is in everyday language ("My parents and I don't communicate any more").

One reason for this lack of precision has been the ambiguous position that the very notion of "communication" has held within the discipline of linguistics. Is the social role of language a nicety one can study if one feels so inclined, or is it basic to the linguistics enterprise itself? Sociolinguists such as Hymes and Halliday argue that an understanding of the communicative context—who is speaker, who is being addressed, what is happening extralinguistically—is part of the linguist's job.

On the other hand, Chomsky takes a position on the status of "communication" in a linguistic theory reminiscent of his position on semantics. While he has no objection to such study, he does not see how a better understanding of semantics (or of communication) will further the construction of a theory of grammar. Throughout his formal writings, the notion of language as social exchange is conspicuously absent. Instead, Chomsky studies the abilities of an idealized speaker-listener with no limits on productive or perceptual performance and no relationship to the actual language community.

Many of his readers have concluded that Chomsky denies the importance of thinking about the communicative role of language. John Searle, who studies language as the performance of (social) speech acts, characterizes the commonly held perception of Chomsky's position as follows:

> There are two radically different conceptions of language . . .: one, Chomsky's, sees language as a self-contained formal system used more or less incidentally for communication. The other sees language as essentially a system of communication. [1974:30]

In his recent work, Chomsky has attempted to refute the assumption that his language theories preclude any serious consideration of social interchange. Thus, in his response to Searle's comments, Chomsky asserts:

> I have never suggested that "there is no interesting connection" between the structure of language and "its purpose," including communicative function, nor have I "arbitrarily assumed" that use and structure do not influence one another. . . . Surely there are significant connections between structure and function; this is not and has never been in doubt. [1975:56]

He further points out that some of the disagreement arises because of confusion over what the term *communication* means:

> It is hard to know just what people mean when they say that language is "essentially" an instrument of communication. If you press them a bit and ask them to be more precise, you will often find, for example, that under "communication" they include communication with oneself. Once you admit that, the notion of communication loses all content; the expression of thought becomes a kind of communication. These proposals seem to be either false, or quite empty, depending on the interpretation that is given, even with the best of will. [1979:88]

This point is illustrated with two examples:

> As a graduate student, I spent two years writing a lengthy manuscript, assuming throughout that it would never be published or read by anyone. . . . Once a year, along with many others, I write a letter to the Bureau of Internal Revenue explaining, with as much eloquence as I can muster, why I am not paying part of my income tax. I mean what

I say in explaining this. I do not, however, have the intention of communicating to the reader, or getting him to believe or do something, for the simple reason that I know perfectly well that the "reader" (probably some computer) couldn't care less. [1975:61]

These points are well taken, but are they as powerful as Chomsky believes? To begin with, he would never have been able to write his manuscript or write to the IRS if he had not first learned language from a community of communicating language users.[2] The claim that monologue or even unarticulated thought does not depend on a linguistically communicative base is as absurd as claiming that alphabetic writing has no strong dependence on spoken language. Moreover, especially in the case of writing to the IRS, it is difficult to believe that Chomsky has no notion of a reader in mind as he composes his letter. In writing letters, we adjust our salutation, level of formality, number of presuppositions, and so forth to the specific reader or class of readers we have in mind. The fact that he bothered to mail the letter would indicate that he believed at least some minimal communication was about to transpire.

Nevertheless, one point implicit in Chomsky's writing should be emphasized in any discussion of language as communication: not all linguistic exchanges between people are intended to *communicate* (whether information, feelings, or needs). We sometimes use language to hide our feelings or to conceal information, as when we engage in small talk to avoid expressing what we actually think. For this reason, it may be more appropriate to speak of language as a means of social interaction (which might include concealment) rather than *necessarily* as a means of communication.

LANGUAGE AS A FORMAL SYSTEM

A third definitional perspective is concerned with the formal (in the sense of "form" or "structure") properties of language (Sapir's "system of voluntarily produced symbols"). Chomsky has been the most forceful proponent of this position, which he clearly presents in *Syntactic Structures:*

I will consider a *language* to be a set (finite or infinite) of sentences, each finite in length and constructed out of a finite set of elements. All natural languages in their spoken or written form are languages in this sense, since each natural language has a finite number of phonemes (or letters in its alphabet) and each sentence is representable as a finite sequence of these phonemes (or letters), though there are infinitely many sentences.

And more important,

> The fundamental aim in the linguistic analysis of a language L is to separate the *grammatical* sequences which are the sentences of L from the *ungrammatical* sequences which are not sentences of L and to study the structure of the grammatical sequences. [1957:13]

One problem which arises in studying language as a formal system is deciding what human activity is properly "linguistic," and what is not. (For simplicity, we may speak of "linguistic" vs. "communicative but nonlinguistic" behavior, keeping in mind the caveats about the term *communication* expressed above.)

Clear delineation between linguistic and nonlinguistic communication becomes increasingly difficult as linguists become less arbitrary and more reflective in their establishment of guidelines for linguistic research. For example, it has traditionally been assumed that linguistic messages can be transmitted and received only through the auditory-vocal channel; gestural communication has typically been excluded as a means of transmitting linguistic information. The underlying assumption is that, while spoken language is divisible into discrete entities whose patternings can be characterized by identifiable rules, gestural (or, more broadly, kinesic) communication is not. (Writing is also excluded, but for other reasons.) Hence, Crystal writes:

> Despite its importance, the visual system of communication in humans does not have by any means the same structure or potential as the vocal —there is nothing really like grammar, for instance, and there is a very finite vocabulary of gestures indeed in any culture—and the linguist does not therefore call it language. [1971:241]

The a priori restriction of language to the vocal-auditory channel[3] has been challenged from two quarters in recent years: from those, such as Birdwhistell (e.g., 1970), who have argued that the paralinguistic behavior with which we supplement (or replace) speech is also "linguistic," and from linguists studying the structure of American Sign Language.

The issue here, as Crystal himself realizes, is not merely one of modality per se. Rather, it is whether a visual mode of expression *necessarily* lacks "the same structure or potential as the vocal," whether there is anything "really like grammar," or whether a visual vocabulary is inferior to that of a spoken language. Underlying Crystal's exclusion of visual communication from the domain of language is the assumption of a clear understanding of the requirements for vocabulary and grammar in spoken languages.

FORMAL CRITERIA FOR HUMAN LANGUAGE

Human language is commonly defined with respect to three structural properties: having a finite lexicon, having a finite set of collocation rules, and combining lexical items grammatically to yield a potentially infinite set of well-formed constructions (e.g., Chomsky, 1957). These criteria seem straightforward enough, and yet, when we try to apply these abstract criteria to languages which people in society use, we encounter a problem: What are the bounds on the conditions we have set? In general, we want our linguistic analysis to account for all the actual well-formed utterances which occur and also say something about those which don't (but might have) and about those which don't (and couldn't). But, in addition, if our linguistic description is to have any concrete relation to the language people are actually using, it will need to be more specific about the theoretical possibilities.

These concerns are reflected in the following quantitative questions about our initial definition of human language:

What is the minimum number of words a language can have? What is the maximum?

What is the minimum number of combination rules a language can have? The maximum?

Is there an actual limit to the potentially boundless number of generated sentences?

To these can be added questions which explicitly ground language in human social experience:

What is the semantic domain of reference of a language? (Are the things, events, or ideas, being talked about present at the time of discussion? Is the language used to refer to only a restricted area of experience, such as religion or sailing ships?)

What is the social context in which the language is used?

Our difficulty in answering the first three sets of questions makes our answers to the last two all the more important.

THE LEXICON

How many words does a human language need? Is there a minimum number necessary? It has been suggested that while bees can, in principle, transmit an unlimited number of messages (e.g., Langacker, 1973:19), their "lexicon" (the round dance, the wagging dance, and the speed and directionality of each—see von Frisch, 1953) is too restricted for their communicative system to be considered a language. We can pose the same question with respect to dialects or historical stages of any human language (insofar as dialects or historical periods are distinguished lexically). How many isoglosses does one need to bundle together before the whole package can be considered a dialect distinct from any other? Similarly, how many words must be different in a language at time A and at time B to decide that times A and B constitute significantly distinct "stages" in the history of that language?

The same problem arises with respect to sublanguages, that is, specialized forms of vocabulary and/or syntax used by restricted groups of people engaged in joint or parallel activity (sailors, astronauts, CB radio operators—see chapter 5). While one can write a dictionary (and, where appropriate, a grammar) of those items which are distinct from the language of the general community, how do we determine whether we are indeed dealing with a distinct language?

Or consider the issue of pidgin languages. Pidgins have a relatively small number of lexical items, relying instead on simple rules of syntax to produce enough terms for labeling the environment. In Neo-Melanesian (currently called Tok Pisin), we find

grass bilong head = "hair"
grass bilong face = "beard"

Yet the presence of a productive means of creating a large lexicon from a comparatively small number of primes cannot be a condition for excluding such a scheme from the domain of language. German, to cite the best-known example, uses a similar principle of lexical productivity, recombining old elements to form new words:

fern = "far," "distant"
Fernglas = "binoculars"
Fernsehen = "television"

The only obvious difference is that Neo-Melanesian retains an analytic structure,[4] while German is synthetic, combining all morphemes into a single word.

Implicit in all of these questions is the equally fundamental question: Is there a minimum number of *types* of words a language must have? (This leads directly into the question of semantic domain of reference.) For example, a human language must have at least some common names (or else participants in a conversation would have to share all the same experiences in order to understand one another). Must a language also have proper names, or can these be adequately replaced by definite descriptions? Empirically based discussions of universals in spoken language have included both proper nouns and common nouns as necessary elements in human language (e.g., Hockett, 1963). However, these universals have resulted from *post hoc* observations rather than deductions from more fundamental conceptions about human language.

Another consideration with respect to naming is the degree of abstraction of class terms. *Chair* and *furniture* are both class terms, yet the latter category includes more items than the former, and is commonly assumed to represent a higher level of abstraction. Should a definition of language place any constraints on the number of superordinate categories? While such a question is rarely posed today (we tend to assume that any language has "enough" superordinate terms to fill its needs), the issue was central to turn-of-the-century discussions of "primitive" languages. It was argued that primitive peoples had primitive mentalities, which were not capable of abstraction:

> The nearer the mentality of a given social group approaches the prelogical, the more do these image-concepts predominate. The language bears witness to this, for there is an almost total absence of generic terms to correspond with general ideas, and at the same time an extraordinary abundance of specific terms, those denoting persons and things of whom or which a clear or precise image occurs to the mind. [Lévy-Bruhl, 1926:170]

Should Lévy-Bruhl's claim of an "almost total absence of generic terms" ever be substantiated empirically, we would need to judge whether or not systems lacking a significant number of generic terms are indeed languages.

Still other questions arise in considering whether there is a minimum number of *types* of words a language must have. For instance, must a system have metaphors in order to be considered a language? Although practically no one has considered metaphor a sine qua non for human language when constructing formal definitions of language,[5] we nevertheless tend to express surprise when a nonhuman exhibits the ability to construct metaphors—for example, the accusation by Koko the gorilla that her trainer was a *dirty bad toilet* (Patterson, 1978) or Washoe's famous nonce form *water bird* for "duck."

How many words can a human language have? Probably no one knows all the words in Webster's Third International. Is this merely a "performance" limitation on human memory, or are there theoretical reasons why this is so? In terms of the questions concerning semantic domain and social context of use, can limitations on vocabulary be derived from practical limitations on the number of areas of inquiry and social contexts a human being normally encounters?

Within the formal purview of linguistic inquiry, the question of a maximum becomes important in determining the feasibility of using a particular mode of representation for encoding linguistic messages. Goody and Watt (1968), among others, have argued that pictographic or ideographic written representation would be impractical as a productive means of written language because such systems would require too many "lexical items" to record everything which needs to be represented. In fact, there is evidence in Sumerian,[6] Hittite (Gelb, 1952:115), and Chinese (ibid., p. 118) that as these forms of writing moved from pictographic to ideographic systems, the number of lexical items (and the variations with which particular items were produced[7]) measurably decreased. However, Goody and Watt's (1968) initial claim that written Chinese has so many lexical items as to render it learnable by only a handful of people, later had to be retracted (Goody, 1968), as there are indeed a large number of literate Chinese. Whether this number is "large enough" (and whether Romanization would make universal literacy possible among the Chinese) is an issue which brings hypothetical questions about lexical maxima into the concrete domain of language pedagogy and use.

GRAMMATICAL RULES

The same questions concerning the content of a language's lexicon also apply to its combination rules. If there is a minimum number of grammatical rules a communication system must have to be a language, does the dance of the bees qualify, since the only "combinations" are the recursive additions of more loops or wags in a given period of time? In the realm of human language, Pig Latin has only three rules of its own: remove the first sound of the word, place it at the end, and add [eɪ]. Is this still English with an added twist, or is it a new language? Precisely the same question can be asked of dialects, sublanguages, or historical stages which are differentiated from their nearest linguistic cousins by only a handful of combination rules.

Is there a minimum number or sets of *types* of grammatical rules a language must have? For example, must every language have definable word order conventions? The issue of whether American Sign Language has such word order constraints has led some linguists to question its linguistic status (e.g., Crystal and Craig, 1978). Further research might reveal that restrictions on word order—whatever they may be—are less stringent in signed languages than in speech. If so, we will need to rethink our understanding of what grammatical rules are necessary conditions for language, and whether word order is among them (see chapter 7).

What about a maximum of combination rules? Because there is no language for which linguists believe they have satisfactorily enunciated *all* the grammatical rules (though their numbers are presumed to be finite), it may seem premature to ask whether there is an upper limit on the number of rules a human language might have. Yet contexts exist in which such a question has been or might be raised. Lévy-Bruhl, in fact, took extreme grammatical complexity as a sign of primitiveness:

> We find that the languages spoken by peoples who are the least developed of any we know—Australian aborigines, Abipones, Andaman Islanders, Fuegians, etc.—exhibit a good deal of complexity. They are far less "simple" than English, though much more "primitive." [1926: 22]

Although his logic is suspect (one wonders, for example, how he would have interpreted the complexities of Sanskrit), his comments do suggest an interesting question. As mentioned above, for a language to be learnable, it must have class terms. If, by analogy, each of our sentences was governed by different grammatical rules (which were potentially productive, yet never yielded more than a single sentence each), the language would, likewise, be unlearnable.

In the discussion so far, I have assumed that there are grammatical rules that can, in principle, be identified and that will generate all (and only all) the well-formed formulas (i.e., sentences) in the language. There are two perspectives from which to challenge this assumption. The first requires us to rethink the generalizability of a single grammar across data, across speakers, or across time. The second is more radical still, for it questions the very "linguistic competence" that has become a byword in linguistic analysis. Let us examine these two perspectives in turn.

One of the most important issues confronting the linguist is how much of a language he can expect to account for by his rules. The Chomskian school, developing an economic metaphor, has implied that exceptions to grammatical rules should be very "costly," and therefore, rules should be constructed so as to yield the smallest number of exceptions possible. Like latter-day counterparts of Karl Verner, transformational grammarians have implied that actual language can be wholly generated by rules; our task is to find them.[8]

There have, however, been many schools of linguistics which have rejected the Chomskian cost-benefit analysis of language. Sapir, while acknowledging that grammar is "a universal trait of language," still recognized the existence of exceptions:

> Were a language ever completely "grammatical," it would be a perfect engine of conceptual expression. Unfortunately, or luckily, no language is tyrannically consistent. All grammars leak. [1921:39]

Jakobson (e.g., 1962) assumed that languages are necessarily always in a state of grammatical imbalance: through historical change, regularity is produced in one part of the linguistic system, which in turn produces irregularity in some other part. Vachek modifies this stance somewhat, arguing that

> the permanently imperfect balance, as we take it, is not exclusively due to the mechanical, "unwanted" consequences of a previous therapeutic change, but simply to the fact that the undeniably present integrating tendency (a tendency whose therapeutic nature is obvious) can never assert itself fully in the system of language. [1966:33]

In more recent American linguistics, studies of language variation (e.g., Labov et al. 1972; Sankoff, 1973) have helped to point up the differences between *regularity* and *homogeneity*. Predictable variation within individual's idiolects and across speakers may provide important clues about comparative social status or prospective historical change.

But what happens when we go a step further and question whether language use is indeed as regular as linguists tend to assume? When we list all the "regular" exceptions, make note of all the predictable variations—is there any language left that defies description? The question is a delicate one, since it immediately raises the specter of prescriptivism. As mentioned in Chapter 1, American linguistics in particular championed the description of languages in their own terms, not as they were presupposed to be. In contemporary times, this position has been echoed by linguists such as Labov (e.g., 1972a), who have argued that Black English is as much a "language" as standard white English in that both are governed by stateable, productive rules.

Our question, though, is different: What if there are no rules? Is grammar really the linguist's reconstruction of our internalized knowledge, or is it, at least in part, a norm imposed by teachers of English in literate societies? We are not suggesting that all—or even most—of grammar is imposed from the outside. Every language which has ever been observed has displayed strong degrees of regularity, and we know that nonlinguistically trained informants are quite capable of making a considerable number of linguistic judgments.[9]

In discussing Wayne O'Neill's political objections to imposing standard, middle-class English upon all speakers (and writers), John Simon (1979) points up an important distinction between prescriptivism and random use of language. O'Neill, apparently, is objecting to the former, yet his own writing is littered with constructions that seem to defy anyone's grammatical arsenal, regardless of its leniency. Grammatical rules should yield consistency; still, as Simon demonstrates, O'Neill sometimes has singular subjects agreeing with plural verbs ("the reader or beholder have"), misuses adverbs ("we do not understand at all well"), and does not identify referents of his pronouns. One might argue that such errors can be explained by performance factors. However, since the examples appeared in print in such documents as the *Harvard Educational Review*, one wonders where competence can be tapped if not in the writing which is presumably edited before publication. The point is not to condemn O'Neill's grammar, but to ask whether the average speaker of English indeed "knows" the rule governing agreement between the verb and a compound subject joined by *or*. We may dismiss this rule as an example of prescriptivism, but we are still faced with the problem of how to decide which verb to use in such instances—apparently many of us exhibit free variation. How much of language, therefore, evades grammatical "competence" rules? I shall return to this issue in chapter 6.

PRODUCTIVITY

Much of what I have already said about lexicon and grammatical rules is pertinent to the question of how few or how many combinations of elements in principle can be, or in practice are, generated by a human language user. The fewer the items and types of arrangements, the fewer the significantly different strings which can be produced. However, the number is still potentially infinite if recursion is admissible (e.g., "the very very very . . . very black cat"), but this type of recursion has little to do with actual language use.

Following the Chomskian model that distinguishes between competence and performance, it has been tempting to assume that, given the appropriate circumstances, all users of a language could make equally productive use of the theoretically available components of the language (the lexicon and combination rules). However, once this hypothesis is tested on actual language users, such a possibility becomes insignificant. To begin with, any measurement of *potential* generativity of communicative significance (such as excluding recursion of adjectives, repeated conjunctions) will reflect education, intelligence, personality, conditions of language acquisition, and mental and physical health—hardly traditional matters of linguistic theory. For example, deaf people who learn to speak "grammatically" typically restrict their sentences to a limited number of syntactic patterns. Such restrictions are not surprising, since these are the patterns on which the deaf have been repeatedly drilled. Similarly, shyness in speaking before others or discomfort in writing may be reflected in constrained oral or written syntax. The extent of the language user's "passive" language skills (e.g., oral comprehension or reading) remains uncertain so long as these skills remain untested; we cannot assume the presence of a skill for which we have no evidence.[10]

Moreover, there may be stable social conditions which affect the amount of productivity possible for an individual or even within a language. For example, the use of phatic communication—talking for the sake of keeping the speech channel open rather than for conveying information (Malinowski, 1923)—does not seem to be universally acceptable in language communities. P. Gardner has observed that the Paliyans of South India "communicate very little at all times and become almost silent by the age of 40. Verbal, communicative persons are regarded as abnormal and often as offensive" (1966:398; cited by Hymes, 1974:32). Another type of restricted productivity is found in pidgin languages (see chapter 5). Pidgins are used by a restricted segment of a population (typically adult males), in a restricted set of contexts (e.g., transacting business with individuals not sharing one's native language), and with very little if any stylistic variation (Labov, 1971). But does this last criterion actually distinguish between *any* pidgin and *any* full fledged language? Although it is difficult to know how to measure stylistic potential, we might hypothesize that language communities which do not prize verbal eloquence (such as the Paliyans) might be just as deficient in stylistic variation as a pidgin which has not moved toward creolization.

MODES OF LINGUISTIC REPRESENTATION

I have suggested that the traditional definition of human language with respect to lexicon, combination rules, and productivity is not sufficiently specific for actual linguistic analysis. I have also explained that the question of how many (or few) words, construction types, or novel utterances a language actually has depends mainly on its use by the language community or the individual user. However, most of my examples have been chosen from spoken language, the traditional domain of linguistic inquiry. I shall challenge this a priori restriction of language to spoken language in order to demonstrate that the criteria for speech—and the inadequacies of these criteria—are similarly applicable to written and sign language. Therefore, we need to drop our presuppositions about which modalities do or do not yield linguistic representations and begin once more with the primary relationship between first-order representation and experience. Only after delineating possible communicative representations can we decide which are and which are not linguistic. Figure 3.3 summarizes the distinctions to be developed in the subsequent discussion.

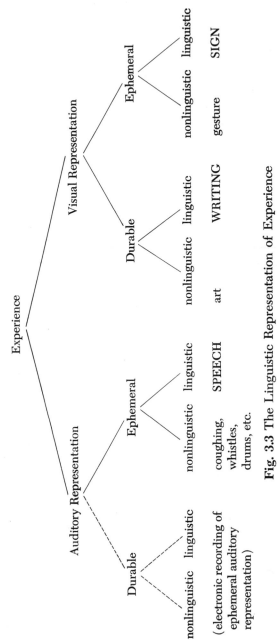

Fig. 3.3 The Linguistic Representation of Experience

The first distinction in Figure 3.3 is between representations which are *perceived aurally* and those which are *perceived visually*. Alternatively, these two types of representation might be described with respect to their production, but the characterization would have become more cumbersome (aurally perceived representations can be produced by the human voice, by computers, by drum beats). For convenience, we will speak of "visual representation" and "auditory representation," by which we will mean "visually perceived representation" and "aurally perceived representation."

A second level of distinction can be made with respect to the *durability* of each representation. In the case of auditory representation, the possibility of a durable representation is only as recent as the phonograph and the tape recorder. Paradigmatically, however, auditory representation is ephemeral (or "rapid fading"—Hockett, 1960). For the representation to be perceived, the percipient must be face-to-face with the message sender.

At first glance, this stipulation might appear to reflect an accidental feature of spoken language exchange—witness dictaphones, telephones, and television. In fact, it is the physical proximity of the interlocutors which defines, in normal situations, the conventions of spoken language and which distinguishes it from writing (durable visual representation). A comparison of written and spoken language will make these differences clear. In the process, I shall also illustrate two points made in Chapter 1: that spoken language is illuminated by contrast with other linguistic modalities; and that the factors that condition linguistic structures are not all formally linguistic.

The critical difference between spoken and written linguistic representation—and the difference from which a number of other defining characteristics can be derived—is the proximity between sender and receiver. Paradigmatically, speech is face-to-face communication, while writing is used when sender and receiver are separated by time, distance, or both (the word *paradigmatically* indicates the exclusion of derivative cases such as spoken language used in telephone calls or tape recordings, or written language used to pass messages during a lecture). If the intended receiver is not present when the message is formulated, the message must be given durable form—which, before the age of electronics, meant inscription on stone, use of a stylus on clay, or drawing with durable material like ink on paper or animal skin. Since the gathering of materials and the composition of a written message is generally more time consuming than speaking, the sender of a written message must determine whether the message is sufficiently important to warrant the extra effort.

On the other hand, the absence of an interlocutor involves several organizational considerations. The most obvious of these is that, since written language cannot exploit the suprasegmental or paralinguistic features which accompany spoken language (Chao, 1968:11), the written code must in some way compensate for the information which would be lost in a so-called transcription of spoken language. Punctuation and paragraphing are typical ways in which this information can be restructured, but so is the use of parallel sentence structure (for instance, to compensate for building excitement in one's voice) or use of foreign words (as the written equivalent of a "stuffy accent"). More important is the fact that writing, unlike speaking, lacks feedback from the receiver.

The vast majority of spoken, face-to-face communication (leaving aside rhetorical speech or ritualized conversation) is not planned. If the speaker says something which is not clear, he can get clues from his audience—a puzzled look; a query, "What do you mean?"—that can set him back on course, or help him clarify his remarks. Spoken language is "essentially a dialogue—a continuing give-and-take interaction" (Wrolstad, 1976:22), in which "possible confusions or misunderstandings can always be cleared up by question and answer" (Goody and Watt, 1968:51). But in writing, no such immediate restructuring is possible. The sender must anticipate the difficulties his receiver may have and engage in all the dialogue internally before committing his message to durable written form. As Socrates put it, "written words seem to talk to you as though they were intelligent, but if you ask them anything about what they say, from a desire to be instructed, they go on telling you just the same thing for ever" (*Phaedrus* 275d; cited by Goody and Watt, 1968:51). Consequently, the writer's presentation is generally more cautiously and reflectively formulated than that of the speaker. It is thus predictable that written language should tend to be stylistically more formal than spoken language.

The difference between speech and writing can be illustrated by analysis of the sentence "Kilroy was here." The first difference we notice is that "Kilroy was here," written by Mr. Kilroy, is not a construction that is possible in a similar context in speech. If we say, "Jones was in London," the utterance refers to an earlier occasion of

Jones's presence and not to a current trip to the British Isles. However, the *writing* of "Kilroy was here" could only be done at the time (in the present) that the event occurred.[11]

Here is a situation in which a single experiential event cannot be described the same way in spoken and written language. If we accept this observation, then we want to explore the difference. To do so, we need to look at the choice of the words *Kilroy, was,* and *here* somewhat more closely.

Kilroy, rather than *we* or *I,* must be used because there is no interlocutor present to know to whom the first person pronoun refers; in spoken language, such a problem of reference would not arise. We write *was* (not *is*) because we are formulating the difference in the speaker-auditor relation between writing and speech, that is, we are envisioning a future auditor who is not now present. The use of *here* is particularly interesting, since it not only distinguishes speech from writing but also distinguishes between different writing technologies. *Here* can be used when the writing is done on a quasi-permanent structure like a rock face or a subway car, but not on a piece of paper which can change location and thus give the future audience no indication as to where Mr. Kilroy had actually been.

This distinction between presence or absence of interlocutor is also critical in the comparison of writing and sign. Writing (a form of durable visible representation) is crafted with the basic premise that the percipient is *not* present when the message is formulated; ephemeral visual representation (which includes sign language) presupposes the interlocutor's presence.[12] The contrast between writing and sign cannot be made so neatly as that between writing and speech, for, although all three systems have some unique characteristics, writing and speech are far more similar than are writing and sign. (The justification for this statement will become clear in chapters 5, 6, and 7).

Speech (the linguistic aspect of ephemeral auditory representation), writing (the linguistic aspect of durable visual representation), and sign language (the linguistic aspect of ephemeral visual representation) will need to be examined to determine which of these aspects constitutes language. My remarks can, at best, be exploratory. Moreover, this book cannot give sufficient attention to nonlinguistic auditory and visual representation. The growing literature on nonspeech messages sent through the auditory channel (e.g., Sebeok and Umiker-Sebeok, 1976, on whistle systems) as well as the rich literature on art as representation (e.g., Gombrich, 1960, 1972; Goodman, 1976) will require careful study before definitive comments can be made about their linguistic counterparts.

Language function as a determiner of language structure is an appropriate subject with which to begin this inquiry. If human language is a means of social exchange, then the purpose of that exchange will have a strong influence on the particular form the linguistic representation takes; it may even affect the choice of modality. An understanding of the term *functional perspective* is therefore critical to our discussion of speech, writing, and sign as particular forms of linguistic representation.

IV

Functional Perspectives on Language

WHAT IS A FUNCTIONAL PERSPECTIVE?

THERE ARE at least five senses in which the word *functional* is commonly used by linguists. Our concern will only be with the last of these. However, so that we have some idea of what is *not* meant by this term in the present discussion, a quick review of all five meanings is in order.

FUNCTIONAL WITHIN A LINGUISTIC SYSTEM

Chomsky has remarked upon the multivocal uses of the term *functional* as it applies to linguistic analysis. Although noting that some linguists have looked upon functionalism as a doctrine which holds that "use of language influences its form" (1979:85), Chomsky himself uses the term rather differently in an early paper with George Miller (Miller and Chomsky, 1963). In a later summary he argues that

> there may be a "functional explanation" for the organization of language with grammatical transformations, which would be a well-designed system corresponding to a certain organization of short- and long-term memory, for example. [Chomsky, 1979:86]

Thus, for Chomsky, the term *functional* is roughly equivalent to "well-designed," and can be applied to the way in which elements of the grammar are put together.

This application of the notion of function to a whole linguistic system is reminiscent of one of the ways in which members of the Prague School understood the idea of function. An example is Martinet's work on historical phonology (e.g., 1952, 1955). Using such notions as the principle of least effort, functional load, and push chains and

93

drag chains, Martinet has argued that once phonological systems fall out of "balance" (e.g., equal number of voiced and voiceless stops, even distribution of stops and fricatives), they "strive" to regain a state of equilibrium. The subsequent discussion of causes of language change ("The Problem of Diversity," below) will return to the Prague School's systemic approach to language function.

THE SENTENTIAL CONTEXT

Another use of the term *functional*—and again one which interested the Prague School—derives from an analysis of individual sentences. Within the Prague School, this approach was initially developed by Vilém Mathesius (e.g., 1964) under the name Functional Sentence Perspective, or FSP, which considers how different languages (or synonymous sentences within a single language) express the same real-world experience through differential distribution of old and new information within the sentence. An example of FSP is the use of optional word order changes in an inflected language such as German or Czech to indicate what constitutes old and what constitutes new information in a sentence. Renewed interest in FSP is reflected in the work of Henry Kučera (e.g., Kučera and Cowper, 1976) and Susumo Kuno (e.g., 1972).

The term *functional* can be applied in other ways at the sentential level of analysis. Fillmore (1968b) speaks of his cases (Agent, Object, Instrument, Locative, etc.) as playing "roles" in the sentences in which they appear, and Dik (1978) intends the term *functional* to label semantic, syntactic, and pragmatic functions as they relate to the formation and utterance of a sentence.

DISCOURSE

It is in the domain of discourse that the idea of function is probably most familiar to linguists. In the discourse interpretation of function, we identify factors within the production and reception of a linguistic message and indicate which role those factors might serve in the act of communication.

By now it is customary to begin any discussion of language function qua discourse with the name Karl Bühler. This Austrian psychologist identified three distinct functions a language might serve, associating each with a factor in the discourse (1934):

emotive: associated with the first person of the addresser
conative: associated with the second person of the addressee
referential: associated with the "third person" of the person or thing
             spoken of

Jakobson (1960) expanded this list to six pairs of factors and functions ("factors" are indicated in capital letters, "functions" in lower case):

CONTEXT
Referential

ADDRESSER   MESSAGE   ADDRESSEE
Emotive   Poetic   Conative

CONTACT
Phatic

CODE
Metalingual

Variations on the discursive theme appear in the work of Halliday (1970, 1973) and Hymes (1974).

The domain of these discussions of language function relating to discourse is the uttering of a message by an addresser to a receiver within some context. Of prime interest, especially in the work of Hymes, is how one determines (or predicts) which of these functions will dominate in a given conversation. Note, however, that these are not questions about how the language system got to be the way it is, but rather, *given* the language system, how it is *used* on a given occasion.

LANGUAGE ACQUISITION

A very different use of the term *functional* has emerged in the literature on language acquisition. The relevant domain here is that of semantic development: Which factors influence the order in which young children learn new words? Eve Clark (1973) has argued that semantic complexity of words, along with perceptual salience of the objects or properties to which these words refer, are the major factors influencing semantic acquisition. Katherine Nelson (1973) has taken a different stance, suggesting that the use of the objects being referred to is the all-important factor in early semantic development. Children first learn names for things that change (location, directionality), not for static things which are merely easy to perceive (color, shape). Other linguists (e.g., Greenfield and Smith, 1976; Bloom and Lahey, 1977) have assumed positions somewhere in between.

In discussions of function within the contemporary language acquisition literature, the major variables are the child and the object whose name must be learned. What is often missing is any notion of *social* function (e.g., the child early on learning the word *more* to get a bigger amount of something). The social and pragmatic origins of such high frequency words as *more* in the young child's lexicon are sometimes acknowledged (e.g., Brown, 1973). However, until fairly recently, work in language acquisition has tended to retain a structuralist bent.[1]

SOCIAL LINGUISTICS

Finally, there is the notion of function with which we will be concerned in this book: that of language being shaped by the social tasks for which speakers use it. The idea of form following function will need to be qualified with many caveats. Chief among them is the realization that a social explanation of linguistic shape can only be applied to a rather circumscribed set of linguistic phenomena. Subsequent sections of this chapter will investigate the kinds of linguistic phenomena which might belong to this set. First, though, the investigation of a functional perspective must be prefaced by considering linguistic diversity. Unless there are alternative shapes languages can choose from, there is no "stuff" to which one or another functional perspective can be applied.

THE PROBLEM OF DIVERSITY

Why are there so many different languages in the world, and why do they keep changing their shapes? These two simple questions lead us rather quickly into territory which is at once provocative and intellectually treacherous. Asking *which* shapes language assumes leads us to construct linguistic models whose appropriateness we can at least test with linguistic data. Asking *why* those shapes arise requires us to introduce a largely new set of variables, many of which go well beyond the linguistic data themselves. As David Hume established, causation of any sort is difficult (he would have said impossible) to prove; and causation in language is every bit as difficult to establish as causation in, say, history or economics.

Why, then, should we venture into a domain fraught with such difficulty? The answer lies in our reasons for thinking about language in the first place. I have argued that human language can be both a source of and a solution for human interpersonal problems. This does not necessarily imply that language users are aware of what they are doing with their language (or what their language is doing to them). Yet it does suggest, at least in the therapeutic aspects of language, that some linguistic processes serve identifiable ends. To recognize such purposiveness is not to imply that the linguistic process was necessary or that an alternative process could not have done the job as well. Languages often hobble along with inadequacies, such as the lack of a common gender pronoun in English to be used in place of *he or she*. Languages are also renowned for arriving at alternative solutions to the same problem. The word *television* is conveniently abbreviated to *TV* in the United States, but to *telly* in Britain. What is relevant is that a generally accepted common gender pronoun would find a ready niche in contemporary American English and that both the English and the Americans have worked out solutions for abbreviating the name of an extremely common item in their experience.

We shall be looking at linguistic diversity as the result of language changes; some of the purposes of these changes can be identified (or at least conjectured), others cannot. The discussions of spoken (chapter 5), written (chapter 6), and signed (chapter 7) systems examine in some detail the hypothesis that linguistic properties (relationships between *signifié* and *signifiant*, choice of modality, range of vocabulary or grammar) may be intimately associated with concomitant non-linguistic events. However, to understand why such arguments have received little attention in contemporary linguistic discussions, we need to look more closely at the notion of language as purposeful activity. Let us begin by way of an analogy.

BOAS AND THE ARMENIANS

In his intellectual biography of Franz Boas, Melville Herskovits describes a lawsuit in which Boas became involved:

In 1923, a suit was instituted in the courts of a western state where Orientals were not permitted to own real estate, asserting that Armenians were not Caucasoid, and therefore were not eligible to hold property. Much of the argument turned on the fact that the characteristic "rounded" head of these people, which gave a high breadth to length . . . proved their Mongoloid racial affiliation. [1953:28]

Characteristically, Boas approached the problem with the same premise on which he based his work with American Indian societies and languages: that genetic differences are not to be confused with cultural or culturally induced differences. In the Armenian case, he distinguished between two groups of Armenians: those born in the United States and those who had emigrated from Europe. He measured the head size of members of each group and found a marked discrepancy, the explanation of which caused the case to be dismissed:

> Armenians who had migrated to the United States had the characteristic lack of the occipital protrusion at the back of the head that marked those born in this country, while those native to the United States exhibited this characteristic. [ibid.]

That is, immigrants had more rounded heads than American-born Armenians. This occurred because

> in Armenia, children are placed in a cradle-board, on which, after the manner of much of Eastern Europe, they lie on their backs, tightly swaddled. Being unable to toss about, the weight of the head suppresses the development of the occiput; but this genetic trait at once asserts itself in Armenians of American birth who are permitted the free movement that allows unrestricted development of the tender bony structure of the head. [ibid.]

The issue at the heart of this case has plagued us for a long time: How many of our human characteristics—both physical and mental—are biologically inherent, and how many are the result of interaction with the environment? The problem appears in many guises, the most common of which are "nature vs. nurture" or "heredity vs. environment." Which side of the argument one advocates may have serious implications for theory and practice within the social sciences. Arguments for and against integration, justification or rejection of social welfare programs, as well as theories of education and of human language—all have been influenced by presuppositions about human malleability after birth.[2]

In linguistics, the question of malleability proves crucial to the study of language function. If we believe, as does Chomsky,[3] that a significant portion of human language is innate, then we immediately restrict the range of variation which is possible within human language. By restricting the range of innateness to such metalinguistic considerations as the ability to learn language or the ability to determine the grammaticality of a simple utterance, we have not lost any of the flexibility relevant to the discussion of language varying according to its social purpose. Once we enter the realm of what Chomsky called "substantive universals" (1965), we have, in principle, added constraints to the actual language that speakers might produce.

There is a second way of looking at the question of what is inherent in human language qua human language and what is malleable. If there are parts of human language which are not innate, how do they come into being—in the individual, or in the linguistic community? This question leads to an even more difficult one: What kinds of change in language are possible?

CAUSES OF LANGUAGE CHANGE

Changes in language can happen for a host of reasons, not all of which are identifiable, and not all of which are interesting. No one really knows, for instance, why the First Germanic Consonant Shift came about, leaving us with English *father* in place of Latin *pater,* or Germanic *broþar* instead of Latin *frater.* (A number of hypotheses have been proposed over the years, but they have been rejected for lack of evidence. One such proposal suggested that the cold climate of northern Europe led to a greater huffing and puffing when speaking, causing stops to become fricatives. Another version claimed that the switch from stops to fricatives reflected the aggressive spirit of the Germanic people.) On the other hand, there are many changes whose origins we can easily document. We do know why English added the word *sputnik* to its general lexicon. However, the conditions are sufficiently straightforward as to arouse but little linguistic interest. And, of course, there are those changes which fall somewhere between these two extremes.

What *types* of changes can languages undergo? The literature on the question is rich and varied,[4] but several concerns seem to stand out. Does the change originate within the language itself, or is its source external, coming either from another language, or from social factors affecting the members of the speech community in question?

A second query deals with linguistic effects rather than causes: Does the change make for a more or less "unified" system than the prior state of affairs yielded? (Obviously, our notion of "unified" depends very much on the particular model of grammar we subscribe to.) Another sort of "effect" which change can bring about concerns the speech community: its power of social identification and its power of expression.

Figure 4.1 summarizes the sources—and outcomes—of change which human language may undergo. Obviously, many combinations of variables are possible. Changes initiating within a given language may yield increased balance or generality within some portion of the grammar (for example, English noun plurals). Alternatively, as Jakobson observed (1962), increased simplification in one portion of a grammar may yield imbalance elsewhere, as in the loss of nasals in some Salishan languages (see Ferguson, 1963). Change originating outside a language typically adds complexity to a grammar (often enforced by prescriptivism), though increasing generality may also result. Simplification occurs in the addition to English of a phonemic distinction between /š/ and /ž/, when /ž/ was borrowed from French. The addition of phonemic /ž/ made the voiced/voiceless distinction a general property of English obstruents. A case of external influence causing increased complexity is seen in the borrowing of certain noun + adjective phrases from French (e.g., *notary public*). These phrases complicate English syntax, since the normal ordering of substantives and modifiers in English is adjective + noun.

In considering outcomes of linguistic change vis-à-vis the speech community, we must introduce a distinction which will prove important in our attempts to understand what it means for a linguistic structure (or a linguistic change) to be functional (see "Complications," below). At the least, we need to ask whether the linguistic construction *itself* is significant in interpersonal linguistic interaction, or whether *social value* is being attached to a fortuitously selected linguistic feature. The latter category has attracted much attention in the recent sociolinguistic literature by Labov and his colleagues (see Labov, 1972b). Several of the examples of both categories of change which are presented in figure 4.1 will be discussed in subsequent chapters.

Without underestimating the importance of language as a marker of social or economic identification (or aspiration), we must not forget

| | Outcome for Linguistic System | | Outcome for Speech Community | |
	Balance/Generality	Imbalance/Lack of Generality	Power of Social Identification	Power of Expression
language internal	e.g., elimination of multiple ways of forming noun plurals in English (use of -s replaces use of -s, -r, or -en)	e.g., merger of nasal with nonnasal consonants in the Salishan languages, creating a violation of the phonological universal that all languages have at least one nasal consonant (see Ferguson, 1963)	e.g., centralization of diphthongs on Martha's Vineyard as a means of identification with the island (see chapter 5)	e.g., progressive loss of iconicity as use of sign language increases (see chapter 7)
language external	e.g., borrowing of phonemic distinction between /š/ and /ž/ from French into English	e.g., borrowing of noun + adjective phrase from French (e.g., *notary public*) in contrast with the adjective + noun order of English	e.g., use of French rather than Anglicized pronunciation of such borrowed words as *crouton* or *Paris* as a status marker	e.g., social conditions fostering growth of specialized vocabulary or syntax (see chapter 5)

Locus of Change

Fig. 4.1 Typology of Linguistic Change

that the particular linguistic construct which bears social prestige is fortuitous[5] and that in most (if not all) instances the use of language as a social marker is itself fortuitous. Patterns of dress, or, as a colleague once quipped, the sporting of handlebar mustaches, might equally well serve to alert the general public to the individual's social intent.

The other type of communal variable, power of expression, is most interesting here because it involves a "necessary" relationship between the linguistic and the social variables initially identified in chapter 1 (figure 1.1). Such a relationship is described as "necessary" not because every language used in a specified social context will *invariably* undergo change of the sort noted, but rather because the change noted is a *logical outcome* of the social conditions specified. If a change does occur, this is the one we predict. Thus, increased use of sign language *logically* leads to a reduction in iconicity (see chapter 7). This does not mean that all sign languages whose use increases become less iconic (prescriptive forces might prevent this). But it does mean that, empirically, we do find a correlation between use and arbitrariness— and that we would be surprised to find either iconicity increasing with use or decreasing with lack of use.

COMPLICATIONS: CLASSIFICATION AND METHODOLOGY

After wending our way through an assortment of types of language change, let us take a serious look at the hypothesis that the shape language assumes may result from nonlinguistic needs of language users. We have reached this point by eliminating whole classes of language change for which we make no functionalist claims, leaving us a more tractable (and plausible) set of linguistic phenomena in terms of which to examine the hypothesis.

WHEN IS A CHANGE SOCIALLY MOTIVATED?

How do we decide which specific linguistic changes might be functionally motivated? We might consider language change according to different linguistic levels (phonology, morphology and syntax, and semantics). While some levels of grammar never admit of functional analysis of the sort we are interested in, others might be very likely domains for functional explanation.

Consider structures (and the changes which created them) on the phonological level. The likelihood of finding functional explanations here is slight—there is nothing inherently "aggressive" about Germanic fricatives, any more than there is anything inherently "indecisive" about languages which distribute equal stress on all syllables. Such associations are after-the-fact notions which, under culturally appropriate circumstances, one might try "reading into" the respective phonologies, but the objective status of such "explanations" is indeed questionable.[6]

On the other hand, the domain of semantics seems particularly ripe for functional explanations. We add new words—or new meanings to old words—as the experiences we need to talk about expand. Twenty years ago, *tripping* was something one could do to a mechanical device ("Please stop tripping all those switches"), while today it is something one might do while with friends at a party. *Meltdown* is no longer only a verb plus a locative, describing what we do with a stick of butter or a ton of iron ore. Now it can also be a noun signifying the process whereby uranium pellets in a nuclear reactor liquefy, causing nuclear havoc ("There was a serious chance of meltdown at the Three Mile Island Nuclear Reactor"). Because language is conventional, it is still up to a linguistic community to determine the meaning of a particular word or phrase. In that sense, meaning is not inherent in a word or phrase. There are, however, precedents within the language which severely restrict the range of likely candidates. *Meltdown* is a logical name for what could potentially happen in a nuclear reactor, while the terms *apple pie* or *Old Black Joe* would not be.

The fact that convention enters into the change process in semantics should not lead us to question the functional base of many semantic constructs. Contrast this circumscribed conventionality in semantics with the open-ended choice speakers have in selecting phonological factors with which to imbue social import. The aspiration to middle-class status might be indicated just as simply by using (or not using) postvocalic /r/, by devoicing final consonants, or by raising one's left eyebrow before initiating a conversation.

The remaining domain to examine is that of morphology and syntax. Like the search for functional explanation in semantics, functional inquiry in syntax has appeared promising to many, and yet, like arguments in phonology, is has borne little fruit. The writings of Karl

Vossler and later of André Martinet exemplify this tradition—and its failures.

Vossler had hoped to demonstrate that grammatical changes between Classical Latin and Vulgar (particularly later Vulgar) Latin reflected changes in the cognitive and cultural style of the population. The Classical Latin passive construction, so he argues, vanished from Vulgar Latin because of a change in the conceptions of personal feeling and personal agency. Speakers began

> to forsake the naïve egocentrism, individualism, and anthropomorphism of the classics. . . . When we say the earth is irradiated by the sun and express this in such a way [that] the earth appears as the bearer of a passive voice of irradiate, we are attributing human characteristics to her. For as a matter of fact she neither suffers nor enjoys the kiss of Helios. . . . Natural events are more and more sharply distinguished from human acts, personal from impersonal. A new *Weltanschauung*, one that is in the main dualistic, is coming into being. [1932:55–56]

Vossler does concede that the link between cognitive, and grammatical shift is not strictly causal:

> The grammatical circumstances that occasioned the downfall of the passive in Vulgar Latin have no immediate connection with the *Weltanschauung*, it is true. [ibid., p.56]

nonetheless,

> mediately, that is, as far as the psychological concomitants are concerned, they have as much to do with it as the tail coat, the bouquet and the patent leather shoes of a loving suitor have to do with his proposal of marriage, which he places at the feet of his beloved according to the customary tradition of his country. [ibid., pp.56–57]

Vossler draws upon similar armchair social anthropology to explain the loss of the overtly marked future tense from Classical Latin:

> The whole temporal conception of the future was weak and it broke down. There is hardly a language in which it is regularly used by the common people. . . . For the ordinary man's attitude towards things is always that of willing, wishing, hoping and fearing rather than that of imagination, thought or knowledge. [ibid., p.61]

In the case of future tense markers, Vossler does hint that cognitive changes hastened the decline of the grammatical forms:

> After the meaning of the future in Vulgar Latin had been deflected into the more practical and emotional direction of willing, wishing, demand-

ing, fearing, etc., the old forms of inflexion could be dispensed with. [ibid., p.62]

The Romance languages later replaced the old future with "several other fresher and stronger means of expressing the new meaning" (ibid.).

A more recent proponent of a similar causal line of thinking is Martinet, whose general thesis is that

> an increasing complexity of social relations will be accompanied by an increasing complexity of syntax. Division of labor will involve the appearance of new forms of human and material relations which will determine the appearance, in language, of new functions. [1962:137]

Martinet attempts to illustrate his bold hypothesis with two examples. First, he argues that the evolution of Indo-European from an ergative to a nominative-accusative system[7] resulted from advances in the cultural and economic level of the Indo-European people (1962:72; 1958). Similarly, Martinet claims that the Latin case system was superseded in modern Romance languages by prepositional constructions because the restricted case system was "no longer capable of taking care of the expression of all the relations needed in Roman society" (1962:138).

Martinet's theses, like Vossler's, are intriguing. There is even the possibility that they are correct. Unfortunately, there seems to be no way of knowing. Without evidence (and it is unclear what such evidence might look like), they have no more credibility than a thesis that English makes heavy use of truncated passives ("The window was broken") because Anglo-Saxon peoples avoid taking responsibility —another logically possible thesis, but not one with much tangible support.

This survey of functional arguments on the phonological, semantic, and grammatical levels leaves us having learned very little. On the face of things, we would need to conclude that our commonsensical intuitions about inappropriateness of functional explanations in phonology (and appropriateness in semantics) are correct, and that the domain of grammar is not much different from that of phonology. But is the analysis accurate? Or perhaps, asking the question differently, will we find that the functionalist hypothesis is indeed supported?

An alternative approach is to ask whether some principle (or principles) of organization other than linguistic level might be associated with functional factors. Consider a principle such as redundancy. When applied to the use of sounds, redundancy might take the form of reduplication. Phonological reduplication appears in a variety of contexts; in many languages, it is a way of deriving new grammatical forms. Indo-European languages sometimes formed perfective verbs through reduplication, as in the Latin

tango = "I touch"
tetegi = "I touched"

In Tagalog, reduplication is used to indicate an agent:

['su:lat]   = "a writing"
[su:-'su:lat] = "one who will write"
['ga:mit]   = "thing of use"
[ga:-'ga:mit] = "one who will use"

[see Bloomfield, 1933:218]

Reduplication is also commonly used in talking to children (the reduction of *stomach* to *tum-tum*), and children themselves frequently reduplicate syllables they are learning to pronounce. Hence, *daddy* becomes *dada*, and *water* might become *wawa*.

In the case of the Indo-European perfective or the Tagalog agentive, there is no obvious reason why reduplication (rather than some other grammatical device) bears the syntactic burden of forming a new grammatical category. However, in language used with and by children, a functional explanation *is* plausible. We know that adults speaking to children simplify their speech in a number of predictable ways: speaking slowly, reducing the range of normal vocabulary, exaggerating intonation contours.[8] We also have good reason to believe that for children just developing a phonological repertoire, reduplicated sequences (e.g., *papa*) are simpler to produce than sequences with dissimilar consonants and vowels (e.g., *pagu*).[9] Lexical redundancy at the grammatical level is another example of redundancy in language. Its use in pidgin languages will be studied in chapter 5 in an attempt to demonstrate a functional basis for this linguistic principle of organization.

In addition to looking at organizational principles (rather than at linguistic levels) as a way of probing the functionalist hypothesis, we might also ask which *domains* of language would be most likely to yield evidence for functionalist arguments. Vossler and Martinet ventured functionalist hypotheses on the basis of the language of adult speech communities. In each instance, it is difficult even to determine what might constitute supporting evidence for a functional hypothesis. On the other hand, when we look at examples of children learning to talk, adults talking to children, or pidgin languages, prospects for productive exploration are far more promising. It seems likely, therefore, that while linguistic constructions which are part of everyday speech may indeed have functional origins, it may be easier to pinpoint such origins by looking at language use which does *not* involve the entire speech community.

We must consider the possibility that a feature of language which was first introduced under functional circumstances may no longer be functionally motivated. Napoleon is purported to have introduced buttons on the ends of coat sleeves to stop his soldiers from wiping their noses on their sleeves. Today's haberdashers have no such motives as they continue the tradition. Within the linguistic domain, the word *penknife* was a logical addition to our vocabulary when writing was still done with quills which needed to be sharpened, and we began speaking of the sun rising and setting at a time when, empirically, we believed such to be the case. Today, quills are no longer used as writing instruments, and our views on astronomy have changed; our locutions have not.

Another reason for placing much of our emphasis on language use which either is not fully developed or is restricted to small segments of a language community is strictly methodological: it is often easier to understand a phenomenon piecemeal than in its entirety. By learning how to make functional arguments for limited uses of language, we discover how to apply our findings to the speech community at large.

Are All Informants Equally Informative?

Once we have identified the domain of language we wish to subject to a functional analysis, how do we collect data? More specifically, What sorts of informants do we need? How many? With what specific qualifications? Examined in which particular circumstances?

The study of language requires the use of a selective sampling of the data. Only a fraction of the potential utterances in a language have actually been uttered, so it is fruitless to attempt to amass a "complete" corpus. Moreover, by the time one managed to poll roughly 200 million speakers of English in the United States alone, one could not be said to be studying the "same" language in the first and the last interviews.

But how do we select *which* informants to study? An answer to this question is apt to be laden with presuppositions about how much of language is "communal" in a speech community, and how much of human linguistic abilities are biologically "built in" (like bookshelves or a fireplace?) at birth. Such presuppositions may themselves be products of social circumstances which appear, at first glance, completely un-related to theories of linguistic abilities.

In chapter 1, the notions of *langue* (Saussure) and *competence* (Chomsky) were introduced. While Saussure's *langue* refers to the linguistic knowledge of an entire speech community (which is mani-fested, through *parole*, to greater or lesser degrees in different indi-viduals), Chomsky's *competence* resides in each member of the lin-guistic group. In both instances, it is assumed that there is a body of linguistic conventions that characterize the language community. In Chomsky's case, this body of information is taken to reside equally in all language users (Saussure is ambiguous on this point). Thus is born Chomsky's "ideal speaker-listener": "Linguistic theory is concerned primarily with an ideal speaker-listener, in a completely homogeneous speech-community, who knows its language perfectly" (1965:3). Chom-sky is well aware that in reality, speech communities are not homo-geneous and that no single individual has perfect linguistic knowledge (1979:55). In practice, though, linguistic inquiry, especially in the United States, has increasingly proceeded as if his idealization held true. There has been a further tendency to assume that if such "com-plete" linguistic data can be found in a single individual, linguistic data need not be elicited in the context in which that language would spontaneously be used. Perfect linguistic knowledge evidenced while participating in a syntax seminar should therefore be no different from that same perfect knowledge displayed in talking to one's in-laws or in shooting pool.

These assumptions of decontextualization and equality among lan-guage users have dominated much of the structuralist and generativist traditions. How did these assumptions arise? Have presuppositions about data collection influenced linguists' attitudes toward the efficacy of searching for functional explanations of linguistic patterns?

The Triumph of Structuralism

In light of the predominant structural biases of American linguists for over forty years (roughly, from 1930 to 1970), the early twentieth-century emphasis on studying language within the context of its use seems particularly refreshing. Franz Boas, pioneering the study of both anthropology and linguistics in America, repeatedly argued for the necessity of studying language naturalistically in order to get the most accurate measure possible of the range of constructions used and the meanings attributed to them. In the words of Robert Lowie, "Boas must be understood, first of all, as a fieldworker" (1937:131). Not surprisingly, Boas was incensed at Bronislaw Malinowski's implication that the doctrine of functionalism constituted a British invention. In a review of Malinowski's *Crime and Custom in Savage Society,* Boas writes: "Dr. Malinowski has a strange impression of what modern anthropology is. He accuses modern anthropologists of a complete disregard of the actualities of life." To the contrary, Boas boasts, Malinowski "will find that the general approach of the modern American anthropologists is quite similar to his own" (cited by Herskovitz, 1953: 67). Were Malinowski's impressions wholly unfounded? Possibly not. The Boasian mystique of the importance of fieldwork seems based, at least partly, in myth. Leslie White (1963) has calculated that of the forty-odd years Boas worked as an ethnographer, only thirty-three and a half months were spent in the field. Where did Boas gather his materials? Largely in major cities. For instance, he writes:

> I had the good fortune to fall in with a party of Eskimo from Port Clarence, Alaska, who stopped in Chicago [where Boas was engaged at the World's Fair] on their way to Washington. [1894:205]

> The following notes on the Tlingit language were obtained from Mr. Louis Shotridge, who spent about six weeks in New York during the winter of 1914–15 [1917:7]

Had Boas (or subsequently, his students) even wished to gather information on indigenous languages from the proverbial Indian seated before his tepee, opportunities diminished as the century wore on. Surviving tribes were relocated on reservations, where traditional activities—and linguistic contexts—no longer were found. Moreover, a number of Indians gravitated to the cities, where job prospects were brighter. Many of these strangers to modernization made their way to the YMCAs. In fact, for several decades, especially in New York, linguistics graduate students searching for an informant frequented YMCAs to make their initial contacts. This phenomenon is recent enough that just ten years ago, a student from Columbia offered to introduce me at the next YMCA open house if I would only agree to work on the language of one of the YMCA regulars.

The results of this decontextualization were predictable. Sociolinguists have shown that individuals' perceptions of what they might say in a given circumstance often bear little resemblance to the language they would actually use spontaneously. A Yana Indian sitting in Horn and Hardart could not be expected to tell the linguist how he would speak at a hunting ritual, or what differences there are between, say, male and female language. He could, however, give enough samples of language to enable the linguist to deduce the phonemic inventory, the basic morphology, some grammatical rules, and some of the lexicon of the language. In the study of indigenous languages, form took precedence over function as a matter of necessity. In ensuing years, however, it might be argued that necessity gave way to virtue; linguists came to view structure as the only aspect of language worth examining. At the turn of the century, Saussure had dismissed the analysis of language use (*parole*) as uninteresting. In striking parallel, decades later, Chomsky argued for the study of linguistic competence. Linguistic performance—that is, language as actually used in real social contexts—was rejected as lying beyond the bounds of proper linguistic theory.

Equality among Language Users

The removal of the native informant from his social milieu contributed to a dramatic shift from the study of structure within the context of situation (Malinowski, 1923) to the study of structure alone. In addition, changes in the demographic status of American Indians resulted in the linguist's increasing reliance upon a single informant for data on a particular language.

In the early years, the use of a single informant was judged to be an unfortunate methodological necessity. The classical case in the literature is Mary Haas's study of Tunica, a language once spoken in the area of what is now Louisiana (1940). By the early 1930s, when Haas began her study, there was only one individual, Sesostrie Youchigant, who spoke Tunica "with any degree of fluency" (ibid., p.9). (Youchigant spoke mainly Louisiana French and English.) No other speakers had sufficient knowledge of the language to converse with him. In fact, Youchigant had had "no occasion to converse in Tunica since the death of his mother in 1915, and even before her death, he preferred to speak French to her" (ibid., p.10). Using data from Youchigant, Haas produced a grammar, a dictionary, and a set of texts in Tunica, despite the fact that at the time the data were collected Tunica "serv[ed] no sociological function whatsoever" (ibid.). Even she admits that

> it is to be assumed that what Youchigant recalls of Tunica is at best a mere remnant of what the language must have been when many speakers used it as the only means of communication. Indeed, I often had the feeling that the Tunica grooves in Youchigant's memory might be compared to the grooves in a phonograph record; for he could repeat what he had heard but was unable to make up new expressions of his own accord. [ibid.]

This tradition of relying on one informant—with all its inherent dangers—has persisted in contemporary grammatical analysis. Underlying Chomsky's hypostatized ideal speaker-listener is the belief in the inherent linguistic equality of all language users. Consequently, any speaker of language X should be as good an informant as any other, *whether or not* additional informants are available.[10]

The issue of linguistic equality in America is complex because it tends to be confused with the idea of sameness. The original Boasian tradition maintained the equality of all linguistic variants, while the exigencies of the ethnographic situation made it convenient to equate "equality" with "homogeneity."

The same confusion arising from the study of American Indian languages has its parallel among Indo-European populations (and their languages). On the one hand, the United States has insisted that diversity is to be tolerated, while in actuality, conformity is typically rewarded. The preponderance of ethnic and linguistic diversity in this country of immigrants caused some Americans to question whether all immigrants (and all of their languages) were to be considered equal in sophistication and worthy of recognition. The tacit but powerful assumption by the majority of the country that equality lies in sameness has been evident in the strong governmental and social pressure to abandon native languages in favor of English. Government-sponsored bilingual education programs are a very recent phenomenon (it was generally assumed that bilingualism lowered a child's intellectual abilities). Even dialectal variation broadcast on radio and television was long seen as detrimental to economic and social progress.

This governmental and attitudinal stance against linguistic diversity was directly at odds with the Boasian insistence on equality of speakers and languages. Despite the efforts of the government and the education system to eliminate linguistic diversity, the linguistics profession actively recorded dialect diversity in America. The best known of the American dialect studies, the Linguistic Atlas of New England (1939–1943), was directed by Hans Kurath. On a more popular level, Henry Lee Smith used his expertise in dialectology as host of a radio program entitled "Where Are You From?" His job was to identify the place of residence of people whom he interviewed. The Providence *Evening Bulletin* writes:

> As a way of keeping awake in [a class he was offering at Barnard on the history of the English language, Smith] began studying the regional dialects as spoken by his girl students. He . . . tried to teach the girls that good usage is good usage in any part of the country and that there was no need to cultivate any particular accent to make themselves socially acceptable. The difference in accents are geographical and historical, not social. [11 December 1950]

Not until the 1960s, however, did linguists' voices begin to be heard by school committees, funding agencies, and the courts. Echoing Boas decades earlier, Labov (1972a) argued that Black English displays the same level of sophistication and regularity as standard (white) American English. Through the efforts of Labov and his colleagues, Black English has become the subject of serious linguistic study. In some instances it has been adopted as a teaching vernacular in schools in which the children's native dialect is Black English. Similarly, bilingual programs have been federally mandated, continuing the prototypically American belief in the equality of peoples, and (linguistically) in the equality of languages and language users.

Implications for Functional Investigations

The first lesson to be learned from looking at contemporary presuppositions about data collection is simple enough: idealization may be useful for armchair linguistics but is not as well suited to an analysis of language as people actually use it. What is more, a linguistic model based on idealizations has less need for functional explorations than does one which is *designed* to study language as a *response* to social needs. Therefore, we should not be surprised at the lack of functional investigations undertaken in the American linguistic tradition, for Chomskians, like their immediate predecessors, were not concerned with the sorts of questions to which functional inquiries might yield answers.

The preamble to this book is now complete. I began by looking (chapter 1) at language as a source—and a solution—to problems of human social interaction. Stepping back from the problem in order to sharpen our perspective, I explored what it means to use language to represent our experiences to others (chapter 2), and what we mean by "language" in the first place (chapter 3). Since I argued up to this point that linguistic representation is strongly governed by human purpose, I then looked more closely at the functionalist framework in terms of which language use, acquisition, and change might be studied and explained (chapter 4).

It is the thesis of this study that the same types of factors that influence the shape spoken language assumes also operate in written and gestural linguistic representation. Let us now examine this proposal in detail.

V

Spoken Language

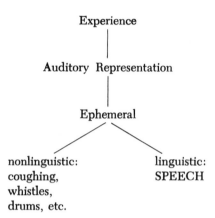

Experience

|

Auditory Representation

|

Ephemeral

nonlinguistic:
coughing,
whistles,
drums, etc.

linguistic:
SPEECH

FACTORING OUT SPEECH FROM OTHER AUDITORY REPRESENTATION

BECAUSE OF ITS familiarity, human speech might appear to be the easiest of the communicative representations to distinguish from its nonlinguistic counterpart. In practice, the line between language and nonlanguage turns out to be as difficult to draw for auditory as for visual representation. Let us see why this is so.

A first step in factoring out speech is to consider the means by which speech is normally produced: the human vocal apparatus. If we look at production rather than perception, we can rule out the clapping of hands, drum "languages," and the like.[1] By adding a further restriction that the message be volitional, we eliminate sneezes, the chattering of teeth, and most coughs. The further criterion of "productivity" (however ill-defined the term may be—see chapter 3) lets us dismiss stylized coughs (e.g., a cough used to catch someone's attention) and perhaps whistling.[2]

The most difficult part of the definitional process, though, is deciding whether the vocal features typically called suprasegmentals are part of language or not. Supersegmentals include accent, voice quality, pitch, tonality, duration. As a number of writers have noted (e.g., Abercrombie, 1972; Crystal, 1974), linguists are not consistent as to which suprasegmentals they include as a formal part of language. Part of the difficulty stems from the fact that a feature which regularly serves to distinguish meaning in one language (e.g., tone in Mandarin) may not in another; thus a unilateral judgment cannot be made as to whether a verbal production is "linguistic."

This point is well illustrated by examining the way in which a single type of semantic information is expressed in different languages. David Abercrombie notes Jules Henry's (1936) findings that

> among the Kaingang of Brazil concepts of degree and intensity are communicated by such things as pitch, facial expression and bodily posture, though we communicate these things by formal linguistic devices. On the other hand in Dakota, an American Indian language, an emotional state such as annoyance, which with us would be communicated in conversation by facial expression or tone of voice, has formal linguistic expressions by means of a particle added at the end of the sentence (of normal phonological structures, and therefore not an interjection). [1972:69]

And Kenneth Pike (1967) observes that there are languages in which speech and gesture interact in what to us might seem peculiar ways. In Papago, for instance, to say "and they are just dropping off to sleep" requires a nodding gesture along with the spoken *čʔabhab aš ʔi*. In Mazatec, the object slot can be filled either by a verbal element or by a nonverbal event in immediate context.

Consider the use of the suprasegmental duration to make semantic distinctions in a language in which duration is not ordinarily distinctive. Must our definition of what is properly "linguistic" therefore vary even within a single linguistic community? A famous case in the language acquisition literature (Velten, 1943) is Joan Velten's use of vowel length (which is nonphonemic in English) to distinguish between words (in the adult model) such as *bad* (Joan's [ba:t]) and *back* (Joan's [bat]). Another case involving duration occurs in Bengali, in which villagers use vowel duration to indicate distance. If a location is nearby, an appropriate response to the question "Where is X?" is [hu-i], accompanied by a pointing finger, but if the place is far, the response becomes [hu:-i] (plus more emphatic gesticulation), the length of the vowel being a function of the distance to the place or object in question.[3]

Leaving aside the question of which verbal productions are to be considered "language," we must come to terms with a problem that the model of representation excerpted at the head of this chapter wholly ignores: the so-called paralinguistic dimension of human communication. The first distinction in this representational model (between auditory and visual representation) implies that spoken language is produced and received exclusively through the auditory-vocal channel. By this token, telephone conversations should be indistinguishable from face-to-face conversations—and they are not. Rather, face-to-face conversation is an auditory message *in the context of* associated body postures, facial expressions, choices of distances between interlocutors, and the like. Linguists have traditionally dismissed kinesic and proxemic behavior as communicative but nonlinguistic. Such a restriction can be maintained if, a priori, we restrict face-to-face spoken language to aurally perceived messages alone. However, looking back at the general criteria established in chapter 3 for human language (having a finite lexicon, having a finite set of collocation rules, and combining lexical items grammatically to yield a potentially infinite set of well-formed constructions), it is not clear that kinesic and proxemic behavior should be eliminated from the domain of language. Continuing research on body movement and position (e.g., Birdwhistell, 1970; Scheflen, 1972; Watson, 1970) suggests that paralinguistic behavior satisfies at least the first two of these conditions. We still have comparatively little understanding of how this kinesic and proxemic communication interacts with spoken language. It *is* clear, though, that a full understanding of human speech as face-to-face auditory representation cannot be complete without the other information that is exchanged in a face-to-face encounter.

CLASSIFICATION OF SPOKEN LANGUAGES

Spoken languages have most commonly been grouped together on the basis of structural similarities—shared vocabulary, similarity of vowel repertoires, presence or absence of tones. It has generally been argued that likeness between languages may be viewed in one of three ways: genetic, areal, or typological.

STRUCTURAL GROUPINGS: GENETIC, AREAL, TYPOLOGICAL

Genetic Classification

Genetic classification groups languages on the basis of their historical connections with one another. Drawing on metaphors in both botany and human kinship, genetic classifications speak of family trees (what August Schleicher labeled the *Stammbaum* theory of languages) that branch off into divisions and subdivisions. Parent languages give birth to daughter languages, which are themselves sisters of one another. Figure 5.1 illustrates the best known of the genetic classifications, that of the Indo-European language family. There is still much debate among historical linguists as to the details of the branchings, but the idea that these languages are historically related is generally accepted.

Through the years, serious objections have been raised to the genetic model as a comprehensive way of describing relationships between languages. As with any metaphor, there are some properties which the literal and metaphoric terms hold in common, and some which they do not. (If *all* properties were analogous, the two objects being described would have to be identical.) The analogy between groups of languages and biological organisms assumes, among other things, homogeneity up to each new branching point on the tree. In biology, we know that conditions of propagation place severe restrictions on which organisms can be considered members of the same species. In the case of human languages, however, such homogeneity is neither necessary nor empirically documented. In nature, the proverbial lion can lie down with the lamb without one having a biological effect on the other because of their biological incompatibility. If genetically unrelated linguistic groups are in close contact, however, their languages tend to rub off on one another. This observation, at least in part, led linguists to supplement genetic classification with a second category.

Areal Classification

In an areal classification, we look for linguistic features held in common across languages that are not genetically related but whose speakers reside in geographically contiguous areas. (For languages which *are* genetically related, an areal classification might reveal linguistic similarities that have arisen since the languages diverged historically.) Language contact is assumed to be responsible for the spread of these features from one language to another.

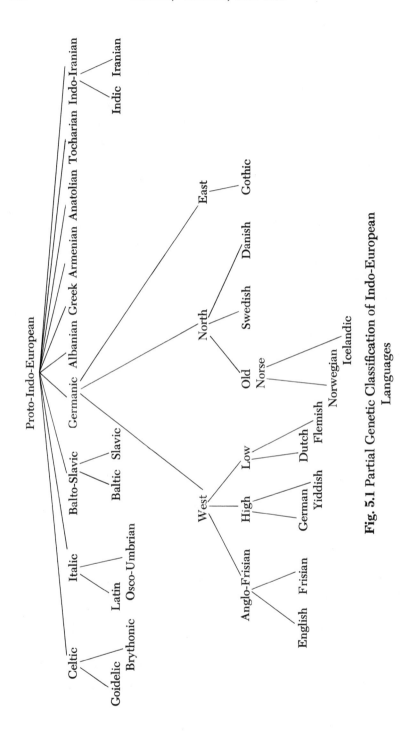

Fig. 5.1 Partial Genetic Classification of Indo-European Languages

A major difficulty in using areal classification lies in determining whether the feature in question was actually borrowed from one language into another or whether it developed spontaneously in each. Take the case of the development of articles (*the, a*) or of compound tenses in western European languages: Lehmann states that because "we find these characteristics spread through mutually unintelligible languages, such as early French, pre-Old High German, and pre-Old English" we can conclude that "speakers of these languages were in close contact, that they belonged to a common 'speech area'" (1973: 233). There is, however, an alternative hypothesis: that these developments occurred independently. The common (genetic) western European syntax from which early French, pre-Old High German, and pre-Old English derived may have made these languages ripe for these syntactic developments, although the actual developments were initiated individually in the three separate languages. Or consider the case of vowel length in Czech. Genetically, it can be argued that the development of phonemically distinctive length is predictable from the rest of the Slavic sound system of which Czech is a part. However, it can also be maintained that the development would not have taken place if speakers of Czech were not geographic neighbors of speakers of Hungarian, a non-Indo-European language in which vowel length happens to be phonemic (see Greenberg, 1968:123).

Typological Classification

The indeterminacy problem in areal classification (as well as the problems of incompleteness in genetic classifications) might be solved by an altogether different approach. Rather than using history or geography as the relevant features with which to correlate linguistic similarities, we can look at the linguistic features themselves.[4] In some instances, one ends up with a set of languages that also would have cohered under a genetic or areal qualification; usually, however, we must juxtapose languages that have neither temporal nor geographic ties. Consider, for example, a typology of languages that use phonemic tone distinctions to mark differences in meaning—included here would be Chinese, Mazatec (spoken in Mexico), and Ewe (an African language). Neither history nor geography can be invoked to explain the common phonological property of all three languages.

It is always possible that a typological analysis will reveal larger numbers of languages sharing a given feature than initially anticipated. In fact, his work on typological classification led Joseph Greenberg to study language universals. In his typological research, Greenberg often found that the feature in question was present in an overwhelming number of languages that he was examining; when it was absent, he could often predict its absence.[5]

Having looked at the three most common ways in which languages are classified, let us step back and ask what we can—or cannot—learn about language from these sorts of analysis. One obvious advantage is that linguistic classification helps us to get some sense of the range of constructions possible (or at least evidenced) in human languages. If we had had to look at every language individually, rather than as a member of a class, generalization would be difficult.

This sort of classification also gives us solid materials for considering how different languages can accomplish similar purposes by alternative structural means. We know, for instance, that agglutinating languages such as Turkish or Chinook string together large numbers of distinct morphemes to form a single word; isolating languages such as Chinese, and to some extent English, typically encode separate units of meaning in separate words. Thus, the Chinook word *inialudam* roughly translates into English as the seven word sentence "I came to give it to her." Sapir identifies the following elements in the Chinook example:

- i-   recently past time
- -n-   the pronominal subject "I"
- -i-   the pronominal object "it"
- -a-   the second pronominal object "her"
- -l-   a prepositional element indicating that the preceding pronominal prefix is to be understood as an indirect object
- -u-   movement away from the speaker
- -d-   radical "to give"
- -am   modifies the verbal content by adding to the notion conveyed by the radical element that of "arriving" or "going (or coming) for that particular purpose"   [1921:70]

In the English translation, the meaning elements and the relationships between them are largely expressed through syntactic linkage of separate words.

Is there any reason to believe that people who speak an agglutinating language are culturally *different* from those who speak isolating languages? Suppose that we hypothesized speakers of Chinook to be abrupt people, as evidenced by the fact that their language compresses many elements of meaning into a single word. To substantiate such a hypothesis, we would need to establish that all communities that speak agglutinating languages share the same cultural trait. (Such evidence is not likely to be forthcoming.) Thus, one of the major values of typological analysis is that it prevents us from pursuing irresponsible hypotheses by forcing us to examine such causal hypotheses in light of other languages belonging to the same typological group.

Are there explanations which *cannot* be drawn from data classified along structural lines? Can genealogical, areal, or typological classifications tell us, for instance, why languages in frequent use develop certain structural characteristics, while those used in more circumscribed contexts develop others? Can these classifications explain why adults who are ostensibly speakers of the same language often cannot understand one another? To find the answers, we need to think about classification of languages in different ways. Rather than taking constructional criteria alone as the basis of classification, we should consider social criteria as well: Is the language used as the basic means of communication between members of a social community, or is its use restricted to a subset of that community? If the use is limited, on what basis does an individual become a member of that subset of speakers? Is the language used in addressing members of other social communities? How much do members of one social community have to say to members of the other group? These sorts of questions are the stuff of which "social linguistics" is made; they also motivate change in "power of expression" (both of which were discussed in chapter 4).

These questions can be formulated with respect to a single speech community or used to contrast language types. The remainder of this chapter will examine the use of socially based classifications, both within and across languages. The first phenomenon is familiar to all of us—the issue of sublanguages. The second phenomenon, exemplifying a cross-societal perspective, concerns the development of "interface" languages, that is, languages that emerge when speakers of mutually unintelligible languages come in contact.

SUBLANGUAGES

As I have previously observed, language communities are heterogeneous; not all speakers of the "same" language understand each other. The reason for this has to do with the reasons we use language in the first place. If we assume that we use (and learn) language to talk about the things we experience, it should not be surprising that people who have different experiences will exhibit differences in their language.

One way of discussing experience is in terms of *activity* or *work*. What sort of things do we *do*? Do these differences in our activities show up as differences in our languages?

Ernst Fischer suggests that it is because humans do work that they have something to talk about. In human evolution,

> the development towards work [i.e., using tools to change one's environment] demanded a system of new means of expressions and communication that would go far beyond the few primitive signs known to the animal world.

In fact, it is work that distinguishes between human and animal communication:

> Animals have little to communicate to each other. Their language is instinctive: a rudimentary system of signs for danger, mating, etc. *Only in work and through work do living beings have much to say to one another.* [1963:23–emphasis added]

Anthropological studies of so-called primitive societies suggest that our earliest ancestors shared most of their activities; idiosyncratic differences between individuals (shyness, self-assurance, bombast) may have yielded differences in speech style or rhetorical abilities, but underlying lexical and grammatical knowledge was probably similar across speakers. Hunting and gathering societies and agricultural societies illustrate this kind of productive homogeneity. While women may engage in different work than men, and a few individuals may be singled out as having distinctive functions (e.g., a shaman or a chief), the division of labor is not so specialized that a linguistic description made by a yam digger will not be understood by someone who mainly repairs canoes.

With the development of religion, basic technology, and social stratification, human society began to see a division of labor. As this division increased, the linguistic needs of society—to paraphrase Fischer, the words people used to talk about their work—were no longer the same for everyone. Instead, there began a development of specialized sublanguages.

Fig. 5.2 Drawing by S. Harris; © 1973 The New Yorker Magazine, Inc. 16 July 1973, p. 24.

Sublanguages are languages (or portions of languages) containing distinct lexicon or syntax and used by a subpopulation (of a larger community) that engages in specialized activities in which the majority of the population does not participate. A sailor, for example, needs to distinguish between spinnaker, mainsail, and jib; scientists must know how to interpret formulae (see figure 5.2); and a printer must know the difference between hot and cold type. As increased diversification and specialization of language use continues, however, language begins to fail in its more general function of creating and maintaining bonds between all members of the social system (see figure 5.3).

There are three specific functions that sublanguages serve. Perhaps the most important of these is the introduction of *precision* to the way

"I can't put it into layman's language for you. I don't
know any layman's language."

Fig. 5.3 Drawing by Dana Fradon; © 1975 The New Yorker
Magazine, Inc. 21 July 1975, p. 31.

one converses with one's fellow workers. If I am crewing on your yacht,
and you simply ask me to "let out the sail," I have no idea whether to
let out the mainsail or the jib.

Intimately connected with the function of precision is that of *brevity*.
In the sailing context you might say, "I'm about to let out the larger
of the two triangular sails, which is attached to the center mast, so
watch out that you don't get hit on the head when it swings over to the
other side of the boat." However, by the time you finish your instructions, the boom may have already knocked me over. An abbreviated
name for an object or a process—like *coming about*—not only saves

effort but reduces the confusion which periphrasis is likely to cause. This kind of abbreviation is no different in kind from the abbreviations entire communities adopt for objects or experiences to which they need to refer often. Most of the time we say *TV*, not *television*, and *IRS*, not *Internal Revenue Service*, precisely because we frequently refer to televisions and taxes.

There is a third, derivative use of sublanguages as well: *exclusion*. Sublanguages can be used to exclude outsiders from participating in a conversation. Addeo and Berger cite an example of stockbrokers engaging in an exclusive form of "Jobspeak" for the benefit of a friend who has no idea what they are talking about:

> "Kinda heavy on the downside, but when you take a muni to make a house call you gotta be ready to end up zero plus tick."
> "Oh, yeah? Sounds like you got a double bottom with a head and shoulders."
> "Right. I was short against the box, only one-eighth away, and next in line, too."
> "Sounds like they squeezed the shorts and then fell out of bed."
> "Not really. When they raid the house, they take all the girls!"
> "What a bucket shop!" [1973:14–15]

Sometimes a dialect of ordinary language unknown to one's interlocutors can serve the same function of exclusion typically filled by sublanguages. On a bus in southern France several years ago, a friend and I were being harassed by several young locals who obviously knew some English. Since there was no place we could move to, I decided to continue my discussion with my companion in a deep (though quite pseudo) Southern drawl. This tactic promptly ended the disturbance, since the youths trying to insinuate their way into our conversation clearly did not have knowledge of English which extended beyond standard English phonology.

Sublanguages, then, are systematic forms of lexicon and syntax that arise paradigmatically to enable a group of people who engage in the same activity to do so more productively than would be possible using only the language of the general speech community. The term *paradigmatic* distinguishes specialized languages that enable their users to increase productive efficiency from languages that, while distinctive, are partially or wholly arbitrary. In the latter, distinctive linguistic features may be created by a subgroup of the population that is socially or productively distinct, but for which much of the new language does not serve a function in the paradigmatic sense defined above. Rather, the primary function of the new language is to set its users apart from the rest of the population. In such cases, the sublanguage itself comes to function less as a tool of social production and more as a tool of social identification. A continuum of sublanguages thus emerges, ranging from those whose structures are determined by their functions, to those whose structures are fortuitously selected and then endowed with social significance.

Activity, Science, and Pseudoscience

I have stated that sublanguages are used, paradigmatically, by groups of people to assist them in carrying out a specialized activity. What kind of activity do I have in mind? Earlier, we mentioned *activity* and *work* in the same breath. And indeed jobs and professions of various sorts typically have specialized vocabularies or syntactic constructions associated with them.[6] *Activity* or *work* can, however, describe any undertaking which evokes or entails linguistic labels. Sports and hobbies are as full of specialized lexicons and syntax as are activities designed to produce profits. Baseball, football, or tennis are obvious examples (admittedly all of these sports have become "professionalized," but the sublanguages associated with them are as necessary in amateur circles as among the pros). *Tight end* or *fifteen–love* are not part of the standard vocabulary of much of the English speaking world. To those who do not follow baseball, a phrase such as "Tidrow walked Yastrzemski" might lead one to surmise that Yastrzemski was a family pet, rather than a batting ace of the Boston Red Sox.

One of the domains in which sublanguages have been most productively developed is science and its concomitant technology. As in other types of activity, sublanguages in science may eventually change the very syntax of ordinary language in order to achieve the degree of precision necessary. This change may entail the creation of a new grammatical construction for a known activity or the transformation of an existing grammatical category to express a new conception of the constitution of the physical world. A famous case in the history of modern science is the development of the concept (and word) *momentum*. The example is clearly set forth by Bhattacharya:

> Consider Newton's famous second law of motion:
> The rate of change of momentum is proportional to the impressed force, and takes place in the direction in which the force acts.

The language, of course, is Newton's and does not exist before him. But back of it lie two centuries of dissatisfaction at the structure of terms available in Latin or modern European languages to describe movement. Why? Because from the Attic Greek *kinein,* all available languages had 'to move (something)' as a transitive verb, which logically gives rise to the Aristotelian formula which was the bane of the Middle Ages: *Omne quod movetur ab alio movetur:* everything that is moved is moved by something else. The difficulty is that this is logically true, given the language, but as Leonardo da Vinci pointed out, demonstrably false. Abandoning the verb as an adequate description, after a lot of trial and error with the newly constructed adjectives and nouns, we finally arrive at a new language: the Newtonian language of momentum and force. What makes the language introduced by physics difficult to understand by the non-physicist is that he is not familiar with the rationale for the new language.

The point here is a fundamental one. The development of science *necessarily* involves coherent language change, a change arising out of the inability of the language to do its work adequately. [1979:315–316]

The development of the word *momentum* illustrates how a specialized activity (in this case, the need to talk about moving bodies) motivates a new use of language. To the extent that the broader population finds cause to talk about the movement of bodies in space, the word may pass from the specialist's sublanguage into everyday parlance. In this way, *momentum* has become part of the vocabulary of the general populace, though its meaning is not as precise as when used technically by physicists. Other words from scientific sublanguages such as *quarks* or *pi mesons* have remained in the domain of specialists.

The effect of scientific sublanguages on everyday language has been at least as important as a means of *social identification* as it has been for increasing power of expression. With the growing prestige of the scientific community, especially after the Second World War, language that *sounds* scientific has acquired high social value. A pseudoscientific use of language has resulted that, in terms of the activity of the speakers, serves no direct function. Its indirect function, though, is to confer a sense of authority upon what is being said. Often the effect is strained (though still intelligible):

The catalogue of a community college in Maryland lists its typing and shorthand courses under "Secretarial Science."

In the midst of the 1974 Arab oil embargo, an advertisement for Buick introduced "an important new concept. Range." *Range* was "what you get when you multiply your gas mileage by the number of gallons your tank holds."

Cash registers at Sears are called "Modular Data Transaction Systems."

At other times, though, the attempt to sound "scientific" results in semantic gibberish. This phenomenon is especially prevalent in college term papers:

> From an undergraduate sociology paper:
> They discovered that both partners are *lower in marriage happiness* when the woman is working out of economic necessity rather than choice and that both husbands and wives are lower in tensions and *high in socioability* [sic] if the wife chooses the labor market over the housework. [emphasis added]

Can "marriage happiness" be measured like the Dow-Jones average?

> From a master's thesis on language development:
> Slobin *proposes the observation* that . . . [emphasis added]

Presumably one proposes *theories*, one *makes* observations.

> From a doctoral dissertation on the history of English:
> If . . . one finds zero instances of a form century after century, we may then say that such a form was for all practical purposes not used—or at least *not used this side of the point of diminishing returns.* [emphasis added]

Can grammatical constructions really be subjected to a cost-benefit analysis?

It might be argued that all these examples are from written, not spoken language and therefore inappropriate in the present discussion. However, to the degree that writing is a representation of spoken language (see chapter 6), we expect to find phenomena such as pseudo-scientific jargon in both written and spoken language roughly comparable, provided that the audience (e.g., a college professor) is held constant. Casual observation of classroom conversation supports this hypothesis. Admittedly, writing tends to be more formal than speech (again, see chapter 6), and it is commonly assumed that formality calls for weighty words. Nevertheless, in formal spoken contexts (e.g., court testimony), the degree of formality—and susceptibility to pseudoscientific jargon—typically approaches that characteristic of writing.

"WIPE THE BUGS OFF YOUR PLATES": TRANSITIONAL CASES[7]

Pseudoscientific language indicates that the primary function of a sublanguage may derive more from its social impact than from its semantic import. There are, in fact, sublanguages expressly created to combine minimal semantic reference with maximal social identification, where such identification implies exclusion of outsiders. High school slangs typically function this way, as does CB radio language.

The character of CB language has changed rather dramatically since its inception in the late 1940s and '50s, when it was modeled after military codes developed for use on two-way radios in World War I. Codes must be *precise, brief,* and *exclusive*—the same three factors essential to paradigmatic sublanguages. In the early use of the citizens band by police, rescue personnel, or ham radio operators, the first two traits were especially important. CB language frequently needs to be more precise than face-to-face spoken communication because of problems inherent in radio transmission; messages can be lost with a weak or fuzzy signal. Consequently, a high degree of redundancy is used to increase the chances of the message being received correctly. Single letters are sometimes encoded as words (e.g., using *Baker* to indicate the letter *B*), and there is a high degree of syntactic redundancy, which strongly resembles the syntactic redundancy in pidgin languages (see "Trade Jargons and Pidgins," below). In both instances, the sender has reason to question whether the interlocutor will comprehend the message transmitted. With CB, the problem may be in the physical transmission, while with pidgin languages, there may be structural uncertainty. (How much of the language does the interlocutor understand?)

Counteracting the high use of redundancy for precision is the feature of brevity, which, in its early days, was functional in transmitting emergency information. Today, the explosion in the number of CBers trying to use the same channel has made brevity a practical necessity. The resulting use of initials to abbreviate the names of familiar places (e.g., *Bronx River Parkway* = *BRP*) is the exact opposite of using full words to be sure a single letter is understood.

The most interesting sociolinguistic development is the use of CB language for social exclusion and social identification. There is a popular belief that its use "protects" the user from being understood by the police—a curious assumption, especially since it was in part modeled after codes used by police. Middle class users of CB language may believe that they are identifying with the world of truckers by learning their lingo. In fact, regular users of CB can easily detect the amateurs' imperfect learning and may refuse conversation with the "nonlegitimate" users. Moreover, some of the truckers' language has evolved away from the forms popularized by amateurs. Among truckers, the proverbial *good buddy* has taken on the meaning of "gay" and has been replaced by *old buddy* or *driver*.

While CB language bears many of the trappings of sublanguages par excellence, it functions, at least among many of its users, as much for social identification as to get work done. Much of the lexicon is self-evident: an expressway is a *superslab*, an armored truck is a *branch bank*, and a gasoline truck is a *thermos bottle*. These are not randomly assigned pairings. At the same time, use of the CB term (rather than the word in everyday language) serves no obvious function other than the identification of the speaker as a member of a group. The logical extreme of this is the use of language as a wholly fortuitous vehicle for social identification, to which we turn next.

Diphthongs on Martha's Vineyard: Form Over Content

The case of diphthongization on Martha's Vineyard is a classic example of the use of an arbitrary linguistic form for social purposes (Labov 1963; reprinted 1972b). Martha's Vineyard is a small island off the coast of Massachusetts. Best-known as a summer vacation haven, it is also year-round home to many people, some of whom identify quite strongly with the island and take pride in distinguishing themselves from people living on the mainland. Labov's study revealed that many islanders pronounced the diphthongs /ay/ and /aw/ in a more centralized position in the mouth than did their counterparts on the mainland. In other words, a word like *five* sounded more like [fəɪv] than the standard English [faɪv]; *house* sounded more like [həʊs] than the standard English [haʊs]—[a] being a lower sound in the vowel space than [ə].

Not all islanders evidenced the same amount of centralization; a study of social factors revealed that the more a speaker identified with the island, the greater the degree of centralization was likely to be. Factors such as age turned out not to be as important. There were cases of younger people who, upon returning to the island after receiving their education, adopted the increased degree of centralization. One woman remarked of her son, "You know, E. didn't always speak that way . . . it's only since he came back from college. Guess he wanted to be more like the men on the docks . . ." (Labov, 1972b:31).

Our discussion of sublanguages has illustrated how the choice of linguistic constructs can be socially motivated among groups of speakers from a single linguistic community. Let us now explore how similar functional explanations can be applied in cross-linguistic situations. The specific cases we shall examine are spoken language systems which are commonly known as trade jargons and as pidgins.

TRADE JARGONS AND PIDGINS

INTRODUCTION

The term *pidgin* is commonly used as a catchall to refer to a vast range of languages linked by two criteria: they contain elements from more than one language, and they are judged not to be as "complete" or "sophisticated" as any of the donors. In the previous attempts to define *pidgin*, we find great variety in the kinds of criteria chosen.[8] Many descriptions have focused on the lexical and syntactic composition of pidgins (it is typically claimed that the vocabulary is predominantly from a European language and the syntax from a non-Indo-European language).[9] Another common characterization is in terms of native speakers: pidgins are said to have none.[10] A few linguists have even commented that pidgins seem to arise in coastal areas.[11] All of these criteria are useful, and, in general, accurate. But, as with the proverbial blind men and the elephant, these isolated characterizations do not leave us with a clear understanding of what a pidgin really is.

Why are pidgins so interesting in the first place? The simplest answer is that they are peculiar kinds of languages—and languages are what linguists are supposed to study—that arise when people who do not share a common language meet under special sets of circumstances. The next logical questions to ask are:

What are the linguistic peculiarities of pidgins?

What are the special circumstances under which they arise?

Do the special circumstances under which people meet account for these linguistic peculiarities? (That is, can we *deduce* the linguistic structure of pidgin from the structure of human interaction?)

In exploring the nature of pidgin, we shall be comparing another peculiar language type—trade jargon. The deductive method can also be applied to creoles, lingua francas, and koinés (although these languages go beyond the scope of the present discussion). All of these are linguistic "interfaces" between speakers not sharing a common language and may therefore be referred to as "interface languages."

This section will examine the hypothesis that the structure of trade jargons and pidgins can be deduced once we know the objects and activities in each original speech community's experience and the relative social and political footing on which the two groups confront each other.[12] Using these two variables, we shall also be able to ask diachronically why these languages arose at the times and places they did and between the groups they did, why many of these languages have died out, and whether such languages will continue to emerge in the future. However, before addressing these specific questions, we need a way of talking about relations between people, their language, and their modes of living.

PEOPLE, LANGUAGE, AND EXPERIENCE

In talking about human language, we can separate the speaker (S), the hearer (H), the language system (L), and experience (E). Three primary relations and one composite relation between these elements can be defined with respect to L. The primary relations are:

between the speaker and the language: SR_1L

between the hearer and the language: HR_2L

between the thing talked about (experience) and the language: ER_3L

The composite relation connecting speaker and hearer may be defined as SR_1LR_2H (this avoids the assumption that both speaker and hearer have the same relationship with the language). A person is said to be *linguistically saturated* when his command of the first two primary relations (SR_1L, HR_2L) and the composite relation (SR_1LR_2H) is such that the community does not correct his linguistic behavior.

Experience

Adult languages may differ from each other with respect to the third primary relation, ER_3L. This relation belongs to the realm of *applicability*—the way in which a linguistic community uses its language to encode experience as well as the adequacy of this encoding. The language of a (single) speech community may change when the language is not felt to encode experience adequately.

This suggests that the daily activity of members of a linguistic community is reflected in their vocabulary and syntax. On one level, this observation is trivial and self-evident: if I dig ditches, I need names for my tools and if I play chess, I need a set of syntactic constructions that lets me describe the movements of the pieces. On another level, the problem is more significant: Are all languages able to talk about all activities? Does the speaker of Navaho have any way of talking about notions like "momentum" or "impressed force," or is the Neo-Melanesian Pidgin word *pairapim* ("explode") adequate for talking about nuclear explosions?[13]

The "experience" of members of a speech community refers both to the material objects in the culture (shovels and chess sets), which I shall represent by the set {M}, and the activities which the people engage in (digging ditches and playing chess), which I shall represent by the set {A}. In order to distinguish between these two aspects of experience, the two relations which make up ER_3L will be identified as MR_4L and AR_5L.

Speakers of a language confront the adequacy problem when they encounter new objects or engage in new activities. As I have just said, one of the ways languages change is by devising ways to talk about new objects and new activities. The adequacy problem also applies to speakers of language L_1 and language L_2 when two speech communities come in contact with each other. If the groups encounter similar objects and engage in the same kinds of activity (if the relationships R in E_1RL_1 and E_2RL_2 are similar), translation or borrowing between L_1 and L_2 will not be particularly difficult. If differences between E_1RL_1 and E_2RL_2 reflect *material differences* between the two groups (i.e., $M_1RL_1 \neq M_2RL_2$), contact between the groups may result in a language interface that centers upon the new material objects encountered. This situation typically lies behind the development of trade jargons. However, if both groups engage in radically different *activities* (if differences between E_1RL_1 and E_2RL_2 reflect incommensurate life styles—i.e., $A_1RL_1 \neq A_2RL_2$),[14] then adequate translation will be difficult, if not impossible. I hypothesize that, under these conditions, a radically different kind of language, a pidgin, arises.

Social and Political "Footing"

If we consider two communities of speakers who come in contact with each other, the first group (G_1) may be either (to oversimplify for a moment) on an equal or an unequal social or political footing with the second group (G_2). By social or political footing I simply mean, Is one group in a position to exert power over the other? In examining interface languages, we shall see various ways in which the sociopolitical relationships between groups in contact determine the kind of language that emerges from the contact situation. When the relative positions of the groups change, we predict concomitant changes in the interface languages linking the two communities.

I have isolated six types of relations—

$$SR_1L \qquad ER_3L$$
$$HR_1L \qquad MR_4L$$
$$SR_1LR_2H \qquad AR_5L$$

and two kinds of variables—sameness or difference of material objects or activities, and relative social and political position. These relations and variables enable us to talk precisely about language used between speakers and hearers from different speech communities that come in contact with one another. It is possible to construct a matrix of relations containing all possible permutations of material objects, activity, and sociopolitical position, and to ask what kind of interface language might arise under each condition. The present investigation is, however, restricted to two cases: difference in material objects and equality of social and political footing; and differences in activity and inequality of footing. Let us begin by looking at the kind of situations that give rise to these collocations of variables, and then we shall examine the sorts of languages that derive from these situations. Finally, we shall come back to the questions posed about the temporal and geographic past and future of interface languages.

Exchange and Empire: The Human Context

Since the dawn of human history, groups of people have been exchanging goods with other groups of people.[15] Humans have exchanged everything from yams for shells, to cows for wives, to missiles for oil, to five days' labor for one week's pay. Exchange may take place under a seemingly limitless variety of circumstances. However, we can identify two ends of an exchange spectrum.

At one end—which includes the vast majority of human trade—two parties confront each other on a relatively equal social footing. Both groups stand to benefit equally from the exchange (although, like the unsuspecting Indians who sold Manhattan, they may be misled), and both groups can choose whether or not to engage in the transaction.

At the other end of the spectrum, which historically includes a much more restricted set of encounters, groups of people come together on an unequal basis. This may take the extreme form of slavery, a more intermediate form like contract labor, or the apparently voluntary form of freely hired labor. However, in each case the group on the short end of the stick has no real choice about participating in the exchange.[16] Moreover, instead of exchanging goods, the subordinate group exchanges labor for subsistence income (or the equivalent) from the dominant group. This labor may entail not only performing new kinds of tasks (e.g., loading large ocean-going vessels) but also living according to a radically different kind of social organization (e.g., a hierarchical society which imposes a regular daily routine on the worker).[17] Frequently, exchange under coercion was preceded by an earlier period of exchange of goods between equals (as in the cases of Hawaii, China, and New Guinea). This change of circumstances is known to historians as the development of colonial empires by western Europe.

What does commerce have to do with language? When two people (or groups of people) who do not share a common language meet for the purpose of exchange, they nearly always need to find some way of talking to one another. It is under these situations that interface languages develop.

We can further specify two types of encounters from which we predict that two very different types of linguistic interfaces will arise. In considering trade between equals who do not share a common language, I shall restrict myself to encounters between representatives of both groups (typically adult males) in which the amount of time spent together is relatively short, and the majority of conversation centers upon the material objects being traded.[18] The opportunity for one group to fully learn the language of the other is limited by amount of exposure and by motivation. This kind of contact gives rise to a linguistic system known as a *trade jargon*, which is not actually a language but an intersection of partial languages.

Subordinate populations exchanging labor for subsistence have a peculiar kind of relationship with the dominant group. As with free trade, the exchange is typically between adult males.[19] Here, however, the subordinate population is compelled to spend large amounts of time with the dominant group (or its intermediaries); and yet, the increased amount of contact does not mean that one group will learn the other's language. By virtue of their differential social position, the dominant group cannot learn the language of the subordinate group, or vice versa.[20] This kind of contact produces linguistic systems we call *pidgins*, which are full fledged languages, although of a strange sort.

FUNCTIONALLY DERIVED DEFINITIONS

What features delimit classes of trade jargons and of pidgins? The following set of structural characteristics are not meant to be exhaustive (e.g., they do not mention the use of reduplication in pidgin), nor do they reflect the fact that many languages that are traditionally called trade jargons or pidgins did not arise under the specific social and economic conditions mentioned above. However, we should be able to explain languages that do not display these structural characteristics in terms of the actual social and economic conditions applicable in those situations.

STRUCTURAL CHARACTERISTICS

TRADE JARGONS

Stability: A trade jargon is not a single, stable language in which speakers are linguistically saturated (see "People, Language, and Experience").

Source of Vocabulary: Lexical items derive from both donor languages.

| Source of Syntax: | Depending on the material on which the grammar is based, the syntax may seem to derive from one or the other donor language, or both. |

| Complexity of Syntax: | Depending on the material on which the grammar is based, the syntax may involve morphological inflection and word order variation. |

| Circumlo-cution: | Where circumlocution (descriptive phrases in place of a single lexical item) appears, it is largely unstable. |

| Redundancy: | Redundancy is high, but it involves (extralinguistic) gestures. |

PIDGINS

| Stability: | A pidgin is a single, stable language in which speakers are linguistically saturated. |

| Source of Vocabulary: | Lexical items derive predominantly from language of dominant population. |

| Source of Syntax: | This is largely irrelevant because most of syntax is unique to pidgin—see the following three points). |
| Complexity of Syntax: | There is very little inflection, fairly strict word order. |

| Circumlo-cution: | Much stable circumlocution exists. |

| Redundancy: | Redundancy is high because of circumlocution in syntax. |

The remainder of this section will explore the extent to which these features of trade jargons and pidgins are directly predictable from the functional needs of the speakers forging these languages.

Functional Definition of Trade Jargon

Trade jargons are linguistic interfaces that arise because the material objects in the language of one group of speakers' experience (M_1) are different from the material objects in another group's experience (M_2). The resulting linguistic interface, however, is not one language but two.[21] Both share some vocabulary but derive the rest of their vocabulary and almost all their syntax from the basic language of the speaker. These shared elements, by themselves, do not constitute a language. We can understand this situation more clearly by introducing some simple formal symbols to talk about the two base languages and the resulting linguistic interfaces.

The base (native) language (L_1) spoken by one group of speakers (G_1) encodes the set of material objects which the speakers normally experience ($\{M_1\}$). Contained within the set $\{M_1\}$ is a subset of objects $\{m_1\}$, which this first group of speakers is trading with speakers of a different language. Similarly, the second group of speakers (G_2) speaks a base language (L_2) which encodes the material objects they encounter in their normal experience ($\{M_2\}$). Contained within $\{M_2\}$ is a subset of items to be traded, $\{m_2\}$.

When the two groups encounter each other, the first group will need to modify its language to incorporate names for the items they are receiving in trade from G_2. In some cases the items being received in trade may already have a native name (e.g., English has a word for "oil"). In these instances, we cannot consistently predict whether the word from L_1 or L_2 will be used in trading either by G_1 or G_2. For the sake of simplicity, all names for received items are assumed to come from the language of the group offering these trade items. The new modified language, L_3, will include most of the structure of L_1, that is, the nouns which are not names of items to be traded, the best of the vocabulary and syntax of L_1, plus the new names for the items received in trade from G_2:

$$L_3 = L_1 + \{m_2\}$$

or, to separate out the items G_1 is trading from the rest of their base language L_1:

$$L_3 = \overline{L_1} + \{m_1\} + \{m_2\}$$

The second group also develops a modified language, L_4, which incorporates names for the items they receive from G_1:

$$L_4 = L_2 + \{m_1\}$$

or

$$L_4 = \overline{L_2} + \{m_2\} + \{m_1\}$$

When we speak about trade jargons, we are really talking about the modified languages L_3 and L_4. However, if we need a shorthand for talking about both L_3 and L_4, we can define a trade jargon as L_0 (the residual lexicon and syntax from L_1 and L_2), plus the vocabulary for the items both groups are trading:

$$L_T = L_0 + \{m_1\} + \{m_2\}$$

This model is, of course, grossly oversimplified in its implication that the only shared vocabularly items in L_T are names for the items being traded. The basic model is constructed this way because the source of other shared vocabulary is, we predict, random (it cannot be deduced from the general structure of trading relationships) and because the vocabulary lists of trade jargons found in the literature are often unreliable (we often do not know whether they reflect L_3 or L_4 or both). Furthermore, because these lists, as in the case of Eskimo or American Indian trade languages, are published for English-speaking audiences, it is highly possible that English words that were used in trading were omitted, since the English-speaking audience already knew them. Stefánsson, for example, prefaces his vocabulary of the Eskimo Trade Jargon of Herschel Island with the admission that

> the vocabulary is briefer by a good number of words through the omission of most common and proper nouns that are only slighty-corrupted English and which would be readily understood by a newcomer in the Arctic. [1909:222]

Most of the confusion over whether trade jargons are actual languages (i.e., Do they have a stable pronunciation, lexicon, and syntax?) has arisen because of the kind of data on which we have based our descriptions. As Silverstein (1972) convincingly established in the case of Chinook Jargon, the use of informants who speak different base languages can lead one to construct radically different grammars for L_T. However, groups trading with each other are not necessarily aware that they are speaking different languages; in fact, they are sometimes convinced that they are speaking not their own base language or even some mixed jargon, but the language of the *other* group. The missionary Paul le Jeune is quoted as saying of the Franco-Amerindian contact vernacular that "the Frenchmen who spoke it supposed it to be good Indian, and the Indians believed it to be good French" (1632; in Hancock, 1971:512). The same phenomenon occurs with other kinds of interface languages; Cole mentions that speakers of Bantu languages who learn Fanagalo "fondly imagine that they are speaking the language of the White man" (1953:7). This belief is not unlike the conviction of the American tourist that he is speaking French when, in fact, he has merely "Frenchified" his pronunciation and added a few French words to his vocabulary.

To what extent are the structural characteristics proposed for trade jargons predictable from the human encounter of groups trading material objects on an equal footing? A trade jargon is not a stable language which is learned in toto (i.e., in which anyone can become saturated) because there are actually as many "languages" as there are base languages spoken by the groups engaging in trade. Because of the multiplicity of language bases, the vocabulary of L_T comes from both donor languages. Similarly, the syntactic structure of the language varies, depending on the base language of the informant. And because each group is using a (modified) form of its own base language, the syntax used may include some of the morphological inflections found in the base language.[22]

Two other grammatical characteristics of trade jargons have been mentioned: unstable circumlocution (if any) and extralinguistic redundancy. If a speaker wants to refer to an object or activity for which he does not have a word in his lexicon, the most normal recourse is to describe the object or activity in terms of other words in his vocabulary; speakers do this all the time. If we want to talk about a particular person whose name we do not know, we might describe his height, weight, hair color, and so forth, hoping that the interlocutor will be able to identify the person from the description. However, if speaker and hearer spend a good deal of time talking to one another, and this nameless person is important in the conversation, by the simple rules of expediency, we shall either find out his name or coin one. In trading encounters, numerous situations arise in which one speaker is at a loss for a word that his hearer will understand. In some cases, the speaker resorts to circumlocution using shared vocabulary, but, because in these situations the period of contact between the trading parties is so limited, few of these spontaneous circumlocutions become crystallized in the language.[23] Frequently, however, when traders need to make their meaning clear, they resort to gesture to accompany their speech.[24] Since the exchange of material objects is the purpose of trade contact, in the early stages of trading, ostension (a form of gesturing) is sufficient to identify such objects. Like verbal circumlocution, gesture makes the total language system highly redundant in the information theoretic sense since a large number of units (in this case, words plus gestures) are needed to express a single piece of information.

Functional Definition of Pidgin

Pidgins arise when a dominant population imposes parts of its life style—which includes material objects (M_1) but, more importantly, particular kinds of activity (A_1)—on a subordinate population with a different life style (M_2 and A_2). A single language emerges whose lexical and syntactic composition reflects the relative power and different interests of the two groups involved.[25] As with trade jargons, the structure of pidgin language is more easily comprehended in terms of a formal representation of the donor languages and the resulting pidgin.

The dominant population (G_1) speaks a language (L_1) that encodes a set of material objects ($\{M_1\}$) and activities ($\{A_1\}$) which people in that group normally experience. Contained within $\{M_1\}$ and $\{A_1\}$ are two significant subsets, $\{m_1\}$ and $\{a_1\}$, which are the objects and activities peculiar to the dominant group, and which the subordinate group will be encountering. Also contained within $\{M_1\}$ and $\{A_1\}$ are objects and activities that the dominant group already has in common with the subordinate population ($\{\mu_1\}$, $\{\alpha_1\}$). If we label as $\overline{\overline{L}}_1$ the remainder of L_1 which is not relevant to contact between the two groups, we can define L_1 as the conjunction of $\overline{\overline{L}}_1$ and the two subsets of $\{M_1\}$ and $\{A_1\}$:

$$L_1 = \overline{\overline{L}}_1 + \{m_1\} + \{a_1\} + \{\mu_1\} + \{\alpha_1\}$$

The subordinate population (G_2) speaks a language (L_2) that also encodes a set of material objects ($\{M_2\}$) and activities ($\{A_2\}$), very small subsets of which ($\{m_2\}$ and $\{a_2\}$) are peculiar to G_2 *and* will be relevant in speaking to the dominant group (e.g., native foods and customs), and other subsets of which ($\{\mu_2\}$ and $\{\alpha_2\}$) are held in common with G_1. Labeling as $\overline{\overline{L}}_2$ the remainder of L_2 which is not relevant to contact, we can define L_2 as $\overline{\overline{L}}_2$ plus the two subsets of objects and activities:

$$L_2 = \overline{\overline{L}}_2 + \{m_2\} + \{a_2\} + \{\mu_2\} + \{\alpha_2\}$$

What kind of language emerges out of this mixture? The characterization of pidgin proposed at the beginning of this section provides a convenient framework for answering this question.

Stability Pidgins are stable languages over which speakers from either the dominant or subordinate group can gain mastery, although it is frequently said that the subordinate population "knows" the language better than the dominant group (e.g., Hall, 1955:22). The stability of pidgin follows directly from the fact that the social situation itself is stable: for years—even decades, day after day, the subordinate population performs the same tasks and maintains the same relationship with the dominant group. In some instances (e.g., Hawaii) this dominant/subordinate relationship has given way comparatively quickly as the dominated group began leaving the plantations and learning the dominant group's language (see Reinecke, 1969:100). In other cases (e.g., New Guinea) the inequality—and the use of pidgin —has persisted much longer.

Source of Vocabulary The majority of the vocabulary comes from the dominant language L_1 because of the position of authority held by speakers of G_1. The dominant group introduces a number of new concepts—$\{m_1\}$ and $\{a_1\}$—which form the basis of the pidgin in that they represent the new kinds of objects and activities that the subordinate group must confront in working for G_1. The subordinate group also has a few items of experience $\{m_2\}$ and $\{a_2\}$ unknown to G_1 that find their way into the pidgin lexicon, but, because the subordinate group must fit its life style to that of the dominant group (and not vice versa), there are comparatively few of these items.

The rest of the pidgin vocabulary refers to experience that both groups shared before contact (eating, birth, death). However, because the dominant group has the upper hand, it can retain its own words for these aspects of experience, thereby forcing the subordinate group to accommodate itself either by learning these parts of the vocabulary of L_1 or by using circumlocution (see below).

Yet despite the overwhelming proportion of pidgin vocabulary taken from the dominant language, the pidgin vocabulary remains much smaller than that of the dominant language itself.[26] The primary reason for this restriction is that, in the typical social situation in which pidgin is used, the laboring population is not given the opportunity to learn L_1[27]—not only because it is felt to be unnecessary, but also because the dominant group may believe that the "natives" are not smart enough to learn the language or because the dominant group wishes to maintain social distance between themselves and the "lower orders."[28]

Source of Syntax Trade jargons exhibit a fairly sophisticated level of syntax that can be traced directly to the base languages. However, in the case of pidgin, the question of syntax assumes a different cast. Pidgin has a novel syntactic structure, chiefly characterized by highly simplified morphology and word order, circumlocution, and syntactic redundancy (the latter two resulting from the paucity of vocabulary).

Nevertheless, many linguists (e.g., Bateson, 1943:138) have commented that pidgin syntax, to the extent that its origins can be traced, seems to derive more from the subordinate language (L_2) than from the dominant language (L_1).

We need to distinguish between the *syntactic structure* of a language (in this case, pidgin), and particular *syntactic features* which are used as surface markers of underlying syntactic and semantic relationships. We must nevertheless remember that these specific syntactic features, however pervasive they may be in texts (e.g., Neo-Melanesian *-im* marking transitive verbs), are not integral parts of the syntactic structure itself. Neo-Melanesian Pidgin would still be a pidgin without its *-im*, because the choice of syntactic features has little (if anything) to do with the new activities of the subordinate population, or with the relationship between the dominant and subordinate groups.

To the extent that the syntax of pidgin delineates common grammatical properties of both L_1 and L_2 (distinguishing between transitive and intransitive verbs, aspectual distinctions, singular and plural number), it is structurally irrelevant whether L_1 or L_2 is the source of explicit syntactic constructions in pidgin (to the extent they exist—see "Complexity of Syntax"). However, there are several reasons which make L_2 (the subordinate language) the logical choice. Since the dominant group (missionaries generally excepted) is primarily interested in using pidgin to get its orders carried out—not in educating the "natives" —they will arrive at the simplest language possible for the hearer (the subordinate group) to comprehend in the shortest amount of time. That is, the relation HRL takes precedence over SRL (see "People, Language, and Experience"). To the extent that vocabulary conveys the dominant group's intentions, there is no time—or need—to worry about niceties of syntax. For the subordinate population—just as for the trader—it is far easier, as hearer, to learn the vocabulary than the syntax of another language. Maintenance of scattered syntactic features from the subordinate group's language is irrelevant to the dominant group since these features play little part in conveying the dominant group's instructions to its subordinates. While these features are equally useless in making the subordinate group understood by the dominant groups (who do not understand the lower group's native language[s]), their use is just as "natural" as the traders' use of syntax from their base languages—which the group with whom they are trading does not understand. Finally, to the extent that syntactic elements of the subordinate language become part of the pidgin, such markers will be easily learnable because of simplicity and high frequency (e.g., Neo-Melanesian transitive verb marker *-im* or predicate marker *i*).

But why does the dominant group not introduce syntactic features from its own language? I hypothesize that, as with their restricted use of vocabulary, the dominant group may either believe the "natives" too stupid to learn their syntax, or that they may wish to maintain linguistic distance between themselves and their laborers. Furthermore, nearly all the dominant languages were, historically, western European languages (especially English), which have comparatively little surface syntactic marking anyway.

Complexity of Syntax As mentioned above, one of the chief characteristics of pidgin is its scarcity of morphological features and syntactic rules. Rather, it is a highly "simplified" language—typically having a set word order, not marking gender or number distinctions, differentiating between aspects but not tenses. These characteristics are predictable from the situations in which pidgins are used. Generally speaking, the simpler the morphology and syntax, the shorter time required to learn (or create) a language. It is advantageous to both parties to understand each other as quickly as possible: the ruling groups stand to increase their profits as they increase the efficiency of their laborers —which requires the laborers to understand what they are being asked to do; and members of the laboring group may expect better treatment from their superiors if they can make themselves understood.[29]

Circumlocution Having just said that pidgin is a very simple language with respect to its limited vocabulary and syntactic machinery, I must now explain the presence of circumlocution. Circumlocution— perhaps the most distinctive characteristic of pidgin—is an extremely cumbersome way of getting one's point across. However, once again the human context in which pidgins are created and used helps explain the usefulness of circumlocution.

The dominant group, as in the case of syntax, is not concerned with the propagation of its mother tongue but that members of the subordinate group understand its desires. If the native doesn't understand the word *never* but comprehends *i no gat wanpela taim* (Neo-Melanesian), simplicity is sacrificed for the sake of comprehension. If, by *tupela han wanpela fut*, the subordinate group understands *fifteen*, there is no reason to extend one's knowledge of the subordinate group's vocabulary.

Consider the similar position of a speaker from the subordinate group, to whom it is of paramount importance to be understood by the overseer who may hold the power of life and death over him. If, for example, while working in the fields, a laborer needs to relieve himself, he must make absolutely sure that his superior understands that he is not running away. It matters little whether both his native language and that of the overseer have simple lexical items for *diarrhea*. If the native does not know the word from L_1 and is not sure the overseer knows the word from L_2, then it is most expedient to describe the problem in no uncertain terms: *pekpek no gut olsam wara* (again, Neo-Melanesian). The circumlocution may save him from a beating —or worse. Likewise, if the laborer injures himself and runs for a tourniquet, he wants to be certain the overseer will understand that he is not shirking his duties but only looking for *strongpela rop bilong pasim rot bilong blut*.

Yet there is a problem with the use of circumlocution. Every language encounters an optimization problem. The fewer the vocabulary items in a language (whether it is a natural language or an interface language like pidgin), the simpler the language. However, if the vocabulary is insufficient for expressing what its speakers want to say (either because no appropriate word exists in the language—as in the case of natural languages—or because the speaker does not know the word in the foreign language and is not certain the foreigner knows the speaker's word—as in the case of pidgin), the speaker may either add a new word, thereby complicating the vocabulary but reducing potential syntactic redundancy—see "Redundancy"), or may resort to circumlocution, which keeps the vocabulary small but increases syntactic redundancy.

It is difficult, if not impossible, to determine which solution the language will select in a particular case. And so, in looking at contact situations which generate pidgin, we can't predict which particular words will be adopted directly from the dominant (or, less often, from the subordinate) language, and which will be expressed phrasally. However, when pidgins are stable for a relatively long time, circumlocutions are often replaced by single lexical items, usually from the dominant language.

Nevertheless, we might ask whether there are any principles governing this vocabulary distribution. Consider first the situation in which the item or activity talked about is part of the previously shared experience of both speech communities and for which both languages already have a single word in their lexicons. At first glance we might hypothesize that, since experiences can here be easily translated, speakers from one group would simply adopt the lexical item from the other (usually from L_1). However, a quick look at Neo-Melanesian disproves this hypothesis. The most mundane objects and activities— for which we assume the native language of the subordinate population has items in its lexicon—are expressed by circumlocution, for example: *deaf* (*i no save harim tok*) or *gratitude* (*pasim bilong givim tenkyu long arapela man*). Thus, it seems that, for pidgin, the optimization balance is weighted in favor of circumlocution—presumably for the reasons we have discussed.

But what about the areas of experience that the dominant population imposes on the subordinate? Should we expect these to be expressed through circumlocution rather than lifted directly from the dominant language's lexicon? Because it is sometimes extremely difficult to translate these new experiences into the indigenous language, and because these are the terms which the dominant population is likely to speak most frequently to the "natives," we would expect words for these new aspects of experience to be borrowed directly from the dominant language. Judging from Neo-Melanesian, this hypothesis generally seems to hold—*automobile* (*motoka*), *battery* (*bateri*), *fountain pen* (*fauntenpen*), *screwdriver* (*skrudraiva*)—although there are some exceptions, e.g., *dynamo* (*masin bilong mekim lektrik*).

Redundancy As we have just seen, pidgin has a high level of syntactic redundancy in that circumlocutions require a large number of items to express a single piece of information. I have already discussed the situational factors that make this syntactic phenomenon highly functional.

In this section and the previous one, I have shown how certain kinds of linguistic structure can be deduced from a small number of nonlinguistic features of human interaction, especially the nature of one's experience and the relative footing on which one confronts speakers of a different language. To test the usefulness of the theory of interface languages I have proposed, it will be necessary to compile data from a large number of trade jargons and pidgins. Before undertaking such research, however, we can benefit from a historical perspective on the actual situations in which interface languages have arisen.

PAST, PRESENT, AND FUTURE

The empirical analysis of trade jargons and pidgins cannot be undertaken by looking under *t* or *p* in an appropriate compendium. Using the above characterizations—either linguistic or nonlinguistic—we find that the names traditionally given many interface languages are misleading. A quick glimpse at Hancock's "Survey of the Pidgins and Creoles of the World" (which appears as an appendix to Hymes, 1971) emphasizes the problem: Pidgin Eskimo and Pidgin Spanish are not pidgins but trade jargons; New Jersey Amerindian Trade Pidgin is a contradiction in terms; Hawaiian Pidgin English and Chinese Pidgin English may have been pidgins at some point in their history, but we cannot be sure until we sort more carefully through the linguistic and nonlinguistic data.[30]

If we can't rely on linguistic labeling to tell us which interface languages are potential trade jargons or pidgins, then we need some other means of finding the right empirical domain to explore. The answer is not difficult to find: if we are correct in saying that trade jargons and pidgins are linguistic responses to conditions under which humans confront each other, we can then ask, historically, when and where these language have arisen. For example, the history of late mercantilism and early capitalism will explain why pidgins (as defined here) did not really appear before the eighteenth and nineteenth centuries, why they almost invariably grew up in coastal regions of non-European countries, and why the dominant language in almost every instance is a western European language.[31]

We can also use history to understand why so many of these languages have died out or have been replaced by other types of languages (specifically, trade jargons giving way to pidgins, and pidgins either giving way to creoles, or dying out completely). By looking at the numerous shifts in the nineteenth and early twentieth centuries from trading relationships to relationships of empire, we can understand the rapid rise of pidgins during the height of Western colonialism; by observing the growing independence of former colonies, we predict the demise of pidgin. Furthermore, unless the structure of the world economy drastically alters in the next decades, trade jargons may continue to emerge on a limited basis between speakers from nonmodernized countries (where speakers do not share a common third language like English, French, or Swahili); pidgins, on the other hand, probably will not. There are no longer the proper mixtures of unprotected "natives," untapped natural resources, and dominant populations who are allowed the upper hand in the expropriation of labor and materials.

VI

Written Language

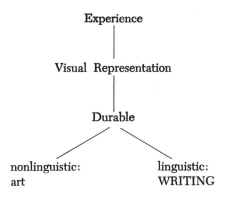

Experience

|

Visual Representation

|

Durable

nonlinguistic: linguistic:
art   WRITING

FACTORING OUT WRITING FROM OTHER DURABLE VISUAL REPRESENTATION

A PICTURE, by conventional wisdom, is worth a thousand words. Given the choice of photographing or describing in words a Hawaiian sunset, few of us would disagree on the choice. We would also probably concur that, while both the photograph and the verbal description are representations of the event, the first is not *language,* while the second is. Moreover, if I should listen to your verbal description and then go home and write it down, my writing would be a second-order linguistic representation of the event, and a first-order (immediate) linguistic representation of your speech (see chapter 2).

How do we decide where to draw the line between durable visual representation which is linguistic and that which is not? How do we know whether a particular representation is a representation of an event or a representation of language? Are pictures and language historically related—ever? sometimes? necessarily?

To understand and answer these questions, let us consider samples

149

of durable visual representation and compare their design, their content, and, to the extent we can determine it, their function. Our goal at this point is to familiarize ourselves with the sorts of visual representation whose linguistic status is problematic. (As we shall see in the section on the uses of written language, the structurally clear-cut cases of writing are interesting for a different set of reasons.)

Most of us have seen photographs of the cave paintings at Lascaux in Southern France and at Alta Mira in Spain. Less well known is that rock art has been found in widely diverse areas of the globe, including Australia (e.g., McCarthy, 1958; Berndt, 1964), North America (e.g., Smith and Turner, 1975; C. Grant, 1967), India (Brooks and Wakankar, 1976), and Africa (e.g., Willcox, 1963; Brentjes, 1969).[1] What is more, despite many differences in detail, there is a surprising degree of overlap in the subjects depicted and even (in some instances) in their manner of depiction.[2] Figures 6.1, 6.2, and 6.3 represent hunting scenes. The animals killed may differ from region to region, but the purpose in painting hunting scenes was probably similar: to induce success in subsequent hunts.

Questions of purpose are always difficult to resolve but especially so when some of our informants have been dead many thousand years.

Fig. 6.1 Horse Surrounded by Arrows, Lascaux Caves, France

Fig. 6.2 Bison Attacked by Hunters, Dharampuri, India (from Brooks and Wakankar, 1976:64)

Fig. 6.3 Man Attacking Buffalo, Concho County, Texas (from Jackson, 1938:281)

One of the most well reasoned analyses of the functions of rock art is that of Brooks and Wakankar (1976). Though written to examine the purposes of rock art in India, much of the theoretical framework is applicable to other regions as well. In their study, the authors identified twenty different "styles" of art, which they group into five historical periods. Styles are characterized by differences in subject matter, coloration, literalness of representation, and manner of drawing (e.g., heavy outline, x-ray style, solid figure). Based on this variation, Brooks and Wakankar hypothesize that alternative styles may serve different representational purposes, among which are religion, magic, secular records, symbolism (directional signals, taboo marks), and decoration. While many of these purposes may have been serious in character, it is also possible that these early artists laced their craft with humor. One mesolithic drawing depicts a nilgai antelope preg-

Fig. 6.4 Nilgai Antelope Pregnant with an Elephant, Hathi Tol Shelter, Raisen, India (from Brooks and Wakankar, 1976:84)

nant with an elephant (figure 6.4), which, according to the authors, "may illustrate a myth or reflect a sense of humor" (1976:84).

But what have rock paintings to do with writing? No one views these pictures as the equivalent of "written words." In terms of the criteria of lexicon, syntax, and productivity identified in chapter 3 as necessary features of any language, we would have great difficulty identifying anything akin to rules of combination (syntax). Yet, with respect to lexicon and productivity, the case is not as clear. Consider the notion of a lexicon: Smith and Turner (1975), for example, present a "catalog" of petroglyphs from Southern California, in which they note similarities between glyphs, thereby hinting at the possibility of similar representational functions. Brooks and Wakankar go a step farther, illustrating striking similarities between the same motifs in rock painting and pottery (figure 6.5). Without some notion of syntax, it is hard to know how to speak of "productivity," and yet it is clear that there was a great deal of combining of figures within a single vignette. Finally, there is the question of function. If Brooks and Wakankar are correct in the range of functions they attribute to rock art, then it appears that some of the purposes that art serves (e.g. secular records, religious ritual), language serves as well. How, then, do art and language differ in the ways in which they accomplish this task?

Let us pursue this question by comparing two types of visual rec-

Fig. 6.5 Comparison of Motifs in Indian Shelter Painting and
Pottery (from Brooks and Wakankar, 1976:32)

ords, both of which look like "art" to the untrained eye. Unlike the cave paintings, they both have an identifiable "order" to them (a crude syntax, if you will), and the motifs used are both more restricted in number and more stylized in presentation than the rock art; and yet, critical differences between the two types of records make us recognize one as art and the other as written language.

What are these differences? They are easier to talk about by first examining examples of both types of pictorial representation. In the first category we have, for instance, Piero della Francesca's "Legend

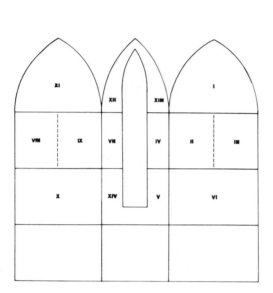

I
THE DEATH OF ADAM

II-III
THE QUEEN OF SHEBA WORSHIPPING THE
WOOD OF THE CROSS
THE QUEEN OF SHEBA BEING RECEIVED
BY KING SOLOMON

IV
THE CARRYING OF THE WOOD
OF THE CROSS

V
THE DREAM OF CONSTANTINE

VI
THE VICTORY OF CONSTANTINE
OVER MAXENTIUS

VII
THE TORTURE OF JUDAS

VIII-IX
THE FINDING OF THE CROSS
THE REVEALING OF THE TRUE CROSS

X
THE VICTORY OF HERACLIUS
OVER CHOSROES

XI
HERACLIUS RESTORING THE CROSS
TO JERUSALEM

XII
A PROPHET

XIII
A PROPHET

XIV
THE ANNUNCIATION

Fig. 6.6 Piero della Francesca, "Legend of the True Cross," Church of San Francesco, Arezzo, Italy. Plan of the Fresco (from Venturi, 1954:56–57)

of the True Cross" (figures 6.6 and 6.7) and the Bayeux Tapestry (plate 1). The "Legend of the True Cross" is a fresco cycle, painted in the mid fifteenth century, in the choir of the church of San Francesco in Arezzo, Italy. The fresco panels, viewed in proper sequence (see figure 6.6), are based upon the legend of the cross found in Voragine's *Golden Legend*, a late-thirteenth-century compendium of saints' lives.

The fresco cycle begins with the death of Adam, over whose tomb his son Seth plants the branch of a tree given to him by the Archangel Michael. From the wood of this tree will be made the crucifix on which the Messiah is to die. King Solomon later has the tree cut down, but the Queen of Sheba recognizes the tree's holy character. The scene then shifts to the conversion to Christianity of the Emperor Constantine. Legend has it that on the eve of battle against the tyrant Maxentius, an angel appeared to Constantine. The angel bore a sign of the cross on which was written *In signo hoc confide et vinces* ("In this sign believe and conquer"). And the story continues—Empress Helena, the mother of Constantine, sets about to find where Christ was crucified, and succeeds in unearthing the true cross. Chosroes, King of Persia, steals the cross, but the Emperor Heraclius succeeds in recovering it and returning it to Jerusalem.

Throughout the fresco cycle, the drawings themselves carry the story. The result is at once transparent and opaque. For the viewer already familiar with the legend, it is possible to "read" the chronicle of events without any written text. And yet, for the uninitiated who fails to recognize the Queen of Sheba or Empress Helena, the representational message is lost.

The Bayeux Tapestry is of the same genre as Piero's fresco cycle in that it tells a story through a series of visual depictions of events. The "tapestry" (it is actually an elaborately embroidered roll of linen, not a woven tapestry) was made in the town of Bayeux, France, sometime during the twelfth century. "Reading" from left to right across more than 230 feet of "text", we learn of the adventures of Harold, Earl of Wessex, and William, Duke of Normandy.

While Edward, King of England, is still on the throne, Harold crosses from England to France. The purpose of this trip is unclear. Harold may have gone to inform William that he, William, has been chosen as Edward's successor; alternatively, Harold might be attempting to re-

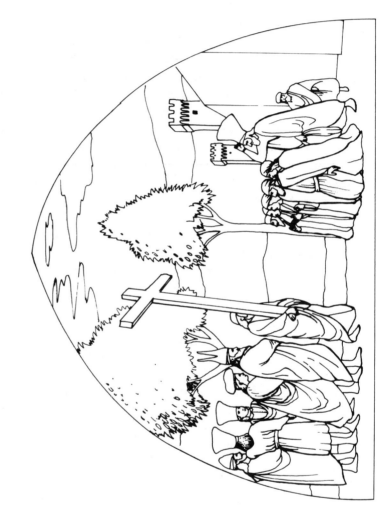

Fig. 6.7 Panels from Top Left-hand Side of "Legend of the True Cross" (VIII, IX, XI)

VIII: The Finding of the Cross

Empress Helena learns in Jerusalem that the only man to know the hiding place of the true cross is a man named Judas. When he refuses to reveal the place, Helena has Judas placed in a dry well. On the seventh day, Judas relents and leads Empress Helena to Mount Calvary, where three crosses have been buried.

IX: The Revealing of the True Cross

Three crosses are unearthed, but it must be determined which is the True Cross. Each cross is lowered over the body of a youth who died that day. When the True Cross is brought down, the youth rises back to life.

XI: Heraclius Restoring the Cross to Jerusalem Chosroes, King of Persia, conquers Jerusalem and carries off the cross. The Roman Emperor Heraclius, incensed, defeats Chosroes in battle (panel X). Panel XI shows Heraclius re-entering the city of Jerusalem, bearing the cross.

claim hostages being held in Normandy, or he might be on a pleasure trip. Harold eventually meets up with William and, after a series of adventures, returns to England. Edward dies, and Harold assumes the throne. On hearing of this, William has ships built and sails with his forces to England. William builds a castle at Hastings, provokes battle with the English, and defeats Harold.

As we see in Plate 1, one striking difference between the "Legend of the True Cross" and the Bayeux Tapestry is that the tapestry adds Latin glosses to the pictorial story line. The viewer need not already know the sequence of events in order to interpret the tapestry. Nevertheless, we must not confuse the two forms of representation on the tapestry. The Latin language provides a written representation of the illustrations, which are a visual representation of the Norman Conquest. If the viewer does not read Latin, he must rely on prior knowledge of the events depicted in order to understand what is actually happening in the tapestry.

The "Legend of the True Cross" and the Bayeux Tapestry contrast with a second type of pictorial representation. This second type is exemplified by the eight extant pre-conquest manuscripts made in Southern Mexico. Some of the best known of these are the Codex Nuttall (housed in the British Museum's Museum of Mankind in London), the Codex Selden and the Codex Bodley (housed in the Bodleian Library in Oxford), and the Codices Becker I and II (now in Vienna's Museum für Volkerkunde). These codices record Mixtec dynastic history from the late seventh century to the time of the Spanish conquest in the early sixteenth century. The manuscripts are made of treated animal hide that is painted and folded into sections. Mixtec "writing" was one of four systems of durable visual representation to develop in pre-conquest Mesoamerica. Other systems are documented among the Maya, the Aztec, and the Zapotec. All four systems are historically linked, but as yet we know little about the actual relationships between them.

Plate 2 is taken from the Codex Nuttall.[3] The codex, which was probably executed in the first half of the fourteenth century, tells the story of 8-Deer Tiger Claw (1011–1063 A.D.), the second ruler of the second dynasty of Tilantongo[4] (I shall come back to the issue of his name below). Alfonso Caso has "translated" the original codex. As Caso explains, the manuscript is read by following the red guide lines from right to left.

The reader begins in the upper right corner and goes down this column, passes to the second column which is between two red lines, ascends this column to where the red line is interrupted, and then descends the left-hand column.

In the first column is a palace in which is seated a lord, called ♂ 5 Crocodile (the 6 is mistaken), and a lady, ♀ 9 Eagle. He is wearing a mask of Tlaloc, the god of rain, and is carrying the sun on his back. His surname would be "Sun of Rain." From her comes her surname, "Garland of Cacao Flowers." Facing each other indicates they are married. The date is the year 6 Stone and the day 7 Eagle. According to our calculations, this year would be A.D. 992. Below appear the three children of this couple: the first son ♂ 12 Motion "Bloody Tiger," born the year following their marriage, in 7 House, A.D. 993; the second son ♂ 3 Water "Heron"; and a daughter ♀ 3 Lizard "Jade Ornament."

Turning to the second column, we see another palace in which is seated a lone lady called ♀ 11 Water "Bluebird-Jewel." She is the second wife of ♀ 5 Crocodile "Sun of Water"; the date of their wedding was the day 6 Deer of the year 10 House, A.D. 1009, or 17 years after his first marriage. In the year 12 Cane, A.D. 1011, in the day 8 Deer, their first son was born, called ♂ 8 Deer "Tiger's Claw," the most famous king of Mixtecs had, who reigned in Tilantongo and Teozacoalco and conquered many places. Then come the births of his younger brother, ♂ 9 Flower "Copal Ball with an Arrow," in the year 3 Cane, A.D. 1015, and his sister ♀ 9 Monkey "Clouds–Quetzal of Jade," in the year 13 Stone, A.D. 1012. Although older than ♂ 9 Flower, she is mentioned last, being a woman.

Descending the third column of this page, we see another palace and in it the lord ♂ 8 Deer "Tiger's Claw" and the lady ♀ 13 Serpent "Serpent of Flowers" who is offering him a bowl of chocolate, symbolic of marriage. The date of this is the day 12 Serpent of the year 13 Cane, A.D. 1051; thus, when "Tiger's Claw" married he was already 40 years old. The page ends with mention of the birth of his two sons: ♂ 4 Dog "Tame Coyote" in the year 7 Rabbit, A.D. 1058, and ♂ 4 Crocodile "Serpent Ball of Fire" two years later in 9 Stone, A.D. 1060. Thus ends page 26 of the Zouche-Nuttall codex. [Caso 1965:960–961]

What, then, is the difference between the pictorial-representations in the Piero fresco and the Bayeux Tapestry on the one hand, and the Mixtec codices on the other? A comparison of the Bayeux Tapestry and the Codex Nuttall makes the point clear.[5]

The Bayeux Tapestry and the Codex Nuttall bear a number of traits in common. Both are linear pictorial narratives of important events involving ruling families. Both order the events in such a way that the reader "knows" where to begin and where to end. Moreover, both employ some clearly identifiable pictorial conventions in the ways they represent their subject matter. In the Bayeux Tapestry, Englishmen have long hair and often wear mustaches, while the Normans are clean shaven. In the Codex Nuttall, stylized hills represent places, while arrows through the hills suggest that the places have been attacked (A.G. Miller. 1975:xv—see figure 6.8).

Fig. 6.8 Hill Pierced with Arrow Standing for Place Militarily Attacked. Codex Nuttall, p. 48 (from A.G. Miller, 1975:48)

But there are differences as well. The first that strikes the eye is that the Bayeux Tapestry depicts many people who are unnamed—footsoldiers, cavalry, royal attendants who assist the major figures in their exploits. In the Codex Nuttall, only the key figures, who are all named, are depicted; there are "no genre figures, no spear holders, no bystanders" (M.E. Smith, 1973:21). The lack of unnamed auxiliary figures in the Codex Nuttall is an important indication that the codex is a linguistic document telling a story, rather than being an artistic rendering of an event, as is the Bayeux Tapestry. Moreover, since the names of the figures in the Codex Nuttall are embedded in the figures themselves (for example, 9-Eagle is accompanied by her name sign, an eagle head with nine dots—see "Phoneticism and Pictorial Writing"), it is possible to "read" the document without going beyond the text. In the case of the Bayeux Tapestry, we must either know the story in advance or rely on the Latin glosses to make sense of the document. Without these, "we would know only that a group of clean-shaven people invaded by sea and defeated a group of people who wear moustaches" (M.E. Smith, 1973:173). The critical difference, though, is generally seen in the connection between the Codex Nuttall and the Mixtec language. Many of the pictures seem to stand for the things pictured (in Plate 2, the three pictures of children appearing under 5-Crocodile and 9-Eagle stand for the actual children the couple had), while others stand for ideas conjured up by pictures (in figure 6.8, the hill stands as a symbol for "place"). There is a third class of signs as well: those which unmistakably stand for sounds or words in the Mixtec language— so-called phoneticism. Caso offers the following example from Mixtec:

> [An] example of phonetics is evidenced by the identity of the Mixtec words for 'plain' and 'feathers'; both are *yodzo*. 'Plain' in the codices is represented by a feather mantle. Thus, the name for Coixtlahuaca, or *Yodzo Coo,* is translated as 'Plain of the Serpent,' and is represented by a serpent on a kind of feather mantle. [1965:951]

A particularly clear example of this is the place sign for the town of Coixtlahuaca as seen in figure 6.9. While Coixtlahuaca is a Nahuatl name, its Mixtec equivalent is Yodzo Coo (Serpent Plain).

I have intentionally begun this examination of written language somewhat informally in order to give a sense of the issues that arise in determining whether a particular durable visual representation is language. If we take cave painting, the Bayeux Tapestry, and the Codex Nuttall as representing a continuum from art towards language, then we might make the following observations about how written language and art differ:

> To be linguistic, a visual representation must have a conventionalized ordering of elements.

Compared with art, the discrete units in a language are:
  restricted in number.
  restricted in how much of the event they represent.
  repeated (or, in principle, repeatable) in a text.
There is some connection between the visual representation and the
  spoken language.

Fig. 6.9 Place Sign of Coixtlahuaca (Mixtec Yadzo Coo).
1580 Map of Ixcatlan (from M.E. Smith, 1973:245)

The following discussion will examine the extent to which these observations dovetail with the criteria for writing posited in the linguistic
literature.

CLASSIFICATION OF WRITTEN LANGUAGE

FORMAL CRITERIA

Treatises on writing have almost unanimously agreed that writing
systems that represent the sound of spoken language, (i.e., alphabetic
systems, syllabic systems, and "modified" hieroglyphic or ideographic
systems like Chinese and Egyptian) historically derive from pictorial
representations of experience rather than representations of language:

Plate 1 Bayeux Tapestry (Bayeux, France)
This portion of the tapestry shows Harold, then Earl of Wessex, leaving his manor house in Sussex and sailing for France ("Here Harold crossed the sea").

Plate 2 Codex Nuttall (The British Museum)
Page 26 of this pre-conquest Mixtec manuscript tells part of the history of the ruler 8-Deer Tiger Claw. See page 158.

Picture-writing is a mode of expressing thoughts or noting facts by marks which at first were confined to the portrayal of natural or artificial objects. It is one distinctive form of thought-writing without reference to sound . . . when adopted for syllabaries or alphabets, which is the historical source of evolution, it ceased to be the immediate and became the secondary expression of the ideas framed in oral speech. The writing common in civilization may properly be styled sound-writing, as it does not directly record thoughts, but presents them indirectly, after they have passed through the phase of sound. [Mallery, 1893:26]

Whenever we are able to trace the origins of a phonetically based script, it seems that we ultimately find pictorial precursors. In many cases, as in the spread of the Phoenician script, the pictorial origins of the script are wholly camouflaged by the time the script is borrowed by another people.

There are also cases such as that of the Ogham script which appear to follow a logic divorced from anything pictorial. Ogham is a script found on stone inscriptions in the British Isles (especially Ireland) and mostly used to represent the old Celtic language. Monuments bearing the script date from the fourth century A.D., although the script probably dates back much farther. Scholars debate its use; most conclude it was a secret script used by Druids, while others contend it served more practical purposes. More to the point is the way in which the script's elements are formed:

The alphabet consists of one to five notches on a central line (short strokes when written) for the five vowels *a, e, i, o, u* and one to five strokes, which stand to the left or the right of the central line, or cross it, for the consonants. In this way $4 \times 5 = 20$ possibilities are yielded. [Jensen, 1970:579]

These twenty possibilities are shown in figure 6.10. Figure 6.11 illustrates how the marks were actually used:

A central line, in tomb inscriptions, an edge of the grave pillar was used as a rule; [figure 6.12] shows a gravestone with a bilingual inscription. The old Irish Ogham inscription runs: *Sagramni maqi Cunatami*, and the Latin: *Sagrani fili Cunotami* '(The grave) of Sagran, son of Cunatam.' [ibid., pp.579–580]

No one knows where this highly stylized phonetically matched system of markings came from. As Jensen points out (ibid., pp.580–582),

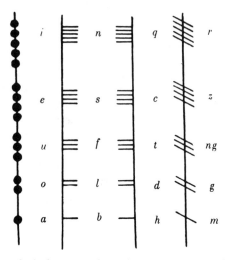

Fig. 6.10 Symbols for Vowels and Consonants in the Ogham Script (from Jensen, 1970:579)

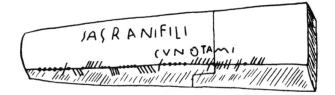

Fig. 6.11 Example of Ogham Inscription (ibid., p. 580)

Ogham has been traced to Latin by some and to Germanic Runes by others. (Still others would derive Runes from Ogham.) Unlike most alphabets, however, the signs in Ogham clearly exhibit a simplicity of organization that wholly belies any earlier pictorial source.

Furthermore, not every durable visual scheme of representation that has a phonetic base is necessarily language. A case in point is the West African system of *oroko* (sometimes called *aroko*), which makes use of homonyms for the names of numbers to get a message across. Jensen cites the following case from Yoruba:

> A group of six cowrie shells has the primary meaning 'six', *efa*. Since, however, *efa* also means 'attracted' (from *fa* 'to draw'), a cord with six cowrie shells sent by a young man to a girl means: I feel myself drawn

to you, I love you. Eight cowrie shells means 'eight', *ejo*. The same
word, however, also means 'agreeing' (from *jo* 'to agree', 'to be alike');
hence the sending of eight cowrie shells on the part of the girl to the
lover means: I feel as you do, I agree. [1970:31]

An example of oroko is shown in figure 6.12. Use of the so-called rebus
principle has, historically, been a central means by which pictorial representations of things are replaced by linguistic representations of
words. We must, however, be careful not to assume that the presence of
rebus implies an incipient written language, or, as we clearly see in the
case of oroko, that rebus can only derive from a representation of things.
Six cowrie shells represent the number "six"—not cowrie shells.

Returning to the issue of an artistic-linguistic continuum: At which
point do we attach the label "writing" (what some authors have
called "true" or "real" writing) to this durable representation? How
much of the representation must be phonetically grounded? Does
Mixtec, which seems to have a restricted amount of phoneticism,
qualify? In fact, must there be phoneticism at all?

We can formulate the problem in terms of the models of representation and linguistic representation presented in chapters 2 and 3. If a
form of representation is to be deemed a language, it must contain discrete elements which are productively combinable by an identifiable
set of rules. This is one criterion of written language.

A second criterion is that writing is a representation of *speech* rather
than of experience. Using the terminology developed in chapter 2,
speech would be a first-order representation of experience, while writing, being a representation of speech, would be a second-order representation. I have not, at this point, specified the type of representation
of speech I have in mind (e.g., lexical, phonological). A third criterion
requires that the second-order representation be based on sound; it
must represent speech on the phonological rather that the lexical level.

Which of these criteria are *necessary* for distinguishing writing from
art and which are arbitrarily imposed (much as the restriction of linguistic theory to the study of messages transmitted through the auditory-vocal channel is arbitrary)? Does the imposition of the second
criterion or of the second and third (n.b. the third implies the second)
place artificial limitations on what we consider to be written language
(limitations that we do not apply to spoken language)? To answer this
question, let us see how these criteria have been used in the literature
on writing.

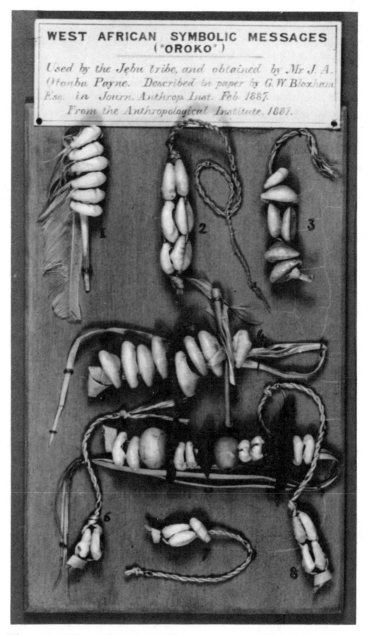

Fig. 6.12 West African Symbol Messages (Oroko). Photograph by V.P. Narracott; from the Pitt Rivers Museum, Oxford.

The literature contains proponents of all three positions. David Diringer, in distinguishing between "embryo-writing" and "writing proper," argues that embryo writing is isolated, arbitrary, and unsystematic

> in the way that [forms of embryo-writing] 'fix' language and ideas, and have little to do with the systematic and (in the fullest sense of the word) *conscious* writing which we find for the first time in the fourth millenium B.C. [1962:16]

Diringer seems to be distinguishing between unordered, nonconventionalized drawings on the one hand (e.g., in petroglyphs) and sequential picture-writing on the other (e.g., North American Indian pictographs):

> *Pictography* or *picture-writing*
> This is the most rudimentary stage of true writing. It is no longer restricted to the recording of single, disconnected images, but is capable of representing the sequential stages of ideas of a simple narrative. . . . Picture-writing can be expressed orally in any language without alteration of content, since the pictures do not stand for specific sounds. [ibid., p.21]

Diringer thus adheres to the first criterion I enunciated but allows his definition of writing to include direct, first-order representations of experience.

Diringer is, however, clearly in the minority in admitting picture-writing to be "true" writing. A somewhat stricter criterion (the second criterion) is adopted by George Trager, who insists that writing must at least represent speech:

> If writing is a symbol system that represents language items, it follows that it may conceivably represent any level of linguistic unit: articulation, sound, phoneme, morphophone, morpheme, syntactic operator, sememe, unit of utterance, unit of discourse. Depending on the perspicacity of the native analyst of the language, any one of these might be recognized and selected for the unit of the writing system. . . . Examination of the known writing systems shows that only some of these aspects of language have ever actually been recognized in writing systems. [1974:382]

(Chao, 1968:101 assumes a similar position.) Under this definition, writing systems may represent either sounds (as with alphabets and syllabaries) or words. However, most linguists and historians of writing insist upon adding the third criterion: that writing must have a phonetic base:

> The early pictograms denote things, but that is all; they cannot make statements, and they cannot convey thought. . . . Pictorial representation ends and true writing begins at the moment when an indubitable linguistic element first comes in, and that can only happen when signals have acquired a phonetic value. [Hawkes and Woolley, 1963:633]

Other proponents of the phonetic position include Gelb (1952), Bloomfield (1933:283), and Goody and Watt (1968:35).

Why this insistence upon a phonetic base for "true" writing? Is the criterion wholly arbitrary, or does it imply unspoken presuppositions about the uses to which speakers (and writers) put their language?

Structural Considerations

What Do the Symbols Represent?

In principle, there are five different types of entities that a durable visual symbol may represent:

> a thing
> an idea
> a word
> a syllable
> a sound

In practice, though, syllables and sounds are more easily discerned than the rest. Many of us are familiar with syllabaries in which each symbol represents a syllable in the language (like Korean, or in older times, Sumerian and Middle Egyptian). Similarly, little needs to be said about alphabets like Roman, Cyrillic, or Greek, in which each symbol represents a single sound. Not unexpectedly, there are minor complications with such straightforward characterizations—alphabetic systems have been known to use one letter to represent two sounds (the x in lox representing /ks/), or two letters for one sound (the ph for /f/ in phone). But the principle is clear enough.

Somewhat hazier are the distinctions between the representations of things, ideas, and words. Chapter 2 discussed the problem of whether the signifié of a linguistic sign was a thing in the objective world or an idea in a person's head. Saussure chose the latter, given our inherent difficulties in finding tangible referents for the sign *unicorn, upside-down,* or *perhaps.*

Traditionally, the attempt to distinguish between signs referring to things and those referring to ideas takes the form of a distinction between *logograms* and *ideograms.* Logograms are said to represent tangible entities such as objects, numerals, or proper names, while ideograms represent abstract notions associated with the item visually depicted. Thus, a picture of a leg would, logographically, stand for a bent leg, while the same symbol, ideographically, would depict the activity of running. The term *ideographic* might mean—but traditionally does not—the use of a symbol to represent a concept (in the Saussurian sense of *signifié*). Under such a definition, the symbol of a bent leg might, ideographically, stand for *either* the concept of a bent leg or the concept of someone running.

The one kind of representation not yet discussed is the use of a symbol to stand in place of a word. Our difficulty is in figuring out when the symbol is standing for either an object or an idea on the one hand, or a word on the other. About the only time we can be sure that a word (rather than an idea or a thing) is the referent is when the pictorial representation is being used because of the homonymic value of the word which names it (recall the example in figure 6.9 of the use of feathers to conjure up the homonym for *plain* in Mixtec). The problem, of course, is that once we understand that the object of representation is a word rather than a thing or an idea, then, necessarily, the real object of representation becomes the *sound* of that word rather than the word itself.

How Much of the System Uses Which Kind of Representation?

All of these issues aside, Is it necessary for the symbols to represent sounds (as with syllabaries or alphabets) in order to consider the system a language? There are three possible answers: either no phonological representation is necessary, some must be present, or the representations must entirely represent sounds. What are the empirical data we must account for, and how do we evaluate them?

From the outset we can eliminate wholly syllabic and alphabetic systems; they clearly fill the bill. The first problematic cases that come to mind are Chinese and Japanese. Japanese is a mixed type, combining the use of *kanji* (word signs borrowed from the Chinese) and *kana* (which are syllabic). This, of course, leads to the question of how to explain the writing of Chinese, which is far too complex to discuss here. Suffice it to say that Chinese writing is neither wholly logographic nor wholly ideographic in the traditional senses of the terms; indeed, it has a rather marked degree of phoneticism.[6]

What about intermediate cases such as Mixtec and Mayan, in which there is limited evidence of phoneticism in the visual representation? Is this degree of phoneticism "enough" to warrant our consideration of these durable schemes as written language?

Gelb epitomizes the traditional position that lack of "sufficient" phoneticism in a durable representation scheme is grounds for denying that scheme the status of language. It is on the phonetic issue that Gelb dismisses Central American systems such as Mixtec and Maya:

> It may shock some scholars to find the highly elaborate inscriptions of Central America classified with the primitive systems of the North American Indians and the African Negroes. Still, the result cannot be otherwise if we look at the problem from an unprejudiced point of view. . . . Although the beginnings of phonetization can be observed among both the Aztecs and the Mayas neither even approximately reached the phonetic stage of writing which we find so well developed already in the oldest Sumerian inscriptions. [1952:51]

What is more,

> the sporadic occurrences of phonetization cannot be taken as evidence of a high level of the Central American system since the principle of phonetization appears sometimes among primitive peoples without any prospects of developing into a full phonetic system. [ibid., p.54]

Recall here the case of West African oroko (figure 6.12).

Gelb's crowning argument belies a curious faith in the inevitability of progress in linguistic science. If the phenomena under consideration are indeed language, language scientists will recognize them as such:

> The best proof that the Maya writing is not a phonetic system results from the plain fact that it is still undeciphered. This conclusion is inescapable if we remember the most important principle in the theory of decipherment: *A phonetic writing can and ultimately must be deciphered if the underlying language is known.* Since the languages of the Mayas are still used to-day, and therefore well-known, our inability to understand the Maya system means that it does not represent phonetic writing. [ibid., p.56]

A curious argument, to say the least. Even if we overlook the fact that the Maya languages we hear today have probably undergone considerable phonological change in the last 500 to 1,000 years since the documents in question were composed, we are still faced with problems. We would hardly be able to defend a thesis that decipherment of a phonetically based script is not only inevitable but inevitable in a predetermined period of time. Success in decipherment seems to entail a curious mix of genius and hard work; Gelb overlooks the former.

However, another factor that may be important is whether the people studying the system are *open* to finding phoneticism. Linda Schele (1979) has argued persuasively that the failure of Maya scholars to find phoneticism may reflect, at least in part, their prior assumptions that it is not there to be found. The general disregard in which Bishop Landa's Maya alphabet has been held (see Pagden, 1975), and the phonetic excesses (according to some) of Yuri Knorozov's work (e.g., 1958) has led many scholars to be highly sceptical of phonetic interpretations. Mayanists such as Tatiana Proskouriakoff (e.g., 1960, 1973) and Heinrich Berlin (e.g., 1963) have developed

> a purely structural approach which makes no assumptions about the nature of the [spoken] language [associated with] the writing system. . . . Within the context of established knowledge about the Maya calendric and arithmetic systems, the inscriptions are studied with the assumption that the content is largely historical and great attention is given to careful study of each grapheme and the relationship of individual glyphs and phrases to the scenes which accompany them [Schele, 1979:14]

Crucial to the issue of decipherment is that

> readings in the original language are rarely and with extraordinary caution suggested and all assignments of meaning are made in the working language of the scholar, not in Maya (except where the field has traditionally used Maya terms as jargon). [ibid, p.14]

As Schele demonstrates in her own work, once one drops one's preconceptions about which factors are relevant in decipherment, one finds a great deal more phoneticism in Maya writing than had earlier been assumed.

And yet we should not attempt to press the issue of phoneticism in Maya writing too far. A great deal of Maya writing *is* pictographic (representing objects, ideas, or words—but not sounds). What is extremely important in deciphering Maya glyphs is understanding that *depending upon the circumstances,* the degree of phoneticism may be greater or smaller. The same glyph may on one occasion function as a logograph and on another as a phonetic sign.

What are the circumstances on which this "degree" of phoneticism depends? By the traditional hypothesis that signs become less pictorial and more phonetic as a representation scheme develops, we would tend to assume that the more phonetic signs in Maya appear in the historically later texts. Not so, says Schele. Rather, she argues that the *needs of the viewers* of the text helped determine the type of visual representation used:

> I suspect that much of the debate about phoneticism in Maya writing may result from the specialty of particular scholars. People who work primarily with texts on public monuments have traditionally believed that the phonetic signs are few in number, while those working with the codices have argued for a high degree of phoneticism. I believe that the Maya had a working set of phonetic glyphs from the beginning of the Classic Period and could have chosen to write phonetically rather than logographically at will. However, those texts on public monuments were intended to function as dynastic records for public consumption in a context where the literacy of the audience was not assured. Most pictographs and many of the more common signs do not require literacy; if we today can recognize a jaguar head, bundle, rabbit, mirror, or deity head, the populace of the Classic Period certainly could. Most of the glyphs on outdoor public monuments such as stelae are logographic and their appearance is remarkably consistent both temporally and geographically. However, when texts move to the interior area of building away from public space as at Palenque, the complexity of the texts and the degree of phoneticism, which does require literacy, expands dramatically. The codices have a high level of phoneticism, but they are designed for use by professional literates. I call to your attention our own growing use of logographic (or pictographic) sign in our own culture when the international sign system is now used in public areas and on highways where literacy is required, but is unexpected in the local language. [1979:16]

The situation is strongly reminiscent of the way in which the message of the Bible was made available in the European Middle Ages. Only priests had regular access to the written holy word. For the illiterate masses (the vast majority of the population), the stories of the Old and New Testaments were learned through sermons, morality plays, and, above all, through stained glass windows in churches.

The data from Maya cast serious doubts on the unexamined assumption that the higher the degree of phoneticism in a writing system, the more "linguistic" that scheme is in some absolute sense. But why have students of written language insisted on a phonetic base in the first place?

The primary assumption behind this insistence is that pictorially based representations are, in principle, unable to represent the full range of referents that can be represented in sounds. Speaking of pictographic means of communication, Goody and Watt state categorically that "however elaborately the system is developed, only a limited number of things can be said" (1968:35). The authors fail to mention, though, that there may be other considerations that make the superiority of phonetically based writing less certain.

Let us return to the aphorism at the beginning of this chapter: a picture is worth a thousand words. There are indeed cases in which a representation of an object or idea is far clearer in conveying a message than is a phonetic representation. Maps (as opposed to written directions) are good examples (at least for most people). The fact that do-it-yourself instructions almost invariably contain drawings—sometimes *only* drawings—suggests that sequences of events whose outcomes *can* be illustrated are sometimes more clearly represented by picturing rather than by describing events.

A second assumption is that pictorially based schemes that represent things, ideas, or words are necessarily iconic, and therefore inadequate to convey things, ideas, or words that are not easily pictured. Another alternative, of course, would be to have each symbol arbitrarily linked with its *signifié*. A good example of such a system is the arbitrary symbol languages used in teaching language to chimpanzees. Premack and Premack (e.g., 1972) had plastic forms arbitrarily paired with such abstract referents as *if-then* and *different* (see figure 6.13), and Duane Rumbaugh's computer lexigrams are associated arbitrarily with referents like *name-of, into,* and *eat* (figure 6.14).

However, is this potential for limitless representation, which phoneticism provides, actually used? Or do many representations that qualify as "true" writing on the grounds of phoneticism actually accomplish no more communicative work than do systems that represent things or ideas? This question is reminiscent of the one posed in chapter 4 about the usefulness of the notion of an ideal speaker-listener. If our concern is with how people *use* language rather than with what

Chocolate

Banana

Give

Wash

?

No-Not

Yellow
                                    Brown

Fig. 6.13 Examples of Signs Taught to Sarah the Chimpanzee. From "Teaching Language to an Ape" by Ann James Premack and David Premack, p.93. Copyright © 1972 by Scientific American, Inc. All rights reserved.

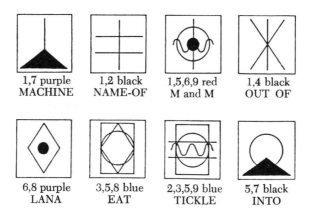

1,7 purple	1,2 black	1,5,6,9 red	1,4 black
MACHINE	NAME-OF	M and M	OUT OF
6,8 purple	3,5,8 blue	2,3,5,9 blue	5,7 black
LANA	EAT	TICKLE	INTO

Fig. 6.14 Sample Lexigrams from Yerkish (from von Glasers-feld, Department of Psychology, University of Georgia, Athens, Georgia, 30601 and Yerkes Regional Primate Research Center of Emory University, Athens, Georgia.

they *might* do under idealized circumstances, then we want to consider what a functional classification of writing might look like.

FUNCTIONAL CONSIDERATIONS

Functional classifications of written language are barely in their infancy. Only one article (Basso, 1974) has appeared in the linguistic literature that directly broaches the question of which functions writing might serve. Basso's classification is an overt attempt to mirror in writing the model of function as discursive competence that Hymes developed for spoken discourse (e.g., 1972). Basso suggests analyzing written language with respect to such categories as *participants, form, topic,* and *function.* If we were to consider the writing of letters, the *participants* would include at least one sender and one receiver; the *form* would take into consideration the quality of the stationery and of the grammar; the *topic* might range from "letter to the editor" to a letter to a friend; and the *function* could be anything from a letter of resignation to a thank-you note for a gift.

As we saw in chapter 4, though, the notion of "function" (and, in the present context, of "functional classification") in which we are interested here takes us far beyond Basso's initial distinctions. To get some idea of the range of issues a functional classification of writing might raise, let us briefly consider an example.

The Mnemonic Function of Writing

One of the reasons we write things down is so that we—or somebody else—will not forget what we have thought or observed or said. We write wills so that our descendants will not squabble over who gets the real estate and who gets the stocks. We keep records of how many seeds germinate in a botany experiment. We take notes in class lectures to help us prepare for final examinations.

If writing serves a mnemonic function (among others), then we can ask the following questions:

Can other nonlinguistic forms of representation serve the same function?

How much of what is to be remembered is represented by the mnemonic device?

Does the form of the written representation have any influence on the extent to which the function of the writing system is mnemonic?

The answer to the first question is obviously yes. We tie strings around our fingers to remind us to pick up the dry cleaning; we leave out empty milk cartons to remind us to pick up more milk. Many societies rely on tally sticks to indicate how many items were processed in some way—they might make notches on a stick rather than writing in a record book "We baked seventeen loaves of bread." Or consider the recurrent practice among high school students of assigning numbers to jokes, so that in the middle of a class someone will call out "Fourteen!" and the whole class will burst into laughter for reasons wholly unbeknownst to the teacher.

Even when the representation takes the form of phonetic writing, the amount of the message to be conjured up varies. This variance appears both when one looks at a single contemporary writing system (I might write *bread* or *buy a loaf of Sunbeam white bread*), as well as when one makes comparisons between systems or across time. Spanish orthography informs us at the beginning of a sentence—and then again at the end—that what we are reading is a question, while English only provides an interrogative marker at the end:

Spanish: ¿Cómo está?
English: How are you?

The *Anglo-Saxon Chronicle* regularly begins its entries with the word *Her*, meaning "in this place," while today we would tend to use a phrase instead of the lexical abbreviation.

It can also be argued that the more ambiguities possible in a system of writing, the more this system serves as a cue for formulaic phrases rather than as a representation of novel thoughts or words. In Eric Havelock's words,

> the range of ambiguity in decipherment stands in inverse ratio to the range of possible coverage supplied by the content. If you want your reader to recognize what you intend to say, . . . you must fit your intended meanings to meanings that the reader will be prepared to accept. [1976:33]

Havelock argues that while syllabic scripts "tend to partake of the formulaic" (ibid.), alphabets permit greater variety in individual expression. In fact, he attempts to establish a causal connection between the development of the Greek alphabet and the emergence of Greek democracy (1976, 1978).

Similarly, Chadwick suggests a causal relationship between formal considerations and the extent to which Linear B was a mnemonic device rather than a record of individual inventions. Commenting upon the apparent limitation of writing to administrative matters, he asks,

> Why should not letters, histories or even poems have been written down? The clumsiness of the script imposes a limitation; we may question how far a document in Linear B would be readily intelligible to someone who had no knowledge of the circumstances of its writing. It is rather like shorthand; the man who wrote it will have little difficulty in reading it back. But a total stranger might well be puzzled, unless he knew what the contents were likely to be. Thus the existence of books and a reading public is unlikely from the outset. [1958:131]

Chadwick's observations seem to follow Havelock's hypotheses about ambiguity and invention: Linear B, like the later prealphabetic Greek script, which was borrowed from the Semites centuries later, was also syllabic.

Thus we see that written languages might be classified with respect to the extent of their literal rendering of what was thought or said (as opposed to conjuring up a precomposed "formula" of words or phrases). In some cases, the mnemonic classification may correlate with structurally based notions of classification (e.g., syllabic vs. alphabetic). Our task, in such cases, is to explain the correlation rather than assume the redundancy or irrelevance of one or another set of features. This situation is precisely parallel to the case study in chapter 5, in which we explored the reasons behind structural and functional properties of trade jargons and pidgin languages.

Our discussion of the varying scale of mnemonic functions is but one example of a functional category by which to classify written languages, yet there are probably dozens of others. In order to get some sense of which functional ranges of written language are possible, we need to probe more deeply into the uses of actual written languages.

USES OF WRITTEN LANGUAGE

Written language, I have suggested, has an existence distinct from that of spoken language, but that, like speech, admits of variation. Nonetheless, speech and writing can, in principle, be used for referring to the same semantic domains. Poetry and legal statutes, genealogies and shopping lists, lectures and cooking directions can be expressed in speech, writing, or both. As we shall see in this section, speaking has typically served a wider range of semantic functions than has writing. Societies are recognized as becoming increasingly literate as they make the functional range of written language more closely approximate that of speech. In fact, the traditional insistence on recognizing as "true writing" only those systems of permanent visual representation that have a phonetic base can be formulated in functional terms: "true writing" (in the Bloomfieldian sense) is that which can be used to fill the same semantic functions as spoken language and can do so with the same lexical and syntactic devices. That is, "true writing" can be *minimally* defined as an approximate transcription of spoken language,[7] without denying that writing may fill additional functions as well. This section will consider this minimal definition of writing, historically examining the extent to which writing has indeed assumed the range of functions commonly attributed to speech.

LINGUISTIC FUNCTION AND THE CONCEPT OF LITERACY

Written language may come to approximate the semantic range of spoken language in one of two ways: either the absolute number of uses to which writing is put can expand, or the number of senders and receivers of written messages can increase—or, of course, both. In principle, there is no reason why a restricted literate class could not increase the range of functions of written language without the size of the literate population increasing as well. Historically, however, the two factors often have gone hand in hand. Therefore, an examination of functional expansion of written language needs to be accompanied by a study of changing patterns of literacy among the populace. That is, we shall need to understand the access people within a society have to the written word, the context of that encounter, and the extent of their proficiency.

Havelock (1976:44) has argued that the Greeks invented literacy since they adapted the Phoenician alphabet in such a way that the Greek language could be easily and unambiguously transcribed and deciphered by any Greek citizen. Gudschinsky's definition of literacy is consonant with Havelock's in that it considers transcription and decipherment as the goals of literacy:

> That person is literate who, in a language he speaks, can read with understanding anything he would have understood if it had been spoken to him; and can write, so that it can be read, anything that he can say. [1968:146, cited in Gudschinsky, 1976:3]

Such a definition of literacy is deceptively simple. If we agree with Hymes (1973) and Bernstein (1971) in the "inequality of speakers"— that (spoken) linguistic abilities of different individuals within a language community are not necessarily comparable—then Havelock or Gudschinsky's approach to literacy would force us to conclude that *literacy* is at once a univocal and a multivocal term.

An alternative approach to literacy is taken by authors such as Schofield, who argues that no single definition of literacy exists which is universally applicable:

> At least for the English industrial revolution it would seem that . . . necessary levels of literary skills varied widely in different sectors of the economy. The meaning of literacy therefore changes according to the context, and it is the responsibility of the historian to specify the appro-

priate level of literary skills consistent with his understanding of the context. [1968:314]

Intimately tied up with the question of individual proficiency in reading and writing are the social and performative issues of whether reading is done silently or aloud and whether it is an individual or a group activity. Our twentieth-century perspective on the functions of reading emphasizes both silence and solitude. Yet these are recent developments: "silent reading as we know it was very rare until the advent of printing—in the ancient world books were used mainly for reading aloud" (Goody and Watt, 1968:42). Steiner observes that

> reading in our sense—"with unmoving lips"—does not predate St. Augustine (who remarked on it) by very much. But I would narrow the range even further. The existence of the book as a common, central fact of personal life depends on economic, material, educational preconditions which hardly predate the late sixteenth century in western Europe and in those regions of the earth under direct European influence. [1972:198–199]

The tradition of oral reading to a group makes written messages available to a segment of the population larger than that which is literate (Schofield, 1968:312–313). Thus, even an accurate count of the literate population (by whatever criterion) will not necessarily reflect the uses of writing within the population.

The "oral" and public character of reading did not begin to give way until printing made possible the private use of books. As McLuhan points out:

> It was almost a century after print from movable type began before printers thought to use pagination for readers. Before then pagination was for bookbinders only. With print, the book ceased to be something to be memorized and became a work of reference. [1960:129]

Similarly, the role of punctuation changed. Nineteenth-century editors of Shakespeare added grammatical punctuation, thinking

> to bring out, or hold down his meaning . . . But in Shakespeare's time, punctuation was mainly rhetorical and auditory rather than grammatical. The fourth century grammarian Diomedes tells that punctuation marks indicate an "opportunity for taking breath." [ibid., p.126]

More generally, printing brings with it a shift from a verbal to a visual approach to the page:

When the eye of a modern copyist leaves the manuscript before him in order to write, he carries in his mind a visual reminiscence of what he has seen. What the medieval scribe carried was an auditory memory of one word at a time. [Chaytor, 1960:124]

SELECTIVE USES OF WRITING

Questions of literacy lead to more general questions about the use of writing. In addition to asking who in the population is involved with written language, we want to know what the writing is used for.

To begin with, we should be aware that knowledge of the possibility of written language does not, in itself, ensure that such writing will ever be used. Hawkes and Woolley, citing Diakonoff, admit that

> the ancient Germans knew of the idea of writing for centuries and even had developed a kind of alphabet of their own (the Runes), but they did not apply their writing system to anything better than magical uses until they had reached the stage of class society. [1963:665]

Even in societies in which writing has been introduced, literacy may initially have highly circumscribed uses. Goody and Watt argue that while Sumerian, Egyptian, Hittite, and Chinese societies were in some sense literate,

> when we think of the limitations of their systems of communication as compared with ours, the term 'protoliterate', or even 'oligoliterate', might be more descriptive in suggesting the restriction of literacy to a relatively small proportion of the population. [1968:36]

Similarly, Havelock (1976:21) speaks of "craft literacy" in Greece for at least 150 years after the adoption of the Phoenician alphabet. Only for the sixth and fifth centuries B.C. does Havelock attribute first semi-literacy, then recitation literacy, and finally scriptorial literacy to the general citizenry.

One of the clearest cases of restricted literacy, with respect to both communicative function and size of the literate population, is Linear B. John Chadwick (1958, 1959) has argued that in Mycenaean Greece, writing was used fairly extensively for administrative purposes, but apparently had little or no use outside of bureaucratic circles.[8]

The recording of a particular kind of communication in writing does not, in itself, guarantee that the population will encounter it in written form. In the case of the Old Testament, for example, the presence of a written text initially had little effect on the people:

In the beginning, the written book is not intended for practical use at all. It is a divine instrument, placed in the temple "by the side of the ark of the covenant that it may be there for a witness" (Deuteronomy xxxi. 26), and remains there as a holy relic. For the people at large, oral instruction still remained the only way of learning, and the memory—the only means of preservation. Writing was practiced, if at all, only as an additional support for the memory. [Gandz, 1935:253–254]

The spread of literacy may be hampered by pragmatic considerations such as complexity of script (Goody and Watt, 1968:35), social stratification (Sumerian and Akkadian kings were illiterate—ibid., p.37), or geographic mobility. In Somali, for example,

the exigencies of the nomadic life allow few nomads to attend . . . schools regularly or over long periods, and teaching is in any case for the most part limited to learning the Qur'ān by heart and not directed towards teaching writing as such. [Lewis, 1968:267]

Equally important is the strength of the existing oral tradition. Again in Somali,

[one explanation of] the surprisingly slight extension of literate Arabic culture notwithstanding the Somalis' long exposure to Islam is the high development of oral communication. The Somali language is a particularly rich and versatile medium and its speakers are very conscious of its literary resources. [ibid.]

Expansion and Decline in Literacy

We have, thus far, been looking at literacy largely in static terms, that is, at selected uses of written language at given periods of time. It is appropriate, however, to "dynamicize" the issue of usage and ask, Under what conditions do the uses of writing spread in a society, and under what conditions do some (or all) uses of writing fall into disuse?

The answer to the question of growth is fairly well documented in the rise of the European middle classes in the eighteenth and nineteenth centuries (cf. Defoe, 1726) and in plans for modernization in emerging countries around the world (e.g., Unesco, 1973). In both instances, the motivations for increased use of writing (and increased literacy) have been largely economic. The proliferation of grammar books in England aided lower class children in acquiring the necessary skills of reading, writing, and arithmetic for improving their station by entering business. In newly developing countries, limited literacy may help a farmer ensure that he is not cheated by traders; more sophisticated written skills may open up a new range of occupational possibilities.

Once a sizable portion of a population becomes literate, written language can, in addition to its more distinctive purposes such as recording laws or serving as a cultural medium, begin to approximate some of the functions of spoken language. A lecturer can jot notes to himself before delivering a speech; friends may exchange letters just to "keep in touch" rather than waiting for a significant event to occur before writing; newspapers can provide the sensationalism that the previously nonliterate classes used to witness in public gatherings.

But the uses of written language may also diminish in number, either when an established writing system is adopted by a previously illiterate people or when the needs of an already literate society change. Just because written representation may historically progress from the potential encoding of a wider range of (phonological) messages to actually doing so, does not ensure that these functions will always be preserved. The data on literacy decline—either in numbers of people or in language function—are, by definition, more difficult to gather than data on the increase in literacy. Yet, disregarding instances in which the decline—or loss—of literacy was brought about by the fall of a civilization (as in the case of Linear B), we can point to at least one case of decline: that among members of cargo cults in coastal and island Melanesia.

The cargo cults, millenarian movements which have grown up in Melanesia at various times during the twentieth century, are Western adaptations of indigenous religions in which a primary purpose is the acquisition of "explicit socio-economic benefits for the practitioners" (Meggitt, 1968:301). Christian missionaries were, by comparison, wealthy and powerful and assured their audience of equality under Christianity. The native population was initially willing to embrace the new religion as a way of sharing in the missionaries' wealth. Such religious participation included schooling:

Men were . . . keen to place their sons . . . in the mission schools to learn the new arts of reading and writing and so penetrate more quickly the mystic secrets which missionaries alleged were contained in the Bibles and prayerbooks. With the esoteric knowledge in their grasp the natives could, so they thought, then directly command the help of the new deity just as they controlled their own gods. [ibid., p.302]

From the beginning, however, literacy did not have the same function in the eyes of the Melanesians as it did in those of their Christian teachers:

> Writing was rarely treated as a straightforward technique of secular action, one whose prime value is repeated and surrogate communication of unambiguous meanings in a variety of situations. [ibid.]

Instead, the Melanesians looked upon written language as "one more of those inherently ambiguous models of communication with the supernatural with which they were already familiar" (ibid.).

Soon, however, the Melanesian faith in the missionaries—and in the benefits of literacy—was shattered, for despite their participation in mission rituals—and despite their sons' learning to read and write—they remained materially poor. The result was a withdrawal from mission churches and schools and from uses of literacy that we would recognize. The native population did, however, retain a ritualized manipulation of writing as a way of understanding the supernatural (ibid., pp. 303–304). Meggitt concludes:

> As long as this kind of chiliastic world view prevails . . . , European-sponsored education has little objective value for the majority of the people, and literacy has a different meaning from that held by the foreigners. [ibid., p.304]

THE MINIMAL DEFINITION OF WRITING AS TRANSCRIPTION

We have been looking at the uses of written language, working under a minimal definition of writing as a transcription of spoken language in order to see variation in the degree to which so-called literate societies have utilized writing as an approximate permanent representation of the semantic domains covered in spoken language. However, as argued earlier, this representation can be, at best, approximate. Not only does writing underrepresent what is spoken (cf. Chao, 1968:110), but it also goes beyond its transcriptive function in that transmission of a message to an absent or unspecified interlocutor creates its own structural and stylistic constraints.

To what extent is this minimal definition of language empirically correct? Is writing *ever* "merely a way of recording language by visible marks," or are there always features that structurally and stylistically set it apart from speech? The answer to this question varies historically: at one extreme lies classical Chinese writing, which has a lexicon, syntax, and diction quite distinct from that of even educated Mandarin speech (Brandt, 1944); at the other extreme lie the phonological transcription systems devised by linguists or missionaries for recording previously unwritten languages. At this same end of the spectrum we find the writings of newly "literate" people who have learned to write the alphabet and to sound out words but have not been trained in a "literary" tradition. Most written languages lie somewhere in between.

The history of written English is an interesting example of how the degree of correspondence between written and spoken language can be repeatedly redefined. If our records accurately reflect the history of writing in the English speaking world, we can identify an early period in which the written style (be it poetic, as in *Beowulf*; historical, as in the *Anglo-Saxon Chronicles*; or ecclesiastical, as in Ælfric's *Homilies*) was clearly distinct from colloquial usage. Colloquial writing (writing approximating a transcription of everyday speech) begins to appear in Middle English (e.g., the Northern mystery plays, Chaucer) and, though not dominant, continues in Early Modern English (e.g., Shakespeare) and Modern English (e.g., Dickens—see Brook, 1970). But does the balance ever shift? Does colloquial speech ever dominate written style? This, I suggest, is precisely what has happened in contemporary American English.

THE FUNCTIONS OF WRITTEN LANGUAGE IN TWENTIETH-CENTURY AMERICA

It is always difficult to be objective when assessing the present—we must be suspicious of perennial Jeremiahs who would have us believe that our age is one of cultural or spiritual decay. Yet it is clear from the popular and academic literature of the past few years that many highly literate people are concerned with what they feel to be a growing illiteracy among school-age—and especially college-age—Americans (e.g., Sheils, 1975; G. Lyons, 1976). Some skeptics (e.g., Stewart, 1976) point out that complaints about declining literacy go back at least a century, leading us to question whether we are indeed falling under the sway of those "perennial Jeremiahs." However, since so many universities and colleges are insisting on English composition or remedial reading courses, the problem merits our attention.

The role of the linguist in American higher education has always been distinct from that of the English composition teacher, partly because of the linguist's preoccupation with speech, and partly because of the structuralist tradition of descriptivism. Yet, in the context of the present approach to writing, perhaps the time has come when the linguist and the pedagogue can join forces.

I have argued that the structures of a language are a function of the uses of that language, that societies differ in their linguistic needs, and that individuals differ in their linguistic abilities as well as needs. Furthermore, I have demonstrated that written language can be analyzed in this same framework. If we encounter a society that has a writing system that can, in principle, express a potentially infinite number of messages, but in which the potentially literate population encounters difficulty in using writing for many of these purposes, then we have two possible explanations. The first is that the functions of literacy themselves remain intact but either the quality of education is deficient or student motivation is flagging. The second is that the functional balance of literacy has shifted. Educators have generally chosen the first alternative. We shall, instead, look at the second.

Have we reason to believe that the functions of writing have changed —or have been changing—over the past century? Steiner, writing independently of the current pedagogical discussion, has argued that during the twentieth century the uses of written language have radically altered. In eighteenth- and nineteenth-century Europe, reading was a private encounter between the individual and the book:

> A man sitting alone in his personal library reading is at once the product and begetter of a particular social and moral order. It is a *bourgeois* order founded on certain hierarchies of literacy, of purchasing power, of leisure, and of caste. [1972:199–200]

Riesman describes roughly this same period in similar terms:

> If oral communication keeps people together, print is the isolating medium *par excellence*. People who would simply have been deviants in a preliterate tribe, misunderstanding and misunderstood, can through books establish a wider identity. [1960:114]

Riesman contrasts "the bookish education of these inner-directed men" (ibid.) with that of their other-directed successors who are "men molded as much by the mass media outside their education as by their schooling; men who are more public relations-minded than ambitious" (ibid., p.115). Similarly, Steiner speaks of the loss of privacy in encounters with the written word. Reading has become a public behavior to be practiced in a university library or in one's office rather than at home. With the coming of the paperback, books have become quasi-disposable. Even highbrow paperbacks carry "no manifest sign of economic or cultural elitism. Mickey Spillane and Plato share the same book rack in the airport lounge or drug store" (Steiner, 1972:200). More important, print has lost much of its communicative value, as it is increasingly being replaced by tape deck or video:

> It is now a commonplace that audio-visual means of communication are taking over wide areas of information, persuasion, entertainment which were, formerly the domain of print. At a time of global increase in semi- or rudimentary literacy (true literacy is, as I have tried to suggest, in fact decreasing), it is very probable that audio-visual "culture packages," i.e., in the guise of cassettes, will play a crucial role. It is already, I think, fair to say that a major portion of print, as it is emitted daily, is, at least in the broad sense of the term, a caption. It accompanies, it surrounds, it draws attention to material which is essentially pictorial. [ibid., p.207]

To Steiner's list of reasons for the retreating functions of print we can add several more. The first of these is the telephone; a vast amount of communication that previously was transmitted in writing can now be done in spoken language. A second factor is the growing degree of geographic mobility; the need for letter writing, if not obviated by a phone call, is likely to be met by a personal visit instead. A third (and admittedly more ephemeral) reason is a growing degree of informality. In a lecture several years ago, I proposed that the growth of a youth-dominated culture in post-World-War-II America was partially responsible for the decline in writing abilities. One of my colleagues countered that literacy was not declining—only the degree of formality was. He argued that it was now acceptable to allow our writing to mirror casual conversation—full of false starts, changes of direction, and so forth. If he is correct, then writing is indeed changing its function from being a reflective medium in which the sender must anticipate his receiver's reaction in constructing his written message, to an idiosyncratic stream of consciousness in which the role of the receiver becomes all but irrelevant.

To say that the functions of writing may be changing is not, however, to give up on making the population "literate." Rather, it is to suggest that before we can hope to solve an educational problem, we should know its systemic causes; and linguistic theory may prove helpful in unearthing that etiology.

PHONETICISM AND PICTORIAL WRITING

We have been looking now in some detail at the range of uses to which written language can be put, and comparing them with the functional range of speech. What remains is to explore how this heightened sensitivity to function assists us in solving some of the definitional problems posed in the beginning of this chapter. In particular, we want to ask whether functional considerations help in deciding whether the requirement that a durable representation have a phonetic base is an arbitrary criterion to impose on written language. Our discussion will center on the representation of proper names in two graphic representational systems that have sometimes been denied the status of "writing": preconquest Central Mexican texts, and North American Indian texts.

The Representation of Proper Names

The argument hinges on the distinction between proper and common names and how such a distinction is recorded in durable representation. All human languages (see Hockett, 1963) have ways of distinguishing between individuals (proper names) and classes (common names). For example, *Albert* belongs to the class of men, *Providence* to the class of cities. Phonetically based systems of writing (alphabets or syllabaries) can represent this distinction unambiguously. In pictorially based systems of representation, the matter is more complex. Yet the pictorial component is not the only—or even the most important —factor to consider.

Paradigmatically, when one represents a proper name nonphonetically, one needs a way of distinguishing between the individual and the class of which it is a member. If I wish to represent my grandfather, I need to be sure that you don't interpret the symbol as "man." Assuming I am a good artist, and assuming further that you, as my audience, know what my grandfather looks like, the problem should be obviated.

However, since writing is, par excellence, a means of communicating with an audience not present at the formulation of my message, I have no way of guaranteeing that the second assumption will hold.

It has traditionally been assumed (e.g., Gelb, 1952:103–104; Goody and Watt, 1963:35) that this problem of distinguishing between class and individual representation has been one of the primary motivating forces behind the introduction of phoneticism into earlier pictographic systems of representation. A man on a throne could be any king, but either the alphabetic "William" or pictures of a will and a yam, interpreted as rebus elements, make it clear that the referent is a specific individual. This formulation of the problem presupposes, I suggest, that the "meaning" of proper names is not transparent (this theory, while appropriate for much of modern western Europe, is highly inappropriate for many other societies). Naming dictionaries may tell us that *Charles* means "man of the common people" or that *John* means "Yahweh is gracious,"[9] but in common usage these meanings are not obvious. Even names that may be transparent on reflection (*Rio Grande, Pennsylvania, Miller, Baker*) we tend to treat as arbitrary labels.

The semantics of naming is, however, quite different in other societies, including the two whose writing will be considered here: North American and Central Mexican Indians. Most of this discussion will deal with personal names, although many of the same points can be made about place names (toponyms) as well. We need to look at what structure these names had, how they were represented in writing, and what happened when additional or foreign names had to be represented. Before beginning, a few comments on the writing systems themselves are in order.

The use of pictography among the American Indians is well documented (see Mallery, 1893, reprinted 1972b). Isolated symbols or chains of symbols were used to keep records, including religious rituals, histories of past events, and censuses of the members of a community. Typical of these mnemonic records were the "winter counts," such as the so-called Lone Dog's Winter Count (figure 6.15). Pictographs were also used for sending novel messages, and after the coming of the whites some of these were even sent through the United States mails (Mallery, 1972b, Vol. I:363). Because of their restricted usage and lack of a phonetic base, American Indian pictographs have not generally been regarded as actual writing (e.g., Gelb, 1952:21).

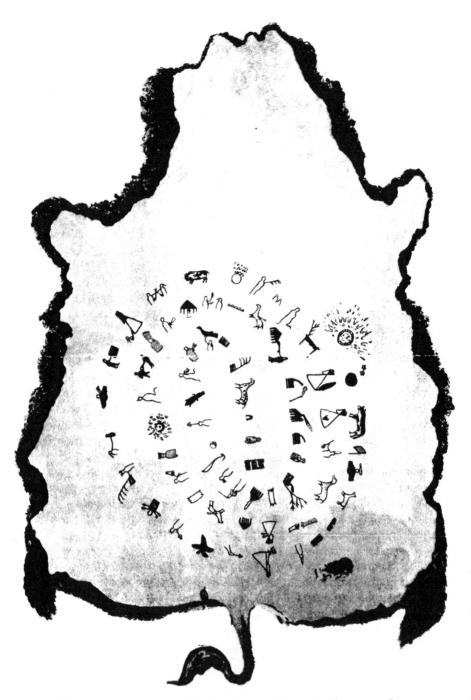

Fig. 6.15 Lone Dog's Winter Count (from Mallery, 1972b, vol. I:266)

On the other hand, Gelb notwithstanding, it is now commonly acknowledged that the Indians of Mesoamerica developed writing systems before the coming of the Spanish (Benson, 1973:v). The best-known (and most sophisticated) of these was the system of Maya glyphs used in what is now the Yucatan, El Salvador, British Honduras, and Guatemala. A different system (although probably connected at some point historically with Maya writing) developed in Central Mexico. Sometimes known as "Aztec," other times more generally as "Mixteca-Puebla" (Nicholson, 1973:1), it was used on monumental stelae and in painted codices to record historical and genealogical information, and ritual. Most of the representations are pictorial, having either iconic or ideographic import (A.G. Miller, 1975:xiv–xv). In addition, they contain some phoneticism through rebus.

NORTH AMERICAN INDIAN "PICTURE WRITING"

Keeping this brief background in mind, let us return to the issue of proper names. In native North America, personal names generally connote an object or attribute with which the person so named is identified. Many of the names refer to animals and attributes or positions of those animals (Spotted-Horse, Sitting-Bull), while others refer to exploits or attributes of the individual himself (Caught-the-Enemy, Spotted-Face, Johnny-Belches-When-He-Eats). The common feature of these names is that they are easily represented graphically; sometimes the figure named is represented with the distinguishing characteristic (Roman-Nose, figure 6.16; Spotted-Face, figure 6.17), while other times the identifying object or characteristic is drawn separately and connected with the human figure by a line (Stabber, figure 6.18; Spotted-Elk, figure 6.19). In some cases the identifying characteristic appears by itself without the generic human figure (Red-Shirt, figure 6.20; Takes-the-Gun, figure 6.21). In all cases though, it would appear that the name is graphically representable and would be recognizable to a member of the tribe "reading" a text.

MIXTEC

Naming in preconquest Central Mexico is more complex, although, in principle, equally amenable to graphic representation. Among the ruling classes, some of whose exploits are described in the surviving

Fig. 6.16 Roman-Nose. Red-Cloud's Census (from Mallery, 1972b, Vol. I:450)

Fig. 6.17 Spotted-Face. Red-Cloud's Census (ibid., p.451)

Central Mexican codices, each individual is given two names. The first of these, a calendrical name, indicates the day on which the person was born. The Mesoamerican calendar had twenty day signs (e.g., alligator, deer, rabbit, and reed—see figure 6.22) and thirteen number indicators.[10] Thus, one ruler's calendar name is "8-Deer" (figure 6.23) and another's "10-Rabbit" (figure 6.24). In addition, each figure has a personal name or nickname. Although we don't know how the personal name was ascribed to the individual (M.E. Smith, 1973: 27), we do know that at least many of the names (those for which we have records) were graphically representable. As with the representation of names in North American Indian texts, the personal name may be incorporated into a generic figure (e.g., 5-Rain Smoking Mountain, figure 6.25, in which a smoking mountain is worn as a helmet) or indicated separately but attached to the generic figure by a line (e.g., 5-Rain Smoking Mountain portrayed in a different manuscript, figure 6.26). From some of the postconquest census cadasters (e.g., Códice de Santa María Asunción, Codex Vergara), we know that common people as well had personal names that are graphically represented.

The Question of Necessity

Graphic representation of proper names in North and Central America appears to be adequate as long as the name to be represented is depictable and the pictorial representation is likely to be understood

Fig. 6.18 Stabber. Red-Cloud's Census (ibid., p.448)

Fig. 6.19 Spotted-Elk. Red-Cloud's Census (ibid., p.456)

Fig. 6.20 Red-Shirt. Red-Cloud's Census (ibid., p.448)

Fig 6.21 Takes-the-Gun. Red-Cloud's Census (ibid., p.454)

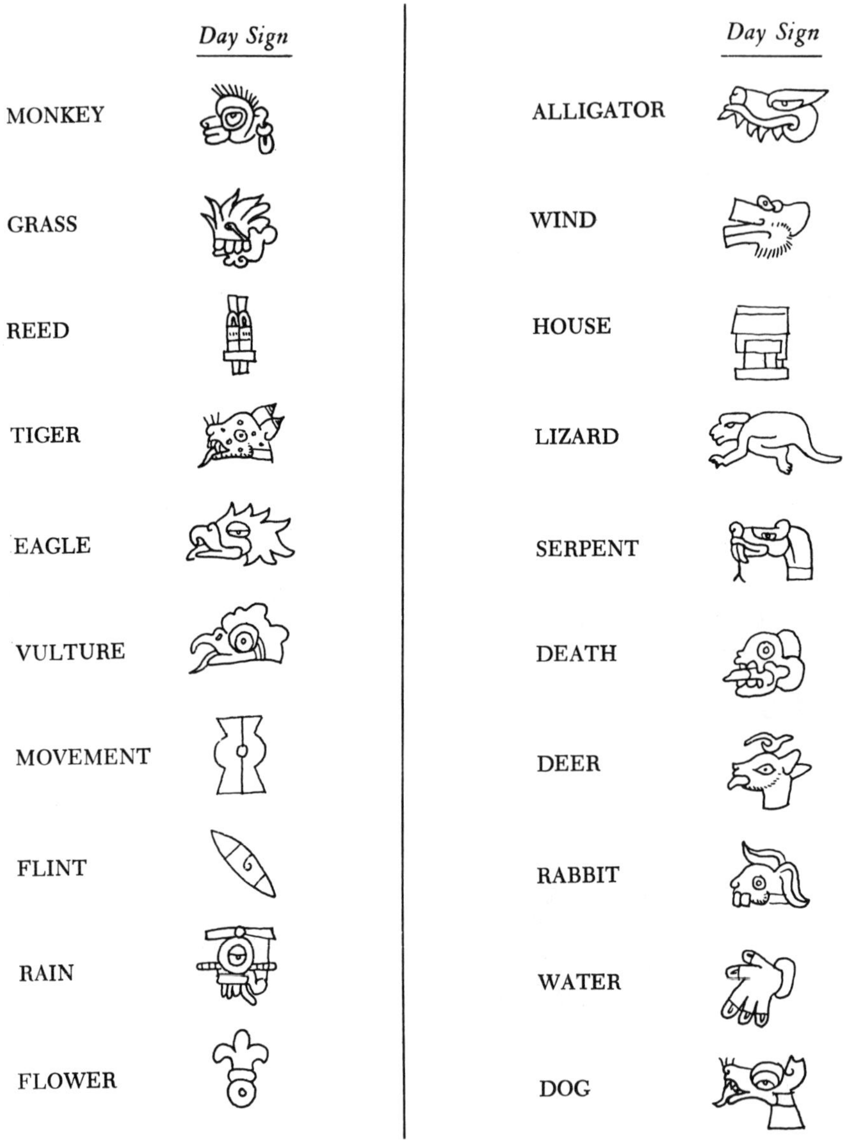

	Day Sign			Day Sign
MONKEY			ALLIGATOR	
GRASS			WIND	
REED			HOUSE	
TIGER			LIZARD	
EAGLE			SERPENT	
VULTURE			DEATH	
MOVEMENT			DEER	
FLINT			RABBIT	
RAIN			WATER	
FLOWER			DOG	

Fig. 6.22 The Twenty Day Signs in Mixtec and Valley of Mexico (from *Picture Writing from Ancient Southern Mexico* by Mary Elizabeth Smith, pp.24–25. Copyright 1973 by the University of Oklahoma Press, Publishing Division of The University. Composed and Printed at Norman, Oklahoma, U.S.A., by The University of Oklahoma Press)

Fig. 6.23 8-Deer. Codex Nuttall, p. 52 (from A.G. Miller, 1975: 52)

Fig. 6.24 10-Rabbit. Codex Nuttall, p. 48 (ibid., p.48)

by the audience. However, what happens when either of these conditions is violated (as is likely when the script must be used to refer to foreigners)?

In North America, there was a consistent attempt to make foreign names fit the graphic mold. European names were regularly "translated" into the local native American language, and could, in theory, be represented by the same graphic principles as indigenous names. William Penn was known as Onas, the word for "feather-quill" in Mohawk; the second French governor of Canada, de Montmagny, was known (in English translation) as "great mountain," a title applied to all subsequent Canadian governors (Mallery, 1972b, vol. I:443). The only exception that Mallery reports to this "translation" process is the representation of a General Maynadier in a text as "many deer," that is, with a graphic representation of near homonyms (figure 6.27). Mallery explains, though, that

> it is not an example of rebus, but of misunderstanding the significance of the word as spoken and heard by such Indians as had some knowledge of English. The official interpreters would be likely to commit the error as they seldom understood more than the colloquial English phrases. [ibid., vol. II:596]

That is not to say that the rebus principle was too sophisticated to be used in native North America—rebus is found in a number of non-

Fig. 6.25 5-Rain Smoking Mountain. Codex Nuttall, p.56b
(from *Picture Writing from Southern Mexico* by Mary Eliza-
beth Smith, p.221. Copyright 1973 by the University of
Oklahoma Press, Publishing Division of The University.
Composed and printed at Norman, Oklahoma, U.S.A., by
The University of Oklahoma Press)

literate societies (e.g., the West African oroko—see Jensen, 1970:31)
whose discursive graphic representation is not as complex as that of the
North American Indians—the North American Indians simply did not
use rebus.

The case was quite different in Central Mexico. Although the extent
to which phoneticism was used to represent proper names (through
rebus) is unclear (Nicholson, 1973)—particularly with regard to how
much of the phoneticism was indigenous and how much reflects
Spanish influence—considerably more phonetic representation was
used than in North America.

Phonetic representation of names was used either by itself or in
conjunction with graphic sumbols. For example, in the Codex Mendoza,

Fig. 6.26 5-Rain Smoking Mountain. Codex Becker I, p.6 (ibid.)

Fig. 6.27 Many-Deer. American-Horse's Winter Count (from Mallery, 1972b, vol. II:596)

the place name *Tochpan* is represented by a rabbit (*tochtli* in Nahuatl) and a stylized depiction of a banner (*pamitl* or *pantli*) (figure 6.28). In other cases, both graphic and phonetic elements are used redundantly for either part or all of the name. So, (again in the Codex Mendoza) the place sign for Tzompanhuacan (figure 6.29), meaning "place of those who possess a skull-rack," is denoted by both a (graphic) skull-rack (*tzompantli*) and "phonetically, by a banner, *pantli*, decorated with hair, *tzontli*, thus *Tzon(m)(tli)-pan(tli)*" (Nicholson, 1973:13).

The use of phoneticism for a proper name, either by itself or re-

 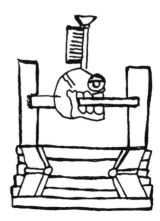

Fig. 6.28 Place sign: Tochpan. Codex Mendoza, fol. 52r (from Nicholson, 1973:10)

Fig. 6.29 Place Sign: Tzompan-huacan. Codex Mendoza, fol. 35r (from Nicholson, 1973:12)

dundantly with graphic representation, varied widely from scribe to scribe.[11] Moreover, although the data have not been properly analyzed by Mesoamerican specialists, it is probable that some genres (e.g., a general census) lend themselves to phoneticism more than others (e.g., the history of the exploits of a few well-known figures). Generally, it seems that "phonetic use of graphemes was considered to be less necessary in the case of especially well-known places and persons" (Nicholson, 1973:35) and "in the case of foreign names (places or persons), their phonetic rendering may have been standard" (ibid., pp. 35–36).

But was the introduction of phoneticism *necessary* in Central Mexico in a way *not* necessary in North America? We would like to answer this question, but like most causal questions dealing with language change, it cannot be settled decisively. Given the systems of naming in both societies—systems that presumably predated any written representation —phonetic representation for proper names was *less* necessary in either society that it would be in, say, modern Europe. That is, were Europe now developing a written tradition, there would be a much greater need for a phonetic component than in pre-European America, despite the fact that the same lexical category (proper names) is being repre-sented in both instances. Thus, in formulating a minimal definition of written language (e.g., must its combination rules include rules of phonetic collocation), we need to consider the social context in which the written language is used.

One type of evidence militates against a simple solution to the question of whether phoneticism is *necessary*: the same name might sometimes be represented phonetically, and sometimes not. In the Códice de Santa María Asunción, for example, the name Oyohuatl or Oyohual is denoted in three different ways: nonphonetically, with a picture of a bell (the Nahuatl for "bell" is *oyohualli*)—figure 6.30; wholly phonetically, with a picture of a road (Nahuatl *ohtli*) and a picture of night (Nahuatl *yohualli*), thus *O(htli)yohualli*—figure 6.31; and both methods used concurrently—figure 6.32. The use of rebus, either by itself or

Fig. 6.30 Householder Andrés Oyohuatl. Códice de Santa María Asunción, No. 316 (from Nicholson, 1973:30)

Fig. 6.31 Householder Antonio Oyohual. Códice de Santa María Asunción, No. 159 (ibid.)

Fig. 6.32 Householder Antonio Oyohual. Códice de Santa María Asunción, No. 82 (ibid.)

in conjunction with a direct graphic representation of the name, may indicate that the name itself is no longer recognized as being associated with "bell" (cf. *John* or *Pennsylvania*), or that the name is not indigenous to the area, and therefore the bell representation, though logical, will be novel to the audience. However, we have no evidence at the moment for either of these hypotheses.

Even if we cannot argue for *necessity* for phoneticism in Central Mexico, several factors make phoneticism more likely to develop in Central Mexico than in North America. It is quite possible that the Indians of Central Mexico had encountered and *needed to refer in their writings* to a larger number of foreigners (either Indian or European) than did their northern counterparts. The point becomes particularly important if the name of the foreign person (or place) is not easily translatable into graphic representation. After the Spanish conquest, the Mexicans regularly had to cope with European names (sometimes assuming them themselves), and it is not obvious that these could be handled as easily as the North American Indians had dealt with *Penn* or *de Montmagny*. Another important factor was potential influence from Maya writing; although the amount of phoneticism in Maya writing is still strongly debated (e.g., Thompson, 1959; Knorozov, 1958; Kelley, 1976), it is clear even to Thompson (1972) that many of the proper names in Maya were represented phonetically.

In comparing two pictorial based systems of representation, North American Indian and Central Mexican, we have seen that the same problems that we found in establishing empirical bounds on the lexicon of spoken languages apply to other representational schemes as well. Only by looking at the actual uses to which a community puts its language can we determine whether phoneticism is a necessary component of a representation system that bears the title *language*.

VII

Sign Language

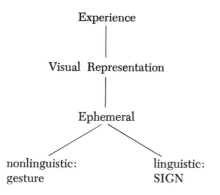

Experience
|
Visual Representation
|
Ephemeral
／ ＼
nonlinguistic: linguistic:
gesture   SIGN

FACTORING OUT SIGN
LANGUAGE FROM OTHER
EPHEMERAL VISUAL REPRESENTATION

THE VERY IDEA that ephemeral visual representation might constitute
language has not sat well with linguists during most of their discipline's
history. In chapter 1, I quoted Bloomfield as saying that "gesture languages are merely developments of ordinary gesture" and that "any
and all complicated or not immediately intelligible gestures are based
on the conventions of ordinary speech" (1933:39). In a similar vein,
Crystal asserts that

> despite its importance, the visual system of communication in humans
> does not have by any means the same structure or potential as the vocal
> —there is nothing really like grammar, for instance, and there is a very
> finite vocabulary of gestures indeed in any culture—and the linguist
> does not therefore call it language. [1971:241]

Crystal's remarks raise two questions: Is there any distinction between gesture in the ordinary language sense of raising one's eyebrows

in surprise or shrugging one's shoulders to indicate ambivalence, and using ephemeral visual representation in lieu of spoken language? And if such a distinction *does* exist, does the latter visual system lack anything "really like grammar," or is the "vocabulary" necessarily small? If our minimal definition of language (chapter 3) entails both lexical and grammatical components (not to mention productivity), then any claim that a gestural system is "linguistic" entails our identification of such components.[1] Of course, the two issues go hand in hand, since the identification of discrete "lexical" elements that can be recombined systematically is one of the primary grounds for distinguishing between linguistic and nonlinguistic gesturing.

Where does gesturing end and sign language begin? The problem becomes particularly complex in that sign languages mainly grow out of "natural" human gesturing, and new signs that derive from pantomime are commonly added to sign languages. To the extent, however, that gestures are modified to conform with an identifiable class of structural conventions, the ephemeral visual representation is no longer mime but language. This process is analogous to the naturalization of a borrowed word in spoken language, whereby a word's phonological or morphological patterning is altered to conform with the patterns of the recipient language. Witness the Anglicization of *Don Quixote* to [dan kwíksət], the replacement of the Latin plural *aquaria* with *aquariums,* or the malapropism *Tempus fugits.*

Sign language does indeed differ from gesture in a number of clearly identifiable ways. And, just as diverse speech communities develop differing structural conventions, sign languages differ in structure from one another. However, neither of these points is wholly accepted in the literature. Rather, it is often claimed that human gesturing is all of a piece, being universal across cultures. Underlying this assumption of universality is the further implication that the imposition of conventions that distinguish among gesturing groups is logically—and pragmatically—unnecessary.

THE ISSUE OF UNIVERSALITY

The purported universality of gestures has long been a favorite target of anthropologists. Weston La Barre explains, for example, that

the American hand-gesture meaning "go away" (palm out and vertical, elbow somewhat bent, arm extended vigorously as the palm is bent to a face-downward horizontal position, somewhat as a baseball is thrown and in a manner which could be rationalized as a threatened or symbolic blow or projectile-hurling) is the same which in Buenos Aires would serve to summon half the waiters in a restaurant, since it means exactly the opposite, "Come here!" [1947:66]

Even the act of pointing with one's finger is not universal:

One day I asked a favorite informant of mine among the Kiowa, old Mary Buffalo, where something was in the *ramada* or willow-branch "shade" where we were working. It was clear she had heard me, for her eighty-eight-year-old ears were by no means deaf; but she kept on busying both hands with her work. I wondered at her rudeness and repeated the request several times, until finally with a puzzled exasperation which matched my own, she dropped her work and fetched it for me from in plain sight: she had been repeatedly pointing with her lips in approved American Indian fashion, as any numbskull should have been able to see. [ibid., pp.51–52]

Gordon Hewes, however, has defended the notion of universality. He has not claimed that all gestures will be universally interpreted the same way; instead, he suggests that, *in an actual communicative context* when it is necessary for humans to understand one another, they will gesticulate in such a way as to get their messages across. Using descriptions of voyages that refer to the use of gestures between peoples who do not speak the same language, Hewes argues that

while it is easy enough to discover that not all seemingly "basic" gestures are human universals . . . where such differences exist, normally intelligent human beings seem to be able to overcome them. [1974:2]

An even stronger stance on universality has been taken by Garrick Mallery, and, derivatively, by Macdonald Critchley. They have argued that sign language itself is universal and perhaps indistinguishable from what others have seen as gestural communication:

Perhaps Garrick Mallery was correct when he proclaimed that 'what is called *the* sign language of Indians is not, properly speaking, one language, but that it and the gesture systems of deaf-mutes and of all peoples constitute together one language—the gesture speech of mankind—of which each system is a dialect.' [Critchley, 1975:72]

Critchley supports his thesis with reports that members of diverse signing communities have been able to communicate with one another with little difficulty:

> Indians can communicate without any difficulty with the deaf of any nationality; according to Mallery there might be initial disagreements between the signs, but they would be mutually comprehensible, and signs of one system were often adopted by adherents of the other. In 1880 [Mallery] took a number of the Indians to the National Deaf-Mute College in Washington, where a very high degree of reciprocal intelligibility was found. From the experience gained from a meeting held in 1873 at the Pennsylvania Institution for the Deaf and Dumb with a number of Indians—Crows, Arapohoes and Cheyennes—the inmates were better understood by the Indians than *vice versa*. [ibid., p.71]

And again,

> In a school for the deaf and dumb in Budapest, a number of children from France, Austria, Czechoslovakia and Italy were admitted as temporary visitors. Within an hour or two they were all communicating freely with each other and at the end of a day it was as though they had been brought up together. [ibid., p.61]

There is some evidence supporting Critchley's position. Deaf signers from diverse cultural communities (e.g., at the Deaf Olympics or at the World Congress of the Deaf) have informally reported that they are able to adapt their signing to be able to understand one another (at least on a basic level) after relatively little contact.[2] However, such observations by no means settle the issue of universality.

As Stokoe points out, conclusions about commonalities between signing systems (e.g., between American Indian Sign and American Sign Language) are dangerous if based only on fragments of each system:

> Selection of data allows proof of almost anything, and semiotic systems like other systems can be proved congruent only by complete system-wide comparison. [1974:354–355]

The fact that a number of members of the American and European deaf communities have felt it necessary to *create* an international sign language, Gestuno (see World Federation of the Deaf, 1975), should suggest that the sign languages of different deaf communities are not nearly as compatible as superficial evidence might suggest.

Furthermore, commonality in *perception* guarantees nothing about commonality in *production*. Just because members of different signing communities manage to understand one another's signs does not mean that the signs themselves are the same. Consider the signs for "tree" in American Sign Language, Danish Sign Language, and Chinese Sign Language. As Bellugi and Klima (1976:522–524) point out, all three signs are iconically based in that they represent a property associated with trees (see figure 7.1). However, this property is different in each instance. In American Sign Language,

> it can be said that the upright forearm represents the trunk of a tree, the outstretched hand represents the branches, and the twisting motion represents the movement of the wind through the branches [ibid., pp.522–523]

With the Danish sign,

> the two hands symmetrically outline the rounded shape of the outer perimeter of a tree and then outline the shape of the trunk [ibid., p.522]

Finally, in Chinese sign,

> the two hands symmetrically encompass the shape of the trunk of a tree and indicate its extent [ibid., pp.523–524]

And yet, despite the differences in production, an American signer—or even a nonsigner—can *understand* the Danish or Chinese sign (and vice versa) with little instruction.

Perhaps the most important factor concerning the universality argument is the lack of evidence that the signs used by interlocutors not sharing a common language are the same ones that signers would employ in signing to a member of their own linguistic community. It is well-documented in spoken language that fluent speakers often speak differently to children or foreigners than they do to people known to be fluent in their language (see Ferguson, 1975). More to the point is the evidence of trade jargons and pidgin languages that arise when interlocuters do not share a common language. We know that such interface languages are not lexically and grammatically equivalent to either of the source languages (see chapter 5). Before using contact language as evidence of the universality of sign, we need careful comparisons of the contact communication with normal, intracommunity language use.

Whatever else it may be, sign language is not universal. Moreover, I have suggested that sign language differs in definable ways from gesture. What are these ways?

Fig. 7.1 Sign for *Tree* in Three Sign Languages (© Copyright Bellugi and Klima 1976:523)

INFORMAL CRITERIA FOR DISTINGUISHING SIGN FROM PANTOMIME

Even to the untrained eye, transmission in sign language and in pantomime of the same message show strikingly different characteristics. Consider the signed and the mimed responses to the instructions, "Explain to someone how to make scrambled eggs." The extent to which the body is involved in the transmission is much greater in mime than in sign. Signing space (at least in American Sign Language) is largely restricted to an area stretching from the head to the midriff, across the shoulders, and not more than about a foot in front of the body. The mime, on the other hand, is free to use any part of his body. Signing is typically done while standing (or sitting) in one place; the mime typically moves from place to place in formulating the message.

Another difference is in the way in which the information is conveyed. In mime, the activity itself is reenacted, while in sign the activity is described. From this, two further differences follow: the movements in mime are more iconic than those in sign (although the amount and the degree of iconicity in sign is also relative—see "Iconicity and Learnability"), and the quantity of contextual detail given in mime is much greater. The mime, for example, must first establish the existence of a cabinet and then open its door and remove a container in order to then indicate "add salt." The signer needs only to convey the instruction "add salt." Thus it generally takes longer to mime a message than to sign it.

FORMAL CRITERIA FOR DEFINING SIGN AS LANGUAGE

Distinguishing sign from gesture is not enough. We must establish not only that signing behavior has distinct properties but also that it constitutes human language.

What are signs used to represent? The traditional denial of the status of "language" to sign systems seems to have arisen, at least in part, from a confusion about what is being analyzed. Linguists have generally assumed that sign language necessarily represents the spoken language of the speech community associated with a signing community. That is, sign has been looked on as a first-order representation of speech and only a second-order representation of experience (chapter 6 discussed the same presupposition with respect to writing). In the case of American Sign Language, the associated spoken language would be English; American Plains Indian Sign Language would be associated with the spoken languages of the tribes using sign. However, sign languages of deaf communities, at least, have distinctive structures that are largely autonomous from the spoken languages of culturally related speech communities (see "Prolegomena to a Functional Typology of Signing Systems").

More serious problems arise when we turn to nonarbitrary criteria for human language. The discussion in chapter 3 (formal criteria for defining human language) identified three properties that any language must have: a finite number of discrete lexical items, a finite number of combinatory rules, and the potential for combining these elements into a limitless number of strings. Do sign languages meet these criteria? In trying to answer this question, I shall use as reference point American Sign Language (ASL), an independent sign language par excellence. If ASL fails to meet these criteria, then other signing systems would be expected to fail as well.

In chapter 3, I noted that, while linguistic theories specify the above criteria for languages, they do not establish a minimum or a maximum number of lexical items or syntactic rules a system must have to be considered a language. This discussion of speech and writing illustrated some of the problems inherent in quantitative criteria. In chapter 5, I argued that trade jargons are not distinct languages (that is, distinct from their contributing languages) because they lack independent syntactic characteristics. On the other hand, in chapter 6, it became evident that there was no way of arguing that a predetermined minimal amount of phoneticism was necessary before a durable visual representation scheme could be considered a language.

ASL has distinct lexical items and its own system of combination rules—but does it have enough of either to be called a language? Crystal and Craig claim that it does not. They judge the lexicon of ASL to be only a fraction of that of English:

> The purely quantitative dimensions cannot be simply dismissed—contrasting the three-quarters of a million items of contemporary English with the 6000 items of Seeing Essential English, the 2500 items of the Paget Gorman Sign System, or the 3000 morphemes of the American Sign Language, for example. [1978:149]

Moreover, the authors believe that such a disbalance is inherent in the visual representational modality itself:

It is not purely a pragmatic question of the number of signs increasing to comparable levels of productivity in the course of time. There is considerable doubt as to whether visual acuity can cope with any increase of such an order—of whether, for example, the signing behavior would not come to contain an intolerable amount of visual formal ambiguity, owing to limitations on the number of visually discriminable items. As Bergman says (1972, p. 22), "Owing to physiological limitations it is doubtful whether the total number of signs in ASL will ever exceed five thousand." [ibid.]

As further evidence for this hypothesis, Crystal and Craig suggest that

as vocabulary increases, it must surely become increasingly difficult to retain an unambiguously iconic relationship between referent and sign, or for visual memory to be able to cope with the number of arbitrary distinctions such as would make the signing behavior comparable to that of speech. [ibid.]

There are several problems with such an argument. Crystal and Craig offer no evidence that human visual perception *is* incapable of discriminating (or of remembering these discriminations) between a much larger number of signs than the presumably current 3000 in ASL. Furthermore, as the level of education and the amount of geographic mobility of the deaf community increase, the lexicon should also. A simple example is the frequent development of new signs at Gallaudet College, necessitated by the confrontation with new subject matter. It is doubtful that the signing vocabulary of a graduate of Gallaudet is limited to 3,000 items.

Another problem concerns Crystal and Craig's covert assumption that in sign languages signs are unrelated to one another, rather than falling into semantic classes. In fact, sign languages *do* use semantic categorization. For example, ASL signs indicating political roles are made with similar movements at similar parts of the body; they are differentiated by handshape. The signs for "king" and "queen" are both made by moving the right hand from the left shoulder across the chest to the right-hand edge of the waist, thus indicating the sash worn by royalty. In the signing of "king," the moving hand assumes an alphabetic "K" handshape, and for "queen," a "Q" (see figures 7.2 and 7.3).

Crystal and Craig appear to assume that the only way to increase the size of the lexicon is to add independent, nonderived words. One of the most productive ways in which the English language increases its vocabulary is by borrowing words outright from other languages

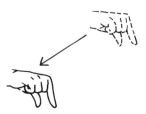

Fig. 7.2 American Sign Language Sign for "King"

Fig. 7.3 American Sign Language Sign for "Queen"

(*sputnik, pajamas, assassin*) or by borrowing elements from other languages and creating nonce forms (*telephone, psychiatrist*). However, as suggested in chapter 5, these are not the only options available to a language. Natural languages such as German and pidgin languages such as Neo-Melanesian create new words by joining together, either as words or phrases, morphemes that already exist in the language. One productive means of creating new signs in ASL is the formation of compounds. For example, the sign for "home" is made up of the signs for "eat" and "sleep" (see figure 7.4). These compounds often become abbreviated with time (see figure 7.5), a phenomenon parallel to the phonological reduction of compounds in spoken language (e.g., *New + found + land* is pronounced as [nufənlən] in American English).

So much for arguments about the size of the lexicon. What about syntax? Are there "enough" syntactic rules in ASL to warrant calling it a language? The arguments here are less easily identified. Perhaps because of the newness of sign language linguistics, along with a predictable degree of differences of opinion in a new undertaking, many linguists persist in their earlier impression that ASL has little or no syntax. Crystal and Craig remind us that

> it perhaps does not need emphasizing that the distance between a communicative system which has two, or three, or ten rules and the syntactic rules of speech is very great. [1978:153]

Furthermore, they reiterate the (by now) familiar assumption that some syntactic rules—word order in particular—are considered to be more critical than others:

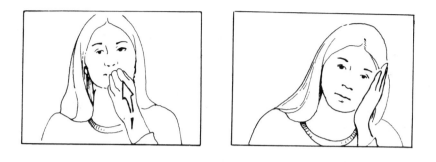

Fig. 7.4 Components of the Formal American Sign Language Sign for "Home" (© Copyright Bellugi and Klima 1976:537)

Fig. 7.5 Abbreviated, Informal American Sign Language Sign for "Home" (© Copyright Bellugi and Klima, 1976: 537)

> There is little evidence in signing of the formal sequential constraints of sign upon sign comparable to the constraints of word order in speech. [ibid., p.152]

This clearly implies that if a representation scheme lacks word order constraints, it is not a language.

The issue of word order in ASL is tricky and has already generated much debate (e.g., S. Fischer, 1975, Edge and Herrmann, 1977). It still remains to be seen which ordering conventions ASL might have, and what means other than linear word order ASL might use in place of the word ordering conventions familiar in spoken languages. Until this is done, it is premature to assume that ASL lacks "sufficient" syntax for meriting the label *language*.

Some linguists working on ASL have confronted skeptics with the argument that ASL is not the only language which lacks the grammatical features that speakers of English presuppose other languages will have. Wilbur (1976) points out that many of the differences between ASL and English are similar to differences between contemporary English and other spoken languages. For example, unlike English, many of the worlds' languages (ASL, Kwa languages in Africa, Thai) do not have grammatically marked passive constructions, and passives are quite uncommon in Japanese and Czech. The absence of the present tense copula in ASL is paralleled by a similar absence in Bengali and Russian; the absence of definite and indefinite articles in ASL is matched in languages like Russian, Yoruba, Hindi, and even Old English.

In addition to lexical and grammatical complexity, there is the issue of productivity. Is ASL potentially as "productive" as bona fide spoken or written languages? Since potentiality cannot be measured by the actual number of utterances produced, we need to ask whether there are *structural* limitations on the kinds of utterances that can be produced in ASL.

Advocates of ASL have argued that there are not. In Stokoe's words:

> Because American Sign Language is the medium of communication used by a community of people . . . , anything expressible in another language can be expressed in it. [1972:63]

Crystal and Craig find this claim to be "premature" and to "hide massive methodological problems" (1978:149). The most fundamental of

these problems, in their eyes, is that ASL lacks an adequate amount of
displacement (the ability to use a sign for a referent that is distant in
time or space) to make indirect reference. Recall that Hockett defines
displacement as one of the essential "design features" of human language (see figures 3.1 and 3.2). Crystal and Craig believe that

> many signs are dependent on the immediate context for a correct inter-
> pretation, i.e. part of the formal identity of the sign resides in the ac-
> companying situation, and the more use that a signing behavior makes
> of this, the more difference from speech one must conclude there to be.
> [ibid., p. 147]

As evidence, the authors observe that many signs

> vary in form depending on the nature of the accompanying object,
> event, etc. (for example, the sign for carry depends on exactly what it
> is that is being carried). [ibid.]

But what relevance does this phenomenon have for the notion of displacement? Displacement is concerned with referring to something
that is not visually present. As long as the object I am talking about
carrying is not physically present—regardless of how its identity affects
the shape of my sign, we still have a perfectly good example of displacement. Moreover, we know that many languages of the world lexically distinguish verbs on the basis of other elements in the sentence.
Russian has two wholly distinct series of movement verbs, one for talking about going by foot, the other for talking about going by vehicle.
Either we could consider the variants in the sign for "carry" as distinct
lexical items (which will help push the size of the ASL lexicon above
3000 items), or we can see these formational variants as the sign equivalent of derivational suffixes indicating a modulation of a word's basic
meaning. In either event, displacement is not at issue.

Crystal and Craig also argue that sign languages lack displacement
because many signs depend on accompanying facial expression or body
movement for their meaning. In Israeli Sign Language, for example,
the sign for "lemon" is manually identical to the sign indicating "to-
mato." The signs are differentiated by accompanying the sign for
"lemon" with a facial expression indicating "sour" (Cohen, Namir, and
Schlesinger, 1977:246–248). Yet what does the use of nonmanual components of signing have to do with the issue of displacement? As long
as the facial expression or body movement does not restrict the range

of referents to things present here and now, the fact that the interlocutor must look at the signer's face and body, as well as at his hands, to comprehend the sign would seem to be irrelevant.[3]

Have Crystal and Craig seriously questioned the linguistic status of ASL on the basis of inadequate lexicon, syntax, or productivity? Probably not; however, until more work has been done on ASL, it will be difficult to know whether their arguments can be permanently laid to rest.

CLASSIFICATION OF SIGN LANGUAGES

I have been speaking, so far, of "sign language" almost as if there is one unified language type. Occasionally I have referred to differences between sign languages (e.g., American Plains Indian Sign vs. sign languages of deaf communities) but have not defined what these differences are.

There are at least four ways of distinguishing among sign languages: two rest upon structuralist principles, a third classification has characteristics of both structuralist and functionalist approaches to typology, the fourth is wholly functionalist in orientation.

STRUCTURAL PERSPECTIVES

Genetic Classification

For sign languages of deaf communities (see "Prolegomena"), it is possible to develop family trees comparable to those used to show relationships between spoken languages (see figure 5.1). Stokoe (1974) has suggested the outlines a genetic classification might take. In the family tree of sign languages shown in figure 7.6, we see that while French and American sign languages are directly connected, ASL and British Sign Language are not.

Such genetic reconstruction has its drawbacks. Attempts at reconstruction largely depend on written information. Given the low status of signs (and signers) in most countries, much of the necessary information is unavailable. Adequate family trees are therefore difficult to develop.

Furthermore, genetic analysis is of limited appropriateness for classifying sign languages of the world. Unlike spoken languages, which can

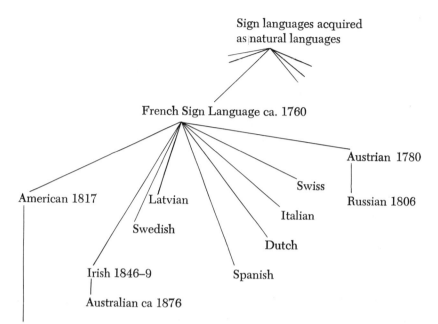

Fig. 7.6 Genetic Classification of Sign Languages:
The French Branch (from Stokoe, 1974:366)

nearly all be traced to some (or many) other spoken languages, certain
sign languages have arisen de novo, unrelated to any other sign systems. Particular gestures may not be universal, but the act of gesturing
is. There is no reason why systematic signing could not have evolved
independently a number of times. If this is so, then an ideal genetic
classification might not go far beyond a list of all known signing systems, yielding little additional information about them.

Formational Classification

Sign systems may also be classified in terms of formational properties. This approach is largely comparable to the typological classification of spoken languages. Some of the formational questions we might
ask are: What are the possible hand configurations? What are the
boundaries of the signing space? What constraints are there on forming
new signs? A different type of formational question, however, concerns
what is being represented: Is it things or ideas (i.e., reality or one's

perception of it), or is it language? In the former case, each hand configuration represents what would roughly be comparable to a single word in speech, while in the latter, speech sounds or grammatical morphemes may be represented as well. In the latter cases, finger spelling is employed (e.g., to spell out the word *perplex* or to indicate with a "D" handshape the past tense of a verb).

Classification Along a Sign-Speech Continuum

Another way of looking at the difference between the use of handsigns and of finger spelling is to view sign languages along a continuum from full autonomy of the sign language to the use of signs as a near "transliteration" of speech. The idea of a speech-sign continuum can be seen as far back as the middle of the eighteenth century, when Abbé Charles de l'Épée "invented" French Sign Language, the system from which American Sign Language has largely derived.

Épée (1776) distinguished between what he called *le langage des signes naturelles* ("the natural language of signs") and *signes méthodiques* (what Stokoe, 1978:5, takes to be a metalanguage). The *signes naturelles* were those which Épée observed already in use among his deaf pupils. They were, however, insufficient for teaching his students French language and culture; he needed an additional set of signs to indicate such grammatical aspects of French as tense and articles. Whenever possible, he adopted (or adapted) natural signs for his purposes. One such case is the *sign méthodique* for indicating tense:

> [Épée] found . . . that the pupils he observed signified that an action or event was in the past by "throwing the hand behind the shoulder once or repeatedly." In his instructional manual he shows how he teaches the past tenses of French verbs. . . . He uses one backward motion of the hand over the shoulder to indicate the simple past, two *coups de la main* for indicating the perfect tense, and three for the pluperfect tense. [Stokoe, 1978:6]

In other cases, Épée invented signs himself:

> He assigned the definite masculine article *le* a crooked index finger, at the brow, *la* the same finger at the cheek. . . . Épée says the crooking of the index finger was a reminder to the pupil that the definite article chooses *one* of many possible instances of its noun; the brow location was chosen because of the masculine custom of tipping or touching the hat brim; the cheek is the locus of the feminine article sign because as he notes the coiffure of ladies of the period often presented hanging curls there. [ibid., p.7]

Épée could, in principle, have taken his manual representation of French one step farther: rather than using signs to indicate grammatical morphemes (not to mention the objects, properties, and activities indicated by natural signs), he could have used finger spelling to represent French letter for letter. In fact, a manual alphabet had been introduced into France by Jacob Rodrigues Pereira (from Portugal) some years earlier. Épée rejected the system because he felt it was possible for deaf students to be taught great skill in encoding and decoding French with a manual alphabet without really understanding any language.

Two points are actually at issue in distinguishing between what Épée identified as *le langage des signes naturelles, signes méthodiques,* and finger spelling: whether manual signs are used to signify experience or spoken language and whether the signs follow the syntactic ordering of the associated spoken language or have their own syntax. The combination of these two variables gives rise to at least the following possible systems:

only natural signs
indigenous syntax

only natural signs
syntax of associated spoken language

natural signs plus grammatical signs which are based on experience
syntax of associated spoken language

natural signs plus grammatical signs which are based on associated
    spoken language
syntax of associated spoken language

finger spelling based on associated spoken language
syntax of associated spoken language

In the United States, all of these possibilities are in use.[4] The first type we commonly refer to as ASL (although see the discussion of ASL in "Types of Signing Communities"). The terms *signed English* or *manual English* are commonly (though inexactly) used to refer to the next three types. The second type is most nearly represented by a form of signing called *Siglish,* which strings together ASL signs in English word order, but makes no attempt to represent English inflectional or derivational morphology. The third and fourth types are represented most nearly by *Seeing Essential English, Linguistics of Visual*

English, Manual English, Signing Exact English, and *Signed English.*

Seeing Essential English (or SEE I, as it has come to be called) was invented in the 1960s by David Anthony and was the first concerted attempt to adapt American Sign Language to English syntax. (Earlier, the Paget-Gorman Systematic Sign Language used British Sign Language in trying to accomplish a similar goal.) Anthony intended his system for deaf people of all ages. For this reason, SEE I currently has about 6000 words and a complex set of syntactic principles and criteria.

Several attempts have subsequently been made to provide a simpler mapping of American Sign Language onto English. Linguistics of Visual English, Manual English, Signing Exact English (commonly known as SEE II), and Signed English are all derivatives of SEE I to some degree. SEE II was explicitly designed to be used with children, and Signed English was created for preschool deaf children. All of these systems derive over half of their signs from American Sign Language, supplementing ASL signs with additional signs for words, as well as with signs for derivational and inflectional suffixes. Some of these suffixes take the form of unitary signs, while others are composed of finger spellings (e.g., indicating the past tense with the finger-spelled letters "E" and "D"). In fact, finger spelling is used, to some degree, in all of these systems except Siglish. The Paget-Gorman system uses finger spelling for proper names; in the SEE systems, it is generally (though not entirely) avoided. Manual English makes somewhat greater use of finger spelling, for example as an alternative way of forming the past tense. In Signed English, the amount of its use varies with the user's fluency in English and with the audience being addressed.[5]

The final type of signing system involves the exclusive use of finger spelling (paralleling the associated spoken language). In the United States this method is known as the Rochester Method, after the area in which it was first widely used. (Ironically, the Rochester Method is no longer common in Rochester.)

The User's Perspective

The discussion of how to classify spoken and written languages suggested that structural classifications by themselves often reveal little about the extent to which the formal properties of a language are actually used or why these formal properties might exist in the first place.

All of the classification schemes we have looked at so far have begun by making distinctions between the languages or language symbols themselves. Another possibility would be to make initial distinctions in terms of the *people* who are using the language, as Rolf Kuschel (1974) does in his study of the language of a single sign language user on Rennell Island in Polynesia. Kuschel distinguishes between signs that can be understood by a member of the same cultural group as the signer, signs intelligible to someone from a related group, and signs that would be clear to anyone. Our next task, of course, is to see the possible correlations between a social and a linguistic classification. If there is an empirical basis for a social approach to sign language analysis, we would expect a high degree of predictability of structural factors from social factors, and vice versa. My earlier analysis of writing and especially of speech provided just such evidence in their respective domains.

As in the case of writing, there have been practically no attempts to compare different types of signing systems with respect to differences among their users. Therefore, these attempts must be seen as only a first step.

PROLEGOMENA TO A FUNCTIONAL TYPOLOGY OF SIGNING SYSTEMS

TYPES OF SIGNING COMMUNITIES

Stokoe distinguishes five kinds of sign systems on the basis of whether or not they are acquired as native languages, whether or not they are associated with specific spoken languages, and if so, what kinds of scripts are used in writing those spoken languages (figure 7.7). This scheme can be simplified—distinguishing only between systems that are used as the primary mode of communication in a deaf community (which normally implies that they are acquired as native languages) and systems used for special purposes by hearing populations. This second subgroup needs to be further divided into sign languages used by populations who share a single spoken language, and those who do not (figure 7.8). An example of a sign language used regularly by a deaf community is American Sign Language (ASL). American Plains Indian Sign Language (PSL) typifies a sign system used by a

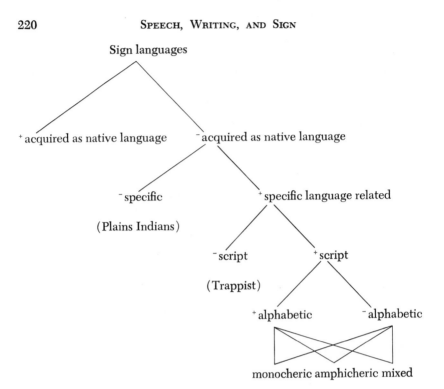

Fig. 7.7 Stokoe Classification of Sign Languages
(from Stokoe, 1974:358)

hearing population that, at least originally, seems not to have shared a common spoken language. And Cistercian Sign Language (CSL) exemplifies a sign system used by a hearing community that shares a common spoken language (although this language may vary, depending on the location of the monastery).

American Sign Language (ASL)

ASL is the primary means of communication used by an estimated

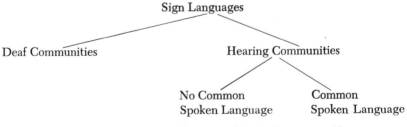

Fig. 7.8 Simplified Classification of Sign Language Types

one-half of the deaf population in the United States. With nearly one million users, it is the fourth most widely used linguistic system in the United States, behind English, Spanish, and Italian (Mayberry, 1978). ASL is commonly used among deaf children and adults and by deaf adults to their children, whether deaf or hearing. Until recently, however, the deaf have commonly hesitated to use it with hearing people (Kannapell, 1977). In addition to its strictly linguistic function, ASL is a mark of social identification, somewhat analogous to the use of diphthongs on Martha's Vineyard to identify with the island (see chapter 5). When interacting with hearing people who know some signs, the deaf tend to switch to a manual system whose structure approximates that of spoken English; this may be one of the reasons that (hearing) linguists have had so much difficulty in obtaining consistent data on ASL.

What about the *other* half of the American deaf population who don't use ASL? Moreover, what about deaf children born to hearing families who do not know sign? Households with a deaf child often work out so-called home signs to permit some rudimentary communication between the child and other family members. Like nicknames or idiosyncratic names that hearing families often develop among themselves (e.g., calling the television set the *idiot box* or the *boob tube*), these signs may be recognizable to outsiders because of the transparent relationship between the sign and its referent. However, because multiple iconic representations of the same referent are possible (recall the three signs for "tree" in figure 7.1), there is considerable variation among home signs that share the same referent. For this reason, home signs have little value for the child entering a classroom.

Some hearing parents of deaf children receive formal training in signing. Note that we have said "formal training in signing" *not* "instruction in ASL." Typically, parents learn signs for objects and activities that are especially important in their children's lives.[6] Depending on the child's age, signs may be selected on the basis of the child's needs for labels relating to home life, the parents' need to know what signs the child is learning at school, or both. It is generally assumed that these signs are strung together in the order of English syntax. Usually, if these children are to sign fluently in ASL, they must learn to do so from their peers at school.

Does attending a school for the deaf assure the hearing-impaired child a model for learning ASL? Hardly. To begin with, the use of ASL in classrooms for the hearing-impaired is far from being universally accepted. The so-called oral method, which aims at teaching the deaf to speak, read, and write English without the use of signing, has dominated deaf education for over three-quarters of a century.[7] As early as 1904, participants in the World Congress of the Deaf proclaimed that

> the oral method, which withholds from the congenitally and quasi-congenitally deaf the use of the language of signs out;ide the schoolroom, robs the children of their birthright; that those champions of the oral method, who have been carrying on a warfare, both overt and covert, against the use of the language of signs by the adult, are not friends of the deaf; and that in our opinion, *it is the duty of every teacher of the deaf, no matter what method he or she uses, to have a working command of the sign language* [*American Annals of the Deaf*, 1904:57– emphasis added]

The call has not been heeded; many educators of the deaf (especially those teaching in oral programs) know few if any signs. Others know and use individual signs with English syntax. This does not, however, mean that they know ASL.[8] Learning 500 words of Russian and then stringing them together with English syntax is certainly not tantamount to knowing Russian.

Until recently, regardless of how much signing educators of the deaf knew, little signing was used by teachers in the classroom. In 1955, 78.6% of the schools for the deaf in the United States used only the oral method for teaching. Another 5.1% of schools used nonoral techniques, while 14.3% combined oral and nonoral techniques (Lunde, 1956; quoted in Stokoe, 1978:22). This, despite the fact that in 1943 an estimated 78.2% of the deaf used sign language and only 1% used speech alone (ibid.). Some schools have strictly forbidden the use of manual communication to the point of slapping hands on playgrounds or making children sit on their hands in class. In recent years, these statistics (and practices) have begun to alter, particularly with the growing acceptance of total communication (simultaneous speech and signing in English syntax) in schools for the hearing-impaired across the country.

What does this suggest about the fluency in ASL of hearing-impaired children in schools for the deaf in the United States? Many deaf children do not learn ASL at all (although, even in oral schools, indigenous systems of signs develop). If a child attends a school in which signing is forbidden and then returns to a household which does not sign, there are no models available from which to learn the language. Only when the child matures and regularly interacts with other deaf people who know ASL does he begin to learn the language. This may happen when a deaf graduate of an oralist school attends an institution such as Gallaudet College or the Rochester Institute for the Deaf, at which signing *is* normally used. It may also happen when the individual begins to participate in local deaf clubs. The question we must ask here is, how fluent can an adult become in a new language? It is typically assumed (e.g., Lenneberg, 1967) that after puberty, normal (hearing) people cannot acquire native competence in a new language. Either we must assume that native competence can be acquired by adults in signed (as opposed to oral) language, or we must conclude that deaf signers of the sort we have characterized never attain native fluency in ASL.

A less drastic case is that of deaf children attending schools in which signing is permitted, although ASL is not the medium of instruction. Since this is the situation in the vast majority of schools for the deaf, it is an important case to consider. In these schools, the children do indeed sign among themselves. However, "signing" is not necessarily the same as using ASL. Students (and teachers) readily acknowledge that some children are "better signers" than others. (It was noted in chapter 4 that some hearing people are more fluent language users than others.) Equally important, if a signing "norm" develops in one school or geographic region, it is not necessarily the same norm as elsewhere. Lexical items and even conventions of syntax may differ from place to place.

Of course spoken languages display considerable geographic variation as well. The item that is called a *bucket* in one part of the country is called a *pail* in another. In the phonological domain, some speakers pronounce the words *Mary, merry,* and *marry* as homonyms, while others make a two- or three-way phonological distinction. Is the amount of variation in ASL significantly different from that in spoken languages? Is it considerably greater than that in spoken languages? The sociological factors dialectologists use in assessing—or predicting—amounts of variability in spoken language (e.g., geographical isolation of speakers) suggest that in contemporary American society, there would be greater variation in ASL than in English. No careful, comprehensive studies have been done, but it seems likely that this prediction will hold. The next issue, of course, will be to decide when a quantitative difference becomes a difference in quality. Is there enough variability among sign language users to deny the existence of a *community* of users sharing the same linguistic system? The problem is familiar: How many participants are required to make up a language community?

In discussing spoken languages, we have found no easy answer. A single speaker of Tunica (and not very proficient at that) served as the only informant for an entire grammar of the language. Moreover, there are still small tribes (such as the Tasadai in the Philippines) who regularly interact only with one another. We expect their languages to differ from those of nearby groups with whom they share a common genetic linguistic source. If, for spoken languages, we are willing to acknowledge that social circumstances may yield high degrees of variation among users of genetically common languages, we should not be surprised to find wide variability among users of ASL, whose social circumstances have prevented signers from forming a more homogeneous linguistic community.

Why have we dwelt so long on the point that ASL is *not* the native language of many deaf Americans? The purpose of this section is to present ASL as an example of a signing system that is used as a primary means of communication for a group of deaf people and to clear up, in advance, some of the misconceptions about this system. ASL is not *the* language of the deaf in America any more than English is *the* language of all hearing people in the United States.

American Plains Indian Sign Language (PSL)

A second type of signing community comprises signing populations whose hearing is normal but who do not share a common spoken language. Our exemplum is American Plains Indian Sign.

What was (and is) the sign language of the American Plains Indians? Where, why, and how did it develop? Who initially used it? What uses does it have now? With the exception of the last question, there is little agreement about the etiology and development of PSL. In fact, as we shall see, the structural characterizations found in the language (see "Comparison of Structural Properties") are also fraught with contradictions. Part of the difficulty derives from the fact that the language flourished in the nineteenth century, before the development of sophisticated techniques of linguistic description in the early and middle parts of the twentieth century. This problem is further complicated by the fact that an adequate study of ephemeral visual representation necessitates the use of movie or video equipment, which has only become technically and economically feasible within the last few years. Hence, the literature on PSL generally resorts to verbal descriptions or sketches to convey the signs' configurations.

Most of what we know about PSL comes from the writings of Garrick Mallery, an Army Colonel who worked for the United States Bureau of Ethnography during the latter years of the nineteenth century. He produced an exhaustive study of pictorial writing in native North America, *Picture-Writing of the American Indians* (1893, reprinted 1972b). Turning his attention to ephemeral signing behavior of the same population, he also wrote extensively of Amerindian sign (1880a; 1880b; 1881). Since Mallery's work, a scattering of ethnologists and linguists, along with some untrained observers, have written on PSL. A substantial portion of these writings have been reprinted in Umiker-Sebeok and Sebeok (1978). Of the group, Allan Ross Taylor's account (1975) is particularly useful, in that it draws together and compares the positions of earlier writers. Therefore, this discussion will rely heavily on Taylor. Equally important, though, is the work of La Mont West (1960), the only formally trained linguist to have conducted extensive field work on PSL. While PSL was not the only signing system used by American Indians, it was the most sophisticated (Taylor, 1975:329) and therefore the most interesting for comparison with our other paradigmatic types.

All that we know for certain about the origins of PSL is that it was commonly used within and between tribes on the American Plains by the eighteenth century (see figure 7.9). Exactly why, where, and how it developed are still issues of debate. Logically, there are at least four ways in which PSL might have developed:[9]

intertribal communication
contextual problems in using speech
origins in sign language used by deaf Indians
intratribal ritual

Intertribal communication. Our very characterization of PSL as a paradigmatic example of a sign language used by hearing people who do not share the same spoken language logically implies that the language was used for intertribal communication when a common spoken language was not shared. There is the further implication that the signing system arose *because* of this need for a lingua franca.

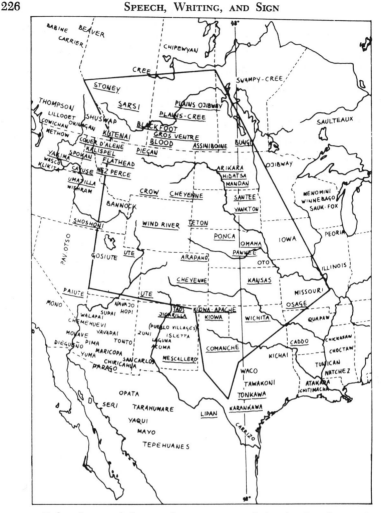

Tribes that used the sign language are underlined. The Plains culture area is outlined by a heavy black line. Note that sign language
use coincides in the main with Plains culture, although tribes in some
contiguous areas also used signs. Not indicated on the map are tribes
not native to the Plains who were crowded onto the Plains from the
East and the Southeast during the late 18th and 19th centuries. Many
of these Indians (e.g., Delaware, Shawnee, Wyandot, Kickapoo, Cher-
okee) also learned and used the sign language. Tribal names requiring
further identification are as follows: Santee, Yankton, and Teton equal
Sioux; Bungi equals Ojibway; Blackfoot, Blood, and Piegan equal
Blackfoot; Jicarilla and Mescalero equal Apache; Wind River equals
Shoshoni. (Map based on Wissler, 1922, p. 221. Tribal entries based
on West, 1960, vol. 2, pp. 61a–61b.)

Fig. 7.9 Distribution of American Plains Indian Sign Language (from Taylor, 1975:368)

Most writers agree that intertribal communication was a central—perhaps *the* central—use of PSL. The relatively high degree of mobility of the Plains population may help in explaining why a visual lingua franca developed on the Plains, but not elsewhere (West, 1960, vol. 2:62). Moreover, trading relationships between tribes may have been a significant factor in the development and spread of the language. Taylor writes that "trade was certainly a principal agent for the diffusion of the sign language throughout the Plains during the nineteenth century" (1975:332). Moreover, he hypothesizes that if the signing system originated in the Gulf Coast of Western Louisiana, Texas, and Northern Tamaulipas (Mexico), as some have suggested, "then trade was probably the catalyst for the spread of the gestures to the Southern Plains tribes" (ibid).

The suggestion that PSL provided a lingua franca for trade between group not sharing a common spoken language invites comparison between PSL and spoken trade jargons, such as Chinook Jargon, which were discussed in chapter 5. Besides the sociocultural context of trade between equals, there are certainly a number of other similarities. In both instances, it was largely men (not women) who learned and used the communicative system (ibid., pp.333–334). Use of the lingua franca was especially common before the adoption of English by the tribes (West, 1960, vol. 2:10). Structurally, both forms of representation display lack of stability across tribes, and both use redundancy extensively (see "Comparison of Structural Properties"). However, there are also differences between the systems—not to mention puzzles —that need explaining.

We know that the use of PSL did not preclude knowledge of spoken languages other than one's native tongue. West (1960, vol. 2:62) dismisses the hypothesis that sign grew up because of "indisposition or inability of the plains Indian to learn a spoken language other than his own" (Dodge, 1882:46; Humfreville, 1897:153) on the grounds that 52% of his PSL informants were fluent in English and 17% knew two or more other Indian languages. One might take issue with West, arguing that the conditions that gave rise to PSL (the need for a lingua franca) cannot explain its use today. As noted before, we still put buttons on the sleeves of men's coats, even though we are no longer trying to prevent the use of coat sleeves as handkerchiefs. The question is, how far back in time does one see the use of sign language among Indians who are bilingual? Clark (1885:218,340) attempts to correlate the *presence* of sign lingua francas with the *absence* of spoken lingua francas. West, however, argues that

> sign language is actually not excluded from two of the areas cited as having lingua francas and it turns out that the area of highest development of sign language also had spoken lingua francas prior to white contact. [1960, vol. 2:63]

What we would like at this point—but lack—is information on the uses of signed and spoken lingua francas one hundred or even two hundred years ago.

A still more important divergence between (spoken) trade jargons and PSL can be seen in the conditions under which they were used. While trade jargons seem to have been used exclusively for intertribal communication, PSL had a number of intratribal uses as well. In fact, many have argued that as early as the nineteenth century heavy use of PSL was made *within* individual tribes who shared a common spoken language. Umiker-Sebeok and Sebeok even state that

> there is good reason to believe that, in fact, [the] primary use [of American Indian Sign Languages] was for communication among members of a single tribe. [1978:xxiii—also see Richard Dodge, 1882, ibid., vol. 2:8]

In the twentieth century PSL is used heavily among speakers of the same language. Half of the 111 informants West surveyed in the late 1950s reported they had learned PSL around home (the other half mentioned extratribal contacts). Moreover, today this sign language is commonly used in story telling, a situation in which the signer and the audience are likely to share a common spoken language.

Contextual problems in using speech. A second possible source for PSL is contexts in which the use of speech is impractical. In hunting and warfare it is often expedient to be able to communicate with one's compatriots without alerting one's prey (see Webb, 1931; reprinted in Umiker-Sebeok and Sebeok, 1978, vol. 2:96). Webb further suggested that the vast, flat open spaces of the American plains themselves facilitated the development of PSL: "On the Plains the eye far outruns the ear in its range." This thesis is highly reasonable but certainly not conclusive. Many hunters and warriors use no sign, and inhabitants of hilly regions often do use sign systems. One of Webb's arguments for his geographical explanation is that of how Indian signs are formed:

1. The Indians, as a rule, made much wider gestures than deaf-mutes. Their gestures tended to "clear" the body so that the signs could be seen against a background of light. . . .

2. The Indians used their arms more than the deaf, and only rarely did the sign depend on the action of a single finger. With the deaf many signs are made largely by the fingers alone. [ibid., p.97]

Taylor counters these assertions, noting that many signs are "not wide and body-clearing" (1975:331). What seems important in determining the physical scope of the signs is the user's degree of formality and fluency in sign:

The plains standard sign users tend to limit the scope of movements, maintain verbal silence and forego facial expression during a dignified and restrained execution of hand signs. *Sign talkers unfamiliar with the standard tend towards larger, freer movements,* exuberant use of facial expression and posture, and frequently voluble running commentary in some spoken language. [West, 1960, vol. 2:75—emphasis added]

This reduction in physical scope with increased fluency is precisely what our theory of language use would predict.

Origins in sign language used by deaf Indians. It is always possible, of course, that PSL developed from a rudimentary signing system created by (or for) deaf Indians. Clark (1885:144) felt it likely that hearing-impaired Indians had always used this sign language, and West (1960, vol. 2:64) confirms that PSL is still used for communicating with the deaf. While authors such as West suggest that PSL is a language system that can be *used* in communicating with the deaf, it is also plausible that deaf Indians themselves (or Indians attempting to communicate with the deaf) may have initiated or at least contributed to the formation of PSL. A parallel process is now going on in Rhode Island, where a group of scuba divers are learning ASL at the Rhode Island School for the Deaf in order to communicate under water.

Intratribal ritual. PSL could, in principle, have arisen in rituals that require silence. These are not activities such as hunting or warfare in which a sign language might be pragmatically expedient, but rather rites in which the tribe's conventions call for silence. There seems to be no evidence for ritual as the origin of PSL, although such origins are documented among other aboriginal tribes (see Umiker-Sebeok and

Sebeok, 1978, vol. 2). More to the point, ritual is clearly the source of the third genre of signing systems we will consider.

Cistercian Sign Language (CSL)

A third category of signing systems contains those used by populations who not only speak and hear but also share a common language. There are many such contexts in which a sign language might, in principle, develop—hunting, scuba diving, working in a noisy factory, sitting in a lecture when someone else is talking. This section is concerned with those sign languages that develop when the use of speech is forbidden for ritual purposes, especially the use of sign in monasteries, and Cistercian monasteries in particular.

To what degree is Cistercian sign representative of ritual sign in general or of monastic sign in particular? Obviously, the extent to which the ritual either necessitates or allows communication between participants will strongly influence the shape of the resulting sign system. If, for example, participants are allowed to communicate only the equivalents of "hello," "come here," and "goodbye," practically any sort of signs would do. On the other hand, if messages are allowed to become complex, I predict rather specific characteristics for the resulting system.

We shall therefore study Cistercian Sign Language (CSL) for two reasons: it has developed to a point where it can encode rather sophisticated messages and, of equal importance, it is well documented. Robert Barakat (1969, 1975) has produced a history, grammar, and lexicon from which the discussion of CSL is entirely drawn.

Since the early centuries of the Christian era, a number of monastic orders have imposed silence upon their members. In the *Rules for Monasteries of St. Benedict,* we learn that

> the Scripture shows that 'in much speaking there is no escape from sin' and that 'the talkative man is not stable on the earth.' [Chapter VII, p. 27; quoted in Barakat, 1975:13]

Visual signs were, however, permitted when communication during hours of silence was necessary. According to Barakat (1975:25), it was with the founding of the monastery in Cluny (in the year 909) that a fixed system of signs first emerged. As the Cluniacs exerted more influence, their signs were adopted in other monasteries in Europe. Each monastery developed its own list of "approved" signs, which differed

widely in number and formation from the signs used in other monasteries.

Monastic sign provides an especially clear example of how functional pressure to communicate creates linguistic change. Barakat relates that

> St. Bernard of Clairvaux . . . noted an abuse of the signs by the monks
> who readily invented "useless" signs to supplement the deficiencies in
> their regular list. The Saint recognized the lack of a sufficient number of
> signs and consequently increased the inventory to 305. [1975:27]

The same phenomenon occurs today at the St. Joseph's Abbey in
Spencer, Massachusetts, where Barakat did his field work. New signs
are created that go beyond the authorized list (Barakat cites, among
others, signs for "all shook up," "sniffles," "electrician," and "pumper-
nickle"). He also explains that some of the authorized signs, such as
those for "bookbinder" or "shoemaker" are "no longer in common use
because less expensive secular sources provide the products these
craftsmen would ordinarily make" (ibid., p.29). Similarly, only functional lexical distinctions are made:

> *Meat* and *fish* have but one general sign each; there are no subdivi-
> sions which indicates that these are either forbidden or restrictions have
> been placed on their consumption in the refectory. *Meat* (pinch the
> flesh of the left hand just below the thumb with right thumb and fore-
> finger), for instance, is never served in the refectory, but only to the
> guests of the monks in a building outside of the monastic enclosure.
> Thus, there is no need for types of meat such as lamb and pork. [ibid.,
> p.31]

A final point about function concerns the use of CSL. In recent times,
the Order has recognized the need to strike a balance between traditional practices and more modern ways, which include the use of some
verbal communication. Barakat observes that

> since brief verbal communication was permitted about five years ago
> [circa 1970], the use of signs among the brothers in some monasteries
> has decreased greatly. The possibility that the signs will be altogether
> eliminated in favor of speech is becoming more real each year. [ibid.,
> p.15]

Even when signs are used, CSL seems to have limited usefulness:

> Silent communication [presumably in CSL] is effective only for short

messages and cannot possibly be as effective and accurate as verbal communication. When speech does take precedence over the sign language it is due to the ineffectiveness of silent communication. [ibid., p.16]

Comparison of Structural Properties

Comparisons of signing systems are not new. West (1960, vol. 2) makes an extensive, albeit rambling comparison of different sorts of sign languages. Stokoe (1974) offers a number of comparative comments, while Crystal and Craig even compare a number of signing systems with respect to a revised version of Hockett's design features for human language (1978:156–159). Lacking is a systematic comparison of sign language types with respect to a consistent set of syntactic and semantic properties of the sort linguists use for comparing and analyzing spoken language.

The following discussion is a first attempt at such a systematic comparison. It is organized to parallel, as much as possible, the structural characterization of trade jargons and pidgins presented in chapter 5. The categories were selected not only for their appropriateness in discussing signing systems but also because they provide a natural bridge for comparing signing systems on the one hand and spoken systems on the other.

Let us consider each of the following structural points in turn:

>   stability
>   source of vocabulary and syntax
>   character of syntax
>   word order
>   circumlocution
>   redundancy
>   sign formation
>   iconicity
>   signing space
>   semantics
>   range
>   dependency on context

Stability.

ASL: relatively stable across fluent users

PSL: wide discrepancies between members of diverse tribes

CSL: stability for signs authorized by order, but diversity among monasteries for unauthorized signs

A sine qua non for any scheme of representation is a body of elements and combination rules whose use is common to a community of language users. Even if users disagree on the meaning of a particular element or combination rule, there must still be a reasonable consensus as to which phenomena belong to the language.

Of the signing systems considered above, ASL most closely approximates the user stability of spoken and written languages. Such stability should increase as the deaf community grows in its level of mobility and, to a lesser degree, education. PSL seems to vary widely from tribe to tribe. Critchley distinguished between two major dialect groups:

> the Northern, where the whole hand and both hands are freely employed; and the Southern, which is largely a unimanual and finger system. The former of these is better suited for purposes of signalling; the latter for conversation. [1975:70]

West, who did not investigate sign language in the southern plains, finds a major split between what he recognizes as "Plains Standard" and local dialects. While the Plains Standard Signing is somewhat restrained, the local dialects—especially in the far northern area—are more free-wheeling (1960, vol. 2:75).

West has also observed in the use of PSL what Charles Ferguson (1959) has called a diglossic situation, in which a user displays different language behaviors with different audiences:[10]

> Many informants know both a local version of the sign language and the Plains Standard, though few who know the latter admit to any knowledge of the former. [ibid., p.57]

Ferguson (1959:330) describes precisely the same phenomenon in the use of local varieties of Arabic as opposed to Classical Arabic or of Haitian Creole as opposed to French: speakers who use local forms of Arabic or Haitian Creole deny even knowing these local languages, which lack social prestige. Moreover, in PSL, the Plains Standard itself does not seem to be known and used by a significant proportion of the population. There is

> considerable dialect diversity within the standard language itself, due in part to the competitive nature of one of its current functions, the display

> of sign language as a tour de force at Pow wows, and in part to the
> fact that those who learn the standard in some school often return home
> and forget or modify the standard until it is quite different both from
> the school version (version used among students, not taught as part of
> the curriculum) and from the local dialect. [West, 1960, vol. 2:58]

West indicates that currently "local dialects can diverge to the point
of mutual unintelligibility and lexical sharing in the range of 20 to 30
percent within the space of one or two generations" (ibid., p.19).

Comparing West's observations about PSL with the previous analysis
of (spoken) trade jargons, both appear to display considerable variation from one group of users to another. Lack of regular contact between users from different tribes probably helps undermine the establishment of a standard that is known and understood across tribes.

The case of CSL is different from that of ASL or PSL. Within a
single monastery, CSL would appear to be highly stable across monks
because monks form a close-knit community (Barakat, 1975:46).
Divergences between varieties of CSL appear when one compares
other monasteries in the United States or in foreign countries (ibid.,
p.45). In America, we find divergences between the signs needed to
handle local conditions. Abroad, the spoken language of the signing
community is also a factor. Because signs in CSL are often intimately
tied to the spoken language (see below), such speech-based signs lose
their significance when transported to a monastery located in a country
in which a different spoken language is used.

Comparing the stability of ASL, PSL, and CSL, similar social factors
appear to work in each case. The broader the social base, the greater
the homogeneity across users. However, ASL is paradigmatically the
most stable of the three because, for the majority of its users, there is
no alternative linguistic modality.

Sources of vocabulary and syntax.

ASL: largely indigenous
PSL: unclear
CSL: heavily dependent upon English

The previous discussion of ASL identified a spectrum of signing systems used by the American deaf population that varied with respect
to the amount of influence English had on their signs and syntax. At
the end of the spectrum which shows the least influence from English

(in signs and syntax) is ASL. Having its own lexicon, ASL directly represents experience rather than a spoken language. As Robbin Battison (1978) has shown, ASL does borrow items from English, such as the finger spellings for English words whose referents are not already named by indigenous ASL signs. However, these signs tend to become "naturalized," losing their distinct finger spelling elements and becoming incorporated into a single sign with an arbitrary link between signifier and signified.

The question of sources for ASL syntax has generated a great deal of debate in the linguistic literature. Of particularly current interest is how much influence French Sign Language has had upon ASL and how much of ASL is indigenous to American signs. Whatever their signing source, though, it is now generally accepted that ASL has its own rules of syntax, which, a priori, have no greater similarity to English syntax than to the syntax of any other spoken language (see Wilbur, 1976; Friedman, 1977; Siple, 1978).

PSL is more difficult to describe because of disagreement over the extent to which PSL is an independent language or a representation of speech. John Harrington takes the extreme position that PSL is merely a visual representation of speech:

> The signs are everywhere based on spoken language and reflect it at every turn. The word order, the syntax, the vocabulary (the peculiar bundles of concepts tied together under the label of each word) of the American Indian sign language all prove it to be based, originally and constantly, on the spoken language of the user, whatever Indian idiom he happens to use as his daily speech [1938, reprinted in Umiker-Sebeok and Sebeok, 1978, vol. 2:117]

Harrington illustrates his case with an example of word-order parallels between sign and speech:

> The sign for *God* is a compound one, consisting of a sign meaning *medicine, mystery,* or *spirit,* according to the various languages, and of a sign meaning *big.* In the Kiowa language the spoken form is *daa'k'ia-'eidl,* meaning *medicine-big,* and the Kiowa makes first the sign for *medicine* and then the sign for *big.* In the Ojibway language the spoken form is *kihtci-manitoo, big-spirit,* and the Ojibway makes first the sign for *big* and then the sign for *spirit.* [ibid.]

Similarly, Kroeber (1958) argues that PSL is a speech surrogate. West assumes the opposite stance, asserting that there is "no evidence that Amerindian sign language is in any sense derivative of spoken language." He does admit, though, that

> the possibility [of sign deriving from speech] is certainly open and will remain so until a detailed comparison has been made between sign and spoken languages for some one American Indian group. [1960, vol. 1:97]

Extending the argument for the autonomy of sign, Taylor points out that the possibility of lexical borrowing must be considered not only from spoken Indian languages to sign, but in the other direction as well:

> The preference for descriptive compounds in the coinage of new terms in the Plains languages may itself reflect the use of the descriptive phrases in the sign language. [1975:349]

Our current state of understanding of the relationship between PSL and spoken language is summarized by Umiker-Sebeok and Sebeok. Speaking for all aboriginal sign languages, of which PSL is but one example, they write:

> It would appear that on the whole aboriginal sign languages act more as a substitute for spoken languages than do sign languages of the deaf (excluding signed English and finger spelling, of course). . . . On the other hand, none of the aboriginal sign language dialects have been described as purely substitutive, and it is to a varying degree 'independent of but translatable into natural language.' [1978:xxiv]

However, the fact that PSL is more closely tied to spoken language than are sign languages of the deaf is the result of *social circumstances* that have held the autonomous development of PSL in check:

> PSL differs from deaf sign language and spoken language precisely because it is used by a restricted number of people . . . and because the variety of communicative contexts in which it was employed was small compared with these other sign systems. . . . We can envision a time when aboriginal sign languages could, given favorable historical circumstances, become as conventional and almost as direct an expression of ideas as the deaf sign languages of today. [ibid., pp.xxiv–xxv]

The fact that social circumstances limiting the use of PSL have helped to maintain its ties with spoken language is reminiscent of our earlier observation that trade jargons do not develop an independent, stable syntax because use of the jargons is socially restricted.

The source of signs and syntax in CSL is much clearer. The large majority—although not all—of the CSL signing system derives from English.

Lexically, there are three groups of signs that do not depend on speech but represent either ideas or experience directly. These include *pantomimic signs,* such as that for "sleep," for which the "palm of hand or hands are placed on one side of the head and then the head is tilted to one side as though resting on a pillow" (Barakat, 1975:36—see figure 7.10). *Pure signs* show arbitrary relationships between signifier and signified. Thus, the sign for "abbot" is made by "placing the tips of the right forefinger and middle finger on the forehead so the tips of the fingers are pointing up" (ibid., p.39—see Figure 7.11); "green" is signified by using the tip of the right forefinger to draw a line from the right ear to the tip of the nose. Barakat's *qualitative signs* are more metaphoric in character, since they define their referents "in terms of

sleep (to)
place palm of right hand on right side of face then lean to right side on that hand with hand still in contact with head

Fig. 7.10 The (Pantomimic) Sign for "Sleep" in Cistercian Sign Language. Reprinted by permission of *Cistercian Sign Language* (Cistercian Studies, No. 11, p.121) by Robert Barakat. Kalamazoo, Michigan: Cistercian Publications, 1975.

abbot
touch the upper right forehead vertically with tips of right
forefinger and middle finger held tightly together

Fig. 7.11 The (Pure) Sign for "Abbot" in Cistercian Sign
Language (ibid., p.93)

what qualities are associated with them" (ibid., p.40). Thus "Irish" is
indicated by either the sign for "green" or the sign for "potato eater"
(see figure 7.12), and the city of Dallas is named by the sequence of
signs for "secular" + "courtyard" + "president" + "K" + "shoot."

In CSL, there are, however, many signs that clearly depend on
speech. Thus, "baloney" is denoted by the signs for "bull" + "O" +
"knee," "cookie" being signed as "cook" + "key" (see figure 7.13), and
the city of Cincinnati being indicated by a reduplication of the sign
for "sin" (hitting the chest with the right hand) plus the signs for "A"
and "T."

Like the lexicon, the syntax of CSL is heavily, but not exclusively,
derived from English. Where deviations exist, they often result from
syntactic circumlocutions that arise from forming derived nouns of the
sort we have already seen. Moreover, since some elements of English,
such as the verb *be* or the expletive *there*, are not represented in CSL,
some syntactic rearrangements are used to convey the desired message.
Finally, the lack of lexical distinctions comparable to the vocabulary

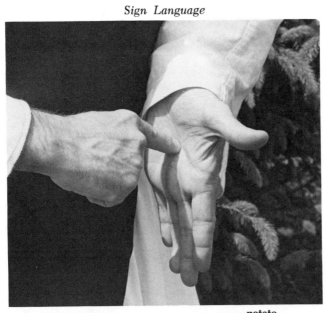

potato
turn tip of right forefinger on palm of left hand

eat (to)
bring thumb, forefinger and middle finger to the mouth
several times; fingers are touching at the tips only

Fig. 7.12 The (Qualitative) Sign for "Irish" (= "Potato" +
"Eat") in Cistercian Sign Language (ibid., pp.103, 115)

cook
extend right hand in front of body as though holding a
pan-handle, then shake from front to back as though
moving a frying pan

key
hold out right hand as though holding a key, then turn
hand as though turning a key in a lock

Fig. 7.13 The (Derived) Sign for "Cookie" (= "Cook" +
"Key") in Cistercian Sign Language (ibid., pp.109, 144)

of English may make for syntactic divergences between CSL and English. Here are some examples of the syntax of CSL:

This is Father Robert. = point to person + "priest" + "R"
He is not here. = name of person + "no" + "around" + "here" + "today"
Is that the abbot? = point to person + "abbot" + questioning look
Rarely does the monk pray in church. = "not" + "two" + "many" + "time" + "religious" + "pray" + "under" + "church"
[Barakat, 1975:56–68]

In sum, the extent to which a signing system draws on spoken language for its vocabulary and syntax depends heavily on the availability of a spoken language and the extent to which the community of users makes productive use of the system. These two factors are also accurate predictors of the other structural characteristics of signing systems considered below.

Character of syntax.

Word order
ASL: may not be as important as in spoken language
PSL: may not be as important as in spoken language
CSL: generally approximates English word order

The existence of grammatically describable word-order constraints has long been considered a necessary property of human language (Saussure, 1959). While recognizing some flexibility in ordering, especially in highly inflected languages, linguists have nevertheless assumed an underlying or unmarked word order in every language (see Greenberg, 1963).[11] In fact, researchers studying chimpanzees who have been taught to sign have considered word order a sine qua non for language. Roger Brown (1970) initially denied that Washoe was using language because of her lack of consistent signing order, while Herbert Terrace (Terrace et al, 1976) has gone to great pains to prove that Nim Chimsky actually does have some notion of sequencing constraints.

It is still not clear whether ASL has such an underlying word order and if so, what that order is. This is also true of PSL. There do appear to be some ordering conventions, such as the placement of negative markers and question markers (West, 1960, vol. 1:90). However, according to West, word order is less important in sign language than in speech. In sign,

> the obligatory grammatical relationships are established not by temporal order of syntax, but by spatial relationships, both within the execution of a single sign and between positions of execution of succeeding signs. [ibid.]

What grammar exists is due "almost entirely to internal sign morphology" (ibid.).

It appears that in visual languages the importance of word-order constraints is directly proportional to the dependence of the visual system on a spoken model. As mentioned above, CSL, which draws heavily upon English, does follow comparatively strict ordering constraints.

Circumlocution
    ASL: low
    PSL: varies
    CSL: reasonably high

The amount of circumlocution in sign is a function of the degree to which members of the signing system are in regular contact with one another and also depends on external constraints upon the size of the vocabulary. We would expect stable circumlocutions to be relatively rare in ASL because it is the primary means of communication for a sizable population. In PSL there appears to be a greater amount of circumlocution, roughly comparable to that found in spoken trade jargons and pidgins. Taylor reports that Indians use circumlocutions when they are not sure of a sign. Thus, although PSL has a sign for "wolf,"

> some tribes not thoroughly conversant with the gesture language make signs for gray, size of animal, large tail, and large, sharp nose. [1975: 340—see also West, 1960, vol. 2:55]

Other documented examples are use of the signs "white" + "soldiers" + "walk" to indicate "infantry," or "female" + "chief" + "big" to indicate "queen." Finally, Webb has commented that "the Indians repeated signs more often than do the deaf" (1931, reprinted in Umiker-Sebeok and Sebeok, 1978, vol. 2:97).

CSL also uses a great deal of circumlocution. We have already seen that the city of Dallas is denoted by "secular" + "president" + "K" + "shoot." Other examples are:

raw = "fruit" + "green"
forest = "all" + "wood" + "courtyard"
freeze = "arrange" + "hard" + "water"

The very presence of such circumlocutions would seem to follow from the fact that the "Cistercian sign language was never intended to expand communication among the brothers but to restrict it to some extent." For this reason, "the administration of the Order has rarely seen fit to increase the sign inventory" (Barakat, 1975:44). Thus, the circumlocution among two radically different groups, the Plains Indians and the Cistercian monks, seems to have arisen for quite different reasons. The Indians' lack of frequent contact made circumlocution necessary to ensure that one was understood. Among the monks, circumlocution was motivated by artificial constraints on the size of the lexicon.

Redundancy

	FACE	SPEECH
ASL:	high	none
PSL:	low	relatively high
CSL:	low	none

In addition to the use of circumlocution as a form of redundancy, let us consider the extent to which redundancy occurs in manual systems through the concomitant use of facial expression or speech. Discussions of ASL have often noted that the amount of facial expression used directly correlates with the degree to which "native" ASL is used. Wilbur (1976) observes that use of the face is more extensive when using ASL than when using some other form of manual or signed English. In the same vein, Stokoe finds that

> manual sign languages [such as ASL] need . . . extramanual means of distinguishing subject from object, statement from question, completion from continuation, connection from separation, and other syntactical operations. [1974:359]

Recalling our discussion of word order in ASL, Stokoe's comment implies that in ASL, facial expressions helps to mark grammatical relations that, in spoken languages, are typically marked by ordering constraints.

Many writers have observed that users of PSL use far less facial gesture to accompany their signs than do deaf signers (see Stokoe, 1972: 108; Taylor, 1975:338; Critchley, 1975:72). On first consideration, the observation seems curious, given Horatio Hale's observation that, when Indians switch from their own languages to Chinook Jargon, they gesticulate actively. Several hypotheses might explain this discrepancy. First (and least interesting theoretically), we may be dealing with two different populations of Indians, one of which gesticulates freely and the other of which does not. Second, the degree of accompanying gesticulation may be a function of one's fluency in signing. Recall West's observation that "sign talkers unfamiliar with the [Plains] standard tend towards larger, freer movements, exuberant use of facial expression and posture" (1960:vol. 2:75). Finally, there is West's hypothesis (ibid., p.77) that the Indians whose signs he observed use little facial gesture because they believe that whites expect them to appear stoical —an interesting case of life imitating art.

What about CSL? While Barakat does not raise the point, we would hardly expect active gesticulation in a religious order that has developed signing as a way of restricting communication.

A second type of redundancy that can occur in signing systems is the use of speech to accompany signs. Such redundancy is used in "simultaneous" or "total" communication, which strings together mostly ASL signs in English word order, accompanying each signed item with its verbal equivalent. ASL proper, however, is entirely silent. So is CSL, for obvious reasons.

PSL, on the other hand, does make frequent use of speech to accompany sign. Use of both modalities is especially common in storytelling. The use of speech alongside signing does not necessarily imply, however, that both modalities convey identical messages. While this is sometimes true, West observed cases in which the speech "involved comments *about* what was being simultaneously signed," and other cases in which the speech constituted "an independent lecture or conversation intended for the writer [presumably West] or some bystander" (1960, vol. 2:76).

Sign formation

Iconicity

     ASL: decreases with time

PSL: currently relatively high

CSL: well-represented

How much do the hand configurations in a signing system resemble the items of experience which they represent? What factors are important in determining the degree of iconicity? In the last part of this chapter, we shall consider this question in some detail, especially with respect to ASL. However, because the issue bears upon our comparison of ASL, PSL, and CSL, I introduce the subject here.

It is generally acknowledged that, while ASL has a number of signs that might be judged iconic, it also has a sizable number of arbitrary pairings between signifier and signified. Moreover, when new iconic signs are introduced, they tend to lose their iconicity over time. In his *Dictionary of American Sign Language*, Stokoe (1965) lists about 25 percent of all entries as currently iconic. (Wescott, 1971:418, hypothesizes that about two-thirds of the remaining 75 percent were originally iconic.)

Signs in PSL are usually considered more highly iconic than those in ASL. The interesting issue here is whether this higher level of iconicity is a necessary property of a signing system used by hearing people or whether it is an accident of history. There seems to be some evidence for the latter position. Dodge (1882, reprinted in Umiker-Sebeok and Sebeok, 1978, vol. 2:4–5) suggests that sign languages of hearing populations historically become increasingly arbitrary. Ljung goes one step farther, attributing the high degree of iconicity found in PSL to its "relatively recent origin" compared to naturally spoken languages. Had PSL "been allowed to develop freely, it would no doubt have become more arbitrary as time went by" (1965, ibid., p. 221). However, because PSL became increasingly a language of ritual rather than one of open-ended communication, such increased arbitrariness in signs did not have a chance to emerge.

There is little to say about CSL on the issue of iconicity; although it has iconic signs (e.g., "sleep" in figure 7.10), it is not clear what proportion of the signing vocabulary they constitute. However, given the heavy dependence of CSL on speech for forming new signs, iconicity is unlikely to be nearly as important in CSL as in ASL or PSL.

Signing space

ASL: generally restricted to rectangular area between head, waist, and shoulders

PSL: more open
CSL: more open

One of the criteria students of sign languages use to distinguish between pantomime and language is the restriction on the physical area in which the movements are performed. The more restricted the signing space, the more "language like" the sign system is assumed to be. The same economy of effort exercised with respect to signing space is responsible, in spoken language, for motivating such abbreviations as TV and SPCA. However, the restrictions on signing space have a theoretically important aspect as well. The very fact that some signs are spatially "grammatical" which others are not further indicates that the system in question is a language governed by rules.

In normal conversation (e.g., when not being poetic or dramatic), the ASL signer generally restricts sign formation to an area between the head and the waist (vertically), and between the shoulders (horizontally). The signing space for both PSL and CSL is less restricted. PSL also utilizes the head, chest, and arm areas but also includes the legs and occasionally the back (Taylor, 1975:38). Signs in PSL are sometimes described as large and expansive, although size may be a function of one's degree of fluency (cf. West's comment that those less familiar with the Plains standard use larger movements). Similarly, in CSL we find signs made by touching the heel (e.g., the sign for "socks") or back (the sign for "back"). Such spatial diversity is possible, at least in part, because the number of signs to be learned is limited in both instances.

Semantics

Range
    ASL: potentially unlimited
    PSL: unclear
    CSL: limited by design

Are there restrictions on the range of topics signing systems can be used for? One answer may lie in the size of the lexicon. Another concerns the exclusion of whole ranges of topics from discussion.

A problem with comparing vocabulary size is the lack of information. While Clark (1885) estimated there were 1,100 signs in PSL, West (1960) puts the number at closer to 3,500 (see Taylor, 1975:343).

Furthermore, we do not always know whether root words or compounds are being counted. (Recall here the cases of German and Neo-Melanesian, in which a large proportion of the vocabularies are formed by combining other elements.) Moreover, since many signs may be unstable through time, especially in PSL and CSL (see Barakat, 1975: 46), a tally of only the basic, stable signs may sharply underestimate the signing options actually available at a given time.

The alternative approach is to ask whether there are any limitations on the topics that can be discussed in the signing system. In ASL the answer, in principle, is no; the issue is less clear for PSL. Some linguists have questioned the semantic flexibility of sign (e.g., Voeglin—see Stokoe, 1974:355). West even writes that some topics were excluded from the sign language texts he collected (1960, vol. 2:76), although the absence of profanity and obscenity and the low frequency of emotive and evaluational terms may be a function of the elicitation situation. On the other hand, Umiker-Sebeok and Sebeok (1978:xx) conclude that the range of topics that could be discussed was "seemingly limitless." It appears likely that such discrepancies result, at least in part, from differing data sources.

In the case of CSL, we would expect, as a matter of principle, that the semantic range of signing would be restricted. It is unlikely that a system that was devised to restrict communication would be as semantically rich as the spoken language it replaces.

Dependence on context
ASL: low
PSL: unclear
CSL: higher

One of the claims that Crystal and Craig (1978) had leveled against signing systems was their lack of displacement (their inability to talk about items of experience not physically present). In the previous discussion of formal criteria for sign languages, I argued that Crystal and Craig failed to make their point for ASL. However, this is not to say that sign languages of deaf communities do not use context when contextual information is available.

One common way of creating proper names in ASL is to denote the person through a characteristic property of that person (using the sign for "mustache" as the name for an individual who wears a mustache).

In this sense, the *origins* of such proper names may be seen as contextually bound. However, the sign becomes acontextual (and the language capable of displacement) if I can make the name sign for my mustachioed friend when he is absent or if I am able to keep using the name sign even after my friend shaves.

The facts about PSL are unclear. We might hypothesize that because PSL is commonly used in storytelling—indirect reference par excellence —it would not be particularly context bound. However, we need more data before drawing any conclusions. In the case of CSL, we do have evidence indicating contextual dependence. Barakat admits that one of the major defects in the system is "the need for context; that is, many messages could not be understood if the persons whom the message is about were not present" (1969:116).

CONCLUSIONS

We have looked in some detail at three signing systems choosen as representatives of three distinct social contexts. As we have seen, none of the examples, perhaps with the exception of CSL, precisely exemplified its type. We have also seen that the structural properties of each of the three signing systems did not neatly cluster so as to yield categorical statements about the linguistic character of each sociolinguistic type. Nonetheless, the following conclusions can be drawn from this comparison:

> The more communicative functions a group of signers uses a signing system for, the greater the divergence between
> that signing system and pantomime.
> that signing system and any spoken language.
> The less accessible a single spoken language, the more a signing system will assume a character of its own.

ICONICITY AND THE LEARNING OF SIGN LANGUAGE

The comparison of ASL, PSL, and CSL touched on iconicity, that is, resemblance between a sign and that which it signifies. Yet the problem of resemblance has repeatedly arisen in previous discussion of representation. For reasons that will become clear, iconicity is an especially important issue in sign language studies.

ICONICITY

The arbitrariness of the linguistic sign, a principle established by Saussure, has dominated linguists' thinking about representation for most of the twentieth century. A word such as *dog* no more looks or sounds like the four legged creature to which it refers than does *chien* or *Hund*; so the idea of arbitrariness seemed reasonable enough.

In recent years, this Saussurian dictum has been questioned, although the challenge has not come on entirely the same grounds from which Saussure took his position. Saussure's concern was with spoken language, while the arguments in favor of iconicity as a significant linguistic parameter have assumed sign languages and written languages to be part of the broader domain of linguistic representation. One proponent of this position, Roger Wescott, has suggested that "as regards iconism . . . the only realistic question we can ask about a given form is not 'Is it iconic?' but rather 'How iconic is it?'" (1971:426).

The importance of "relative" iconism has emerged most fully in studies of ASL. Sign language research, only recently accepted within the fold of legitimate linguistic inquiry, has taken great care to establish that criteria used for judging and analyzing spoken language can be applied to sign data as well. This quest for legitimation seems, in part, to underline attempts to establish that sign languages are *not* overwhelmingly iconic after all, and therefore, by the principle of the arbitrariness of the linguistic sign, qualify as languages.

Yet it is clear that visual signs are different from signs in spoken languages. Admittedly, mature signers might not typically exploit or even be aware of the iconic roots of a sign any more than a speaker of German, in using the word *Handschuh* ("glove"), is conscious of the literal etymology—"hand" + "shoe." Nonetheless, the average level of iconicity in sign languages is higher than in speech.

The place of iconicity in sign language has typically been considered in light of what we might dub the "progressive loss of iconicity" hypothesis, which suggests that the longer either a sign or a sign language user is linguistically "active," the less important iconicity becomes. Nancy Frishberg's work on historical change in ASL (e.g., 1975) has established this principle diachronically. Bellugi and Klima (1976) make a similar point about the changing shape of signs in the course of a conversation: if a novel iconic sign is introduced, the sign loses its iconicity with continued use in the conversation.

A third dimension to the "progression" hypothesis, as seen in Roger Brown's work (1977), suggests that, ontogenetically, iconicity is initially an important aid in learning signs; as the signer becomes more fluent, iconicity becomes less valuable. As we shall see, this generalization is far too sweeping. The assumption that *all* beginners in sign language acquisition—children of deaf parents, adult learners acquiring sign as a second language, autistic children, retarded people, even chimpanzees—make use of iconicity is not verifiable. This is true because the *types* of learners that Brown groups together are sharply distinguishable along functional lines that he overlooks.

DIMENSIONS OF DISCOURSE

This book has shown that linguistic structures are significantly (though clearly not entirely) derivable from the social and communicative needs of the language users. The remainder of this chapter demonstrates the relevance of this thesis to the issue of iconicity in language.

Four variables are important in predicting the role of iconicity in visual language:

the character of the language learner
the character of the message sender and receiver
the character of the message itself
the character of the community in which the linguistic transaction
    takes place

Most of what I have to say about iconicity concerns characterization of the language learner. (My comments on the other three parameters are meant only to be suggestive.) Therefore, I shall reserve discussion of the language learner till last.

The Character of the Message Sender and Receiver

The degree of iconicity contained in an actual message may be affected by the relationship between the interlocutors. Is the interlocutor deaf or hearing? Is the interlocutor conversant either in some form of manual English or in ASL? We have a good deal of evidence that deaf people tend to use ASL with members of the deaf community but a form of manual English with hearing people who sign—whether or not the hearing interlocutor knows ASL. The amount of iconicity should be greater in using ASL than in using manual English, although we lack appropriate studies. The amount of iconicity should also increase (regardless of the base sign system) if the interlocutor is perceived as knowing little or no sign. We have anecdotal evidence here but lack carefully controlled studies.

The Character of the Message

It is with respect to the nature of the linguistic message that we probably know the most about the iconic properties of sign. The work of Klima and Bellugi (1979) has established not only that "poetry and wit" are quite possible in ASL but also that it is in the use of figurative language that the iconic properties of signs tend to be most fully explored. Again, however, we need careful studies comparing how the same signer communicates with the same interlocutor in different linguistic genres before we can hope to understand the effects of genre on iconicity.

The Character of the Community in which the
Linguistic Transaction Takes Place

Our third variable is the linguistic community—especially the *number* of active signers. How many individuals are needed to constitute a linguistic community? Obviously, at least a single message producer and a single receiver. But is that enough? Even if it is, does the language that develops in such a restricted milieu differ in any significant way from language used by multiple producers and receivers?

We are fortunate to have data from which to make comparative studies of levels of iconicity in signing communities of differing sizes. Kuschel's study of Kagobai, the only deaf person on Rennell, a small Polynesian island, uniquely documents the communication system that has evolved between a single deaf message sender and a sizable hearing population. Kuschel reports that many of Kagobai's signs are highly iconic (at least with respect to his cultural milieu); he hypothesizes that this may be a function of Kagobai's unique position and that iconicity might decrease as the number of signers increased (1974:37).

A strikingly similar finding has been reported by Heidi Feldman (1975) for the deaf children of hearing parents that she and Susan

Goldin-Meadow (1975) studied in Philadelphia. While the parents were raising the children in oralist schools, the children independently created their own signing systems. Feldman predicted that the highly restrictive size of the knowledgeable signing community (the children themselves) would generate a highly iconic set of signs:

> The children will not invent a set of arbitrary forms because arbitrary gestures would be inefficient for communication purposes. Since the children will be using these gestures with partners who do not know the system, the receivers are more likely to understand the gestures which relate to their meaning. [1975:15]

Feldman's study bore out the hypothesis. In both Kuschel's work (on the one hand) and Feldman and Goldin-Meadow's (on the other), it would be interesting to see under what conditions such signing begins to lose its strong iconicity. Is it, in principle, necessary to increase the number of deaf signers in a community before iconicity diminishes, or is an increase in the number of comprehending message receivers sufficient?

THE LANGUAGE LEARNER

As stated before, one goal of studying linguistic representation is the solution of problems in communication. Perhaps the most serious problem we can envision is never learning a system of linguistic representation. It has recently become fashionable to teach elements of ASL to populations who either will not or cannot learn spoken English. As we shall see, one of the major reasons for the choice of ASL is its high degree of iconicity, which is believed to facilitate learning. Our beliefs about the correctness of this hypothesis will, understandably, influence our pedagogical techniques; therefore, it becomes a pragmatic imperative to examine the hypothesis in some detail.

In his paper "Why are Signed Languages Easier to Learn than Spoken Languages?" (1977), Roger Brown hypothesizes not only that the underlying premise in his title is true but also that the reason for the greater ease of learning sign, at least in its early stages, is its greater degree of iconicity.[12] Well aware of the strenuous efforts of sign language researchers to establish arbitrariness as a significant factor in sign language *use*, especially among fluent signers, Brown suggests that the significance of iconicity should nevertheless not be overshadowed, a conclusion he reaches through the collection of several kinds of data, some of which he has gathered himself, and some of which he has drawn from other researchers. I shall be questioning this collection of sources, suggesting that an understanding of the role of iconicity in learning language requires a much more fine-grained analysis of what is being learned and by whom than Brown's single generalization would lead us to suspect.

To summarize his paper briefly: Brown surveys the literature on autistic children, mentally retarded children, and chimpanzees being taught sign language (actually in most cases, lexical items from ASL). He finds the lexicon of all three groups to be (at least impressionistically) highly iconic, and hypothesizes that such iconicity might have been perceived by the learner and actually utilized in acquiring the sign. His own data derive from an entirely different population: four- and five-year-old normal children learning signs as a game. In his first experiment, six children were taught eight signs for concrete objects ("chair," "ball"), the experimenter pairing the sign in ASL with the English gloss. Another six children were taught eight other ASL signs but given inappropriate glosses. Brown's second experiment replicated this design, but used more abstract (and generally less iconic) signs. In both instances, the results clearly showed that when a sign was paired with its appropriate gloss (i.e., when the child had a reasonable chance of deriving an iconic interpretation of the sign), comprehension far exceeded that of inappropriate pairings (in which iconic hypotheses would be hard to make).

Brown relates his findings to Rosch's work concerning the Basic Object Level (e.g., Rosch et al, 1976). In normal first language acquisition, according to Rosch, the earliest words learned are usually on the Basic Object Level (the level of generality at which language users most naturally form class terms—*chair* as opposed to the superordinate *furniture* or subordinate *kitchen chair*). Generally speaking, there are more characteristic attributes and movements for Basic Object Level terms than for superordinate or subordinate terms. Moreover, attributes and movements are the principle sources of iconicity in ASL. Therefore, Brown concludes, "there is a greater potential at the Basic Object Level for the creation of iconic signs than at any other level" (1977:21). Since the words in the initial experiment with normal children were largely at the Basic Object Level, he hypothesizes that iconicity is useful in the early stages of sign language acquisition.

This hypothesis is interesting, particularly because it is stated in sufficiently strong form to be dissected and tested. That dissection will be undertaken here by stepping back from the issue of iconicity and considering the particular kinds of language learning we are talking about. Only then shall we be in a position to understand the role of iconicity in different types of language and to determine if it is the same in each instance, as Brown's hypothesis would seem to suggest.

Who are we talking about when we speak of sign language learners? Is there any reason to believe that the spectrum of individuals or classes of individuals involved will all learn language—of any sort—in the same way? Research on the acquisition of first and second *spoken* languages has made us aware that the process by which a person learns additional linguistic systems is not necessarily a recapitulation of native (first) language acquisition (Dulay and Burt, 1974; Politzer, 1974). Similarly, experience with language-deficient children makes it clear that language therapy programs cannot merely attempt to make children pass through "the same" stages of language acquisition as normal children (assuming such an idealized sequence of stages exists) (e.g., Menyuk, 1964; Leonard, 1972).

Therefore, in considering whether iconicity is an aid (at least potentially) to early lexicon building in sign, the first question we need to ask is, Lexicon building by whom? There are at least four different groups of learners to be examined separately:

children learning sign as a first language (normally from deaf signing parents)
oral language users learning sign as auxiliary information
autistic children
mentally retarded children

There may be other significant subgroups (including nonhuman primates), but these four give us a place to begin.

Children Learning Sign as a First Language
It is commonly observed (e.g., Schlesinger and Meadow, 1972) that children of deaf signing parents start acquiring first words earlier than their counterparts who are acquiring speech. First signs have been reported as early as four and one-half months.[13] This observation clearly supports Brown's hypothesis that "the first steps in language learning must be easier with signs, than with words" (1977:1), but does it necessarily imply that iconicity is the key to learnability?

In answering this question, it may help to distinguish three facets of any language acquisition: the structure of the sign to be learned, the linguistic and cognitive abilities of the learner at the time of acquisition, and the process by which the sign is taught or modeled by a mature language user. Empirically, many, if not most, of the early signs children learn when acquiring sign as a native language may be highly iconic—but that does not imply that either the child or the pedagogue is conscious of that iconicity. Donald Moores (1977) reports that extensive longitudinal observations of deaf parents interacting with their young children have yielded no examples of adults using iconicity to explain the meanings of signs, even though the signs were often objectively iconic. We know that signing children do invent signs, often from a clearly gestural base. Bellugi and Klima mention a three-year-old deaf child who "invented a nonce form for 'cinnamon roll' which she made with a cupped hand representing the roll, and an active pointing hand indicating the swirls of cinnamon sugar on top of the roll" (1976:515). Carl Kirchner at the Kendall School in Washington, D.C., reports that his son, at age nineteen months, invented a sign for "doorbell" by pressing in on his nose with one finger. A use of the iconic properties of signs? Obviously so. Yet we have no reason to assume that because iconicity is used by the child in *invention* it will necessarily be *perceived independently in an existing word*, or *understood as a teaching device in the hands of a pedagogue.*

Studies of children's unfolding metalinguistic abilities in spoken language have shown that unconscious linguistic behavior typically precedes its conscious counterpart (Gleitman, Gleitman, and Shipley, 1972; Cazden, 1975). Children can, for instance, correct their errors before they can respond to corrections from others, or comment on the grammaticality of a model which is presented. There is no reason to question that the awareness of iconicity (either through one's own perceptions or through the instruction of another) may indeed be important in somewhat more mature children learning sign, but this does not constitute evidence for Brown's hypothesis about iconicity in the early stages of the acquisition of sign as a native language.

Oral Language Users Learning Sign as Auxiliary Information

There are two types of learners we can include in the category of language users who have some command of a spoken language: young children of the sort Brown studied and adults who take part in similar studies with isolated signs—n.b., we can also include in this latter category the "early stages" of sign acquisition by mature (spoken) language users who set about learning sign as a foreign language. In these cases of auxiliary language acquisition iconicity does prove an important asset to learning. Brown's experiments clearly indicated that iconicity was a significant factor in children's memory for signs. Mark Mandel (1977), using a different experimental design with adults, reached a similar conclusion. In neither case can we really be sure whether is was the presence of a prior spoken language which allowed the subject to conceptualize the iconic relationship between the object and its referent or whether general cognitive maturity was the key to making productive use of iconicity. Perhaps there was some altogether different feature, inasmuch as iconicity may also prove significant for certain socially normal but mentally deficient children (see below).

Autistic Children

A population recently highlighted in sign language research is autistic children. A growing number of studies (e.g., Creedon, 1973; Webster et al. 1973; Bonvillian and Nelson, 1976; Fulwiler and Fouts, 1976; Baron and Isensee, in press) has confirmed the viability of simultaneous communication (signing and speaking) as an entrance into language for many autistic children for whom speech therapy has failed. While most of these programs were conceived and carried out independently, their derivative findings have been surprisingly similar. Many autistic children who learn signing begin using language (in this case sign language) spontaneously for the first time (e.g., Webster et al. 1973); Bonvillian and Nelson, 1976). Some children who become good signers start to speak spontaneously—i.e., with no special oral language therapy (e.g., Creedon, 1973; Oxman et al. 1976), even to the point of dropping the manual communication and only speaking (e.g., Miller and Miller, 1973; Oxman et al. 1976). Finally, in many cases, a decline in destructive activity and growth in social behavior has been observed as the ability to use language (in this case, sign language) develops (e.g., Bonvillian and Nelson, 1976; Fulwiler and Fouts, 1976).

Why has sign language (or at least teaching lexical items from ASL) been so successful with many children who have been unable—or unwilling—to learn to speak? John Bonvillian and Keith Nelson (1978) have conjectured that the comparative ease with which these children learn manual signs (as opposed to oral speech) may be attributable to one of three factors: ease of molding the child's hand and clarity of visual feedback, general superiority of visual and motor skill or auditory-vocal skills in autistic children, or iconicity of the signs themselves. Existing studies using sign with autistic children do little to help us distinguish between these hypotheses.

A study at Brown University (Baron and Isensee, in press) bears on the possible role of iconicity in the learning of signs by autistic children. The study itself was designed to assess the effectiveness of sign language versus spoken language as a means of testing the lexical and syntactic abilities of an autistic child. We worked extensively with a twelve-year-old hearing but mute girl who was clinically diagnosed as autistic.

One of our pretests was designed to determine the subject's ability to apply a class term to different instantiations of the same referent. For example, if we taught her the sign for "mailbox" in the context of a picture of a mailbox, we wanted to know if she would be able to produce the sign for "mailbox" when shown a toy mailbox or an actual mailbox on the street corner. The testing procedure involved a total of nine items (the signs for "shovel," "umbrella," "kite," "mailbox," "fence," "saw," "guitar," "scissors," and "iron"). The subject was first taught the sign in one context (with a criterion of three consecutively correct trials for each item) and then exposed to each item in the two experimental contexts in which it had not been presented initially. The subject was required to produce the sign when the stimulus item was shown (which, as Mandel, 1977, and others have demonstrated, is more difficult than providing a gloss for a sign that is shown or selecting an appropriate picture for a sign).

The results were somewhat unexpected, especially since the subject had earlier been diagnosed as having practically no productive or receptive linguistic abilities. In the testing session that immediately followed training, she scored 100 percent correct. She again scored 100 percent correct when retested after two days, and once again after another six days, with no additional training being given. Although we did not collect comparable data on normal children or adults learning sign for the first time, both Brown's and Mandel's data seem to suggest that it is doubtful that normal subjects would match this performance.

Are these results surprising? Yes and no. They were unexpected in light of previous diagnoses of our subject's linguistic and cognitive abilities but consonant with the behavior patterns typical of autistic children: fixation on objects, insistence on sameness, and eidetic imagery (e.g., Kanner, 1943).

But where does iconicity enter the picture? We have no evidence that the subject did *not* use the iconic properties of the signs, to the extent they existed. Moreover, we did not explicitly control for iconicity in selecting the signs. However, there was no evidence whatsoever that she was aware of iconic properties that might have been transparent to the experimenters.

One study explicitly examined the role of iconicity in the learning of ASL signs by autistic children. The authors hypothesized that iconic signs would be learned more easily by the subjects than noniconic signs. In fact, the authors conjecture that

> no doubt iconic signs may be easier to acquire by everyone but this may not be *as crucial* for sign language acquisition [e.g., by deaf children of deaf parents] as with severely impaired children acquiring language for the first time. [Konstantareas et al. 1978:221n]

The subjects were five autistic and autistic-like children with a mean chronological age of 9 years, 1 month. Unfortunately, since four out of five children were also diagnosed as retarded, it is impossible to determine whether autism or retardation was the characteristic being tested.

The children were taught a total of sixty signs, half of which were judged to be iconic and half noniconic by an independent group of normal children. One-third of the test items were grammatically labeled as nouns in English, one-third verbs, and one-third adjectives:

	Iconic	Noniconic
Noun	10	10
Verb	10	10
Adjective	10	10

Subjects were tested by pointing to appropriate pictures, imitating signs which the experimenter made, or producing signs when shown pictures.

The results of the experiment are ambiguous. While iconicity played no significant role for items grammatically labeled as nouns, iconic signs for verbal and adjectival items were learned significantly better than their noniconic counterparts. However, since the overall learning of nouns (iconic and noniconic) was inferior to learning of verbs or adjectives (a result which the experimenters had not predicted), there is reason to question the choice of the ASL signs and illustrative pictures used in the experiment. Before any conclusions can be drawn about the possible use of iconicity in the learning of ASL signs by autistic children, considerably more research needs to be done.

Mentally Retarded Children

Mentally retarded children have successfully learned at least some lexical elements from ASL when spoken language therapy has failed (e.g., Wilson, 1974; Bricker, 1972). Studies summarizing the results of sign language programs with language-deficient children have tended to group together children with social, mental, and, we might add, physical handicaps. It is often difficult to determine that a given child is autistic but not retarded, or vice versa. However, to the extent that we can distinguish, at least in principle, between syndromes—and learning strategies and behavior patterns characteristic of these syndromes—it is helpful to do so.

Until recently, there has been little attempt to determine whether iconicity helps mentally retarded children to learn sign. In practice, as Brown observed, the early signs that both autistic and retarded children are taught are predominantly iconic (again, in the eyes of the instructor); but this guarantees nothing about the actual *use* either set of children might make of iconicity in learning signs. Because of this lack of data, we decided to collect our own data.[14]

The population we studied was composed of six largely nonverbal handicapped children, ranging in chronological age from 6 years, 3 months to 14 years, 11 months. Their mental ages ranged from 2 years, 7 months to 10 years, 1 month. Two of the children were diagnosed as having Down's Syndrome and were in a classroom for the trainable mentally retarded. Two others were in classrooms for the educable mentally retarded. The fifth child was in a classroom for the learning-disabled, and the sixth was diagnosed as being neurologically and orthopedically impaired. (Despite concerted efforts, it was not possible to locate a homogeneous subject population.)

The children were taught a total of thirty-six signs. The signs were taken from Signing Exact English (as presented in Gustason, Pfetzing, and Zawolkow, 1975), rather than from ASL because a clear set of standardized pictured signs were readily available for Signing Exact English. As in the Konstantareas study with autistic children, one-third of the signs were for referents labeled by English nouns, one-third for verbs, and one-third for adjectives. The signs were also chosen to represent highly iconic, partially iconic, and noniconic signing relationships, as determined by extensive testing with a large group of college undergraduates. In sum, the thirty-six signs were distributed as follows:

	Iconic	Partially Iconic	Noniconic
Noun	4	4	4
Verb	4	4	4
Adjective	4	4	4

Examples of the signs used appear in figure 7.14.

Signs were taught in association with pictures illustrating the object, action, or property to which the sign referred. Examples of the pictures used appear in figure 7.15. Testing was done by having the experimenter show a sign and ask the child to select the correct picture (out of four) which went with the sign, and showing the child a picture and asking him to produce the manual sign associated with it.

Test results revealed that iconicity had no overall significant effect on the ease with which the mentally retarded children learned the manual signs. (Iconic signs for referents grammatically labeled by adjectives were learned slightly better than their noniconic counterparts, but the results were not highly statistically significant.) Can we therefore conclude that iconicity plays no role in the learning of signs by mentally retarded children? Unfortunately, not yet.

All subjects did well in the experiment, averaging nearly 80 percent correct or better in most categories of test items. The test may have been too simple. A more challenging test might have revealed a more significant role for iconicity. Moreover, the subject population was far from ideal. In addition to being heterogenous, its members all had some oral language skills, both in production and comprehension. Ideally, one would like to study sign acquisition by retarded children who neither produced nor showed evidence of comprehending spoken language. Realistically, it is quite difficult to find, much less conduct, controlled experiments with such a group.

Meanwhile, some highly suggestive evidence that retardates do *not* need iconicity to learn visual language has been coming from the Georgia Retardation Center, which has been experimenting with symbols from Yerkish (the language Duane Rumbaugh devised for use with chimpanzees) with nonverbal retarded children.[15] As shown in chapter 6 (see figure 6.15), the symbols are explicitly designed to be noniconic. The fact that nonverbal retarded children have been able to use arbitrary durable visual symbols to participate in their first rudimentary form of communication suggests that iconicity may also be unnecessary for retardates learning an ephemeral visual set of signs.

Iconic	Partly Iconic	Arbitrary

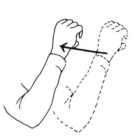

N **TREE** Elbow on back of hand; shake 5

QUEEN Right Q on left shoulder, then on right

CAR Right C behind left C; right moves backwards

V **DRINK** Thumb on chin, drink from C

TALK Index fingers move alternately to and from lips

EMPTY E brushes along back of hand and off

Adj **HAPPY** Brush middle of chest upward twice

BALD Circle Middle finger on head

WRONG Palm-in Y on chin

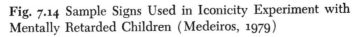

Fig. 7.14 Sample Signs Used in Iconicity Experiment with Mentally Retarded Children (Medeiros, 1979)

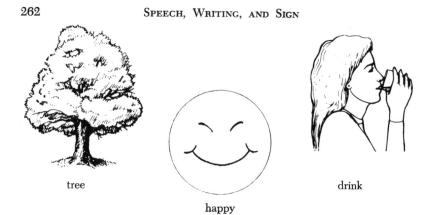

tree

happy

drink

Fig. 7.15 Sample Pictures Used in Iconicity Experiment with Mentally Retarded Children (Medeiros, 1979)

CONCLUSIONS

It is difficult to draw conclusions about the role of iconicity in language learning within a heterogeneous population about which we still know relatively little. Even at this stage of investigation, though, it is clear that iconicity is not equally important for all sectors of the population. Those who already have reasonable command of one linguistic system (e.g., normal five-year-olds or normal adults) can perceive and make use of iconicity in learning signs. At the other end of the spectrum, iconicity has little or no value in the normal acquisition of signs as a native language. What remains to be seen is which role iconicity may play among people being taught signs as a delayed first language.

VIII

Coda

In the European Middle Ages, it was assumed that any piece of literature could be read on four levels—literal, metaphorical, allegorical, and
eschatological. This book is intended neither as a work of literature nor
as a piece of theology. Yet, like texts viewed through medieval eyes, it
has intentionally been written to be read on several levels.

The most basic of these is the literal level, as an introduction to the
study of human language. Like its contemporary counterparts, this
book considers what a human language is and how languages are constructed. It addresses issues of language universals, language acquisition, and language change. However, unlike many of its contemporaries, it broadens the domain of linguistic inquiry from spoken language
to linguistic representation more generally. What is more, this book
suggests that questions of teleology—*why* languages have the shapes
they do—are legitimate issues of linguistic analysis.

The reasons for these departures can be seen as stemming from the
critical level, which approaches the study of human language with the
pedagogue's red pen. It considers contemporary approaches to language and asks whether the ways in which we analyze language have
any structural problems. In chapter 3, we considered standard attempts
to define human spoken language, and found them inadequate. The
case studies of speech, writing, and sign in chapters 5, 6, and 7 revealed
that the same vagueness of definition plagued written and gestural language as well. There is an object lesson to be learned from pursuing
this definitional theme, through its oral and visual variations, to its indecisive end: structural approaches to language that attempt to cir-
cumvent the people by whom and for whom the language was created
are subject to a priori decisions as to what should be studied and how

263

the investigation should proceed. Wholly lacking is any sense of *why* such an investigation should take place in the first place.

This search for a *reason* for studying human language underlies the third level at which the book can be read. Having suggested that a study of human language can help us to understand how language both creates and solves problems in social interaction, I deduced a *method* for examining language that could complement the familiar structural approaches. This method asked *why* languages assume the particular shapes they do. Just as we saw that definitional criteria are no more useful in categorically identifying written or signed language than they are in identifying spoken language, we found that functional explanations for structure are as rich in dealing with visual language as they are in explaining oral language structures.

From chapters 5, 6, and 7, it should be clear that the third level of meaning is as much the outlining of a research program as it is the presentation of a research *problematique*—this text has repeated such phrases as "it seems that" or "more research needs to be done before." For this reason, I have called this final section the *Coda* rather than *Conclusions*. It is much too soon to draw conclusions about an approach to language that has barely begun. Like a large jigsaw puzzle, we have bits and pieces that we have been able to fit together; yet there are vast areas about whose content we can only make rational conjectures.

Some of the puzzles posed herein will require no more than hard work and patience to solve. Concerted sociolinguistic efforts will provide sharper profiles of the deaf signing community or of the potential value of iconicity in language learning for autistic or retarded children; other battles will be harder to win. We may never succeed in deciphering enough of the Maya glyphs to completely understand the extent of phoneticism in Maya writing. More topically immediate, we may fail to comprehend the extent to which our habits of spoken language are responsible for our persistent failures in teaching our students to write lucid English prose.

This book began with an anecdote illustrating the communicative impasse to which our uses of written language may lead us. These misunderstandings continue to plague even the most articulate among us. At a recent Brown University commencement, the president was reading a prepared text of laudatory remarks about a prominent lawyer and judge who was being awarded an honorary degree. The president solemnly intoned that "Mr. X has led a long and distinguished career at the bar." An audience of already slightly giddy celebrants responded with peals of laughter. The embarrassed president haltingly continued his address to the yet more embarrassed lawyer.

Over half a century ago, Malinowski pointed out that language has no meaning outside the social context in which it is used. This book has endeavored to give theoretical and empirical significance to this truism.

Bibliography

Abercrombie, David (1972). "Paralanguage." In J. Laver and S. Hutcheson, eds., 64–70.

Addeo, Edmund and Robert Berger (1973). *EgoSpeak*. Radnor, Pa.: Chilton Book Company.

Akerblom, K. (1968). *Astronomy and Navigation in Polynesia and Micronesia*. Stockholm: Ethnographical Museum, Monograph No. 14.

Alleyne, M.C. (1971). "Acculturation and the Cultural Matrix of Creolization." In D. Hymes, ed., 170–186.

Anttila, Raimo (1972). *An Introduction to Comparative and Historical Linguistics*. New York: Macmillan.

Aristotle. *The Organon*. Octavius Freire Owen, ed. 2 vols. London: George Bell and Sons, 1908.

Arnauld, Antoine (1662, reprinted 1964). *The Art of Thinking*. Indianapolis: Bobbs-Merrill.

Arnheim, Rudolph (1967). *Art and Visual Perception*. Berkeley: University of California Press.

Arnheim, Rudolph (1969). *Visual Thinking*. Berkeley: University of California Press.

Bach, Emmon and Robert Harms, eds. (1968). *Universals in Linguistic Theory*. New York: Holt, Rinehart and Winston.

Bacon, Francis (1863). *Works*. Collected and edited by James Spedding, Robert Leslie Ellis, and Douglas Denon Heath. Cambridge: printed at the Riverside Press.

Bailey, C.-J. and R. Shuy, eds. (1973). *New Ways of Analyzing Variation in English*. Washington, D.C.: Georgetown University Press.

Baker, Charlotte and Carol A. Padden (1978). "Focusing on the Non-Manual Components of American Sign Language." In P. Siple, ed., 27–57.

Barakat, Robert (1969). "Gesture Systems." *Keystone Folklore Quarterly*, Fall, 105–121.

Barakat, Robert (1975). *Cistercian Sign Language*. Kalamazoo: Cistercian Publications.

Baron, Naomi S. and Laura M. Isensee (in press). "Effectiveness of Manual versus Spoken Language with an Autistic Child." *Sign Language Studies*.

Basso, Keith (1974). "The Ethnography of Writing." In R. Bauman and J. Sherzer, eds., *Explorations in the Ethnography of Speaking*. Cambridge: Cambridge University Press, 425–432.

Basso, Keith and Ned Anderson (1973). "Western Apache Writing System: The Symbols of Silas John." *Science* 180:1013–1022.

Bates, Elizabeth (1976). *Language and Context.* New York: Academic Press.

Bates, Elizabeth, with Laura Benigni, Inge Bretherton, and Luigia Camaioni (1979). *The Emergence of Symbols.* New York: Academic Press.

Bateson, Gregory (1943). "Pidgin English and Cross-Cultural Communication." *Transactions of the New York Academy of Sciences,* series 2, vol. 6: 137–141.

Bateson, Gregory (1972). *Steps to an Ecology of Mind.* San Francisco: Chandler Publishing Company.

Bateson, Gregory, Don D. Jackson, Jay Haley, and John H. Weakland (1956). "Toward a Theory of Schizophrenia." *Behavioral Science* 1:251–264.

Battison, Robbin (1978). *Lexical Borrowing in American Sign Language.* Silver Spring, Md.: Linstok Press.

Battison, Robbin and I. King Jordan (1976). "Cross-Cultural Communication with Foreign Signers: Fact and Fancy." *Sign Language Studies* 10: 53–68.

Beaufront, Louis de (1919). *Complete Manual of the Auxiliary Language Ido.* London: Sir I. Pitman and Sons.

Bell, Alexander Graham (1894). "Growth of the Oral Method of Instructing the Deaf." *Annual Report of the Committee on the Horace Mann School,* School Document No. 12.

Bellugi, Ursula and Edward Klima (1976). "Two Faces of Sign: Iconic and Abstract." In S. Harnad, ed., 514–538.

Benveniste, Emile (1971). "The Nature of the Linguistic Sign." In *Problems in General Linguistics.* Coral Gables: University of Miami Press, 43–48.

Benson, Elizabeth (1975). "The Quipu: 'Written' Texts in Ancient Peru." *Princeton University Library Chronicle* 37:11–23.

Benson, Elizabeth, ed. (1973). *Mesoamerican Writing Systems.* Washington, D.C.: Dumbarton Oaks Research Library and Collection.

Bergman, E. (1972). "Autonomous and Unique Features of American Sign Language." *American Annals of the Deaf* 117:20–24.

Berlin, Heinrich (1963). "The Palenque Triad." *Journal de la Société des Americanistes,* tome 52. Paris.

Berndt, Ronald M., ed. (1964) *Australian Aboriginal Art.* London: Collier-Macmillan.

Bernstein, Basil (1971). *Class, Codes, and Control.* London: Routledge and Kegan Paul.

Bhattacharya, Nikhil (1978). "The Context of Language Use." *Proceedings of the Twelfth International Congress of Linguists,* Vienna. Innsbruck: Innsbrucker Beiträge Zur Sprachwissenschaft, 730–733.

Bhattacharya, Nikhil (1979). "Signs and Experience: Steps towards a Semiotic Theory. In N. Bhattacharya and N. Baron, eds., *Theory and Methodology in Semiotics* (*Semiotica* 26:311–354).

Birdwhistell, Ray L. (1970). *Kinesics and Context.* Philadelphia: University of Pennsylvania Press.

Black, Max (1949). "Vagueness." In *Language and Philosophy.* Ithaca: Cornell University Press, 25–58.

Bloom, Lois and Margaret Lahey (1977). *Language Development and Language Disorders.* New York: John Wiley and Sons.

Bloomfield, Leonard (1933). *Language.* New York: Holt, Rinehart and Winston.

Bloomfield, Leonard (1939). *Linguistic Aspects of Science*. Chicago: University of Chicago Press.

Boas, Franz (1894). "Notes on the Eskimo of Port Clarence." *Journal of American Folk-Lore* 7:205–208.

Boas, Franz (1911, reprinted 1966). "Introduction," *Handbook of American Indian Languages*. Washington: Government Printing Office; reprinted as *Introduction to Handbook of American Indian Languages* (J.W. Powell, ed.). Lincoln: University of Nebraska Press.

Boas, Franz (1917). "Grammatical Notes on the Language of the Tlingit Indians." *University of Pennsylvania, University Museum Anthropological Papers*, vol. 8, no. 1.

Bolinger, Dwight (1968). *Aspects of Language*. New York: Harcourt, Brace and World.

Bonvillian, John and Keith Nelson (1976). "Sign Language Acquisition in a Mute Autistic Boy." *Journal of Speech and Hearing Disorders* 41:339–347.

Bonvillian, John and Keith Nelson (1978). "Development of Sign Language in Autistic Children and Other Language-Handicapped Individuals." In P. Siple, ed., 187–211.

Bornstein, Harry (1973). "A Description of Some Current Sign Systems Designed to Represent English." *American Annals of the Deaf* 118:454–463.

Bornstein, Harry, Lillian Hamilton, Karen Luczak Saulnier, and Howard Roy (1975). *The Signed English Dictionary for Preschool and Elementary Levels*. Washington, D.C.: Gallaudet College Press.

Bower, T.G.R. (1977). *The Perceptual World of the Child*. Cambridge, Mass.: Harvard University Press.

Brandt, J. (1944). *Introduction to Literary Chinese*. New York: Frederick Ungar.

Brentjes, Burchard (1969). *African Rock Art*. London: J.M. Dent.

Bricker, D.D. (1972). "Imitative Sign Training as a Facilitator of Word-Object Association with Low-Functioning Children." *American Journal of Mental Deficiency* 76:509–516.

Brook, G.L. (1970). *The Language of Dickens*. London: André Deutsch.

Brooks, Robert R.R. and Vishnu S. Wakankar (1976). *Stone Age Painting in India*. New Haven: Yale University Press.

Brown, C.M. (1974). *Wittgensteinian Linguistics*. The Hague: Mouton.

Brown, Roger (1970). "The First Sentences of Child and Chimpanzee." In *Psycholinguistics*. New York: The Free Press, 208–231.

Brown, Roger (1973). *A First Language*. Cambridge, Mass.: Harvard University Press.

Brown, Roger (1977). "Why are Signed Languages Easier to Learn than Spoken Languages?" Keynote address, First National Symposium on Sign Language Research and Teaching, Chicago, May 30–June 3.

Brum, Raymond de (1962). "Marshallese Navigation." *Micronesian Reporter* 10:1–10.

Bühler, Karl (1934). *Sprachtheorie*. Jena: Gustav Fischer.

Carpenter, Edmund and Marshall McLuhan, eds. (1960). *Explorations in Communication*. Boston: Beacon Press.

Carr, E.B. (1972). *Da Kine Talk*. Honolulu: University Press of Hawaii.

Caso, Alfonso (1965). "Mixtec Writing and Calendar." In *Handbook of*

Middle American Indians, vol. 3, part 2. Austin: University of Texas Press, 948–961.

Cazden, Courtney (1975). "Play with Language and Metalinguistic Awareness." In C. Winsor, ed., *Dimensions of Language Experience.* New York: Agathon Press, 3–19.

Cetto, Anna Maria (1969). *La tapisserie de Bayeux.* Bern: Payot Lausanne, Editions Hallwag.

Chadwick, John (1958). *The Decipherment of Linear B.* Cambridge: Cambridge University Press.

Chadwick, John (1959). "A Prehistoric Bureaucracy." *Diogenes* 26:7–18.

Chafe, Wallace (1970). *Meaning and the Structure of Language.* Chicago: University of Chicago Press.

Chao, Y.R. (1968). *Language and Symbolic Systems.* Cambridge: Cambridge University Press.

Chaytor, H.J. (1960). "Reading and Writing." In E. Carpenter and M. McLuhan, eds., 117–124.

Chomsky, Noam (1957). *Syntactic Structures.* The Hague: Mouton.

Chomsky, Noam (1965). *Aspects of the Theory of Syntax.* Cambridge, Mass.: MIT Press.

Chomsky, Noam (1968). *Language and Mind.* New York: Harcourt Brace.

Chomsky, Noam (1975). *Reflections on Language.* New York: Pantheon Books.

Chomsky, Noam (1979). *Language and Responsibility.* New York: Pantheon Books.

Chukovsky, Kornei (1965). *From Two to Five.* Berkeley: University of California Press.

Clark, Eve (1973). "What's in a Word?" In T.E. Moore, ed., 65–110.

Clark, William Philo (1885). *The Indian Sign Language.* Philadelphia: L.R. Hamersly.

Cohen, Einya, Lila Namir, and I.M. Schlesinger (1977). *A New Dictionary of Sign Language.* The Hague: Mouton.

Cohen, L. Jonathan (1954). "On the Project of a Universal Character." *Mind* 63:49–63.

Cohen, L. Jonathan (1962). *The Diversity of Meaning.* London: Methuen.

Cole, D.T. (1953). "Fanagalo and the Bantu Languages in South Africa." *African Studies* 12:1–9.

Couturat, Louis, O. Jespersen, R. Lorenz, W. Ostwald, and L. Pfaundler (1910). *International Language and Science.* London: Constable.

Cravens, Hamilton (1978). *The Triumph of Evolution.* Philadelphia: University of Pennsylvania Press.

Creedon, M. (1973). "Language Development in Nonverbal Autistic Children Using a Simultaneous Communication System." Paper presented at the Biennial Meeting of the Society for Research in Child Development, Philadelphia.

Critchley, Macdonald (1975). *The Silent Language.* London: Butterworths.

Crystal, David (1971). *Linguistics.* Harmondsworth: Penguin.

Crystal, David (1974). "Paralinguistics." In T. Sebeok, ed., *Current Trends in Linguistics,* vol. 12, part 1. The Hague: Mouton, 265–295.

Crystal, David and Elma Craig (1978). "Contrived Sign Language." In I.M. Schlesinger, and Lila Namir, eds., *Sign Language of the Deaf.* New York: Academic Press, 141–168.

Daws, G. (1968). *Shoal of Time: A History of the Hawaiian Islands.* New York: Macmillan.

Defoe, Daniel (1726). *The Complete English Tradesman.* London: Charles Rivington.

DeMott, Benjamin (1957). "Science versus Mnemonics." *Isis* 48:3–12.

Dempsey, Don (1962). "The Language of Traffic Policemen." *American Speech* 37:266–273.

Deregowski, Jan B (1973). "Illusion and Culture." In R.L. Gregory and E.H. Gombrich, eds., 161–191.

Deregowski, Jan B., E.S. Muldrow, and W.F. Muldrow (1973). "Pictorial Recognition in a Remote Ethiopian Population." *Perception* 1:417–425.

Dik, Simon (1978). *Functional Grammar.* Amsterdam: North-Holland Publishing.

Diringer, David (1962). *Writing.* New York: Frederick A. Praeger.

Dodge, Colonel Richard I. (1882, reprinted 1978). *Our Wild Indians.* Hartford: Hartford Publishing Co.; reprinted in Umiker-Sebeok and Sebeok, eds., vol. 2:3–18.

Dulay, H. and M. Burt (1974). "A New Perspective on the Creative Construction Process in Child Second Language Learning." *Language Learning* 24:253–278.

Edge, Vickilee and Leora Herrmann (1977). "Verbs and the Determination of Subject in American Sign Language." In L. Friedman, ed., 137–179.

Emery, Clark (1948). "John Wilkins' Universal Language." *Isis* 38:174–185.

Épée, Charles Michel, Abbé de l' (1776). *L'Institution des Sourds et Muets, Par la Voie des Signes Méthodiques.* Paris.

Epstein, A.L. (1968). "Linguistic Innovation and Culture of the Copperbelt, Northern Rhodesia." In J. Fishman, ed., 320–339.

Fantz, R.L. (1961). "The Origin of Form Perception." *Scientific American* 204:66.

Feldman, Heidi (1975). *The Spontaneous Creation of a Lexicon by Deaf Children of Hearing Parents.* Ph.D. dissertation, University of Pennsylvania.

Feldman, Heidi, Susan Goldin-Meadow, and Lila Gleitman (1978). "Beyond Herodotus: The Creation of Language by Linguistically Deprived Deaf Children." In A. Locke, ed., 351–414.

Ferguson, Charles A. (1959). "Diglossia." *Word* 15:325–340.

Ferguson, Charles A. (1963). "Some Assumptions about Nasals." In J. Greenberg, ed., 53–60.

Ferguson, Charles A. (1975). "Toward a Characterization of English Foreigner Talk." *Anthropological Linguistics* 17:1–14.

Fillmore, Charles J. (1968a). "The Case for Case." In E. Bach and R. Harms, eds., 1–90.

Fillmore, Charles J. (1968b). "Lexical Entries for Verbs." *Foundations of Language* 4:373–393.

Fischer, Ernst (1963). *The Necessity of Art.* Baltimore: Penguin.

Fischer Susan (1975). "Influences on Word Order Change in American Sign Language." In C.N. Li, ed., *Word Order and Word Order Change.* Austin: University of Texas Press.

Fishman, J., ed. (1968). *Readings in the Sociology of Language.* The Hague: Mouton.

Fouts, Roger S. (1973). "Acquisition and Testing of Gestural Signs in Four Young Chimpanzees." *Science* 180:978–980.

Fraser, Colin, Ursula Bellugi, and Roger Brown (1963). "Control of Grammar in Imitation, Comprehension, and Production." *Journal of Verbal Learning and Verbal Behavior* 2:121–135.

Friedman, Lynn, ed. (1977). *On the Other Hand.* New York: Academic Press.

Frishberg, Nancy (1975). "Arbitrariness and Iconicity: Historical Change in American Sign Language." *Language* 51:696–719.

Fromkin, Victoria and Robert Rodman (1978). *Introduction to Language.* New York: Holt, Rinehart and Winston.

Fulwiler, R.L. and R.S. Fouts (1976). "Acquisition of American Sign Language by a Non-Communicating Autistic Child." *Journal of Autism and Childhood Schizophrenia* 6:43–51.

Gandz, Solomon (1935). "Oral Tradition in the Bible." In S. Baron and A. Marx, eds., *Jewish Studies in Memory of George A. Kohut.* New York: Alexander Kohut Memorial Foundation, 248–269.

Gardner, Beatrice T. and R. Allen Gardner (1969). "Teaching Sign Language to a Chimpanzee." *Science* 165:664–672.

Gardner, P. (1966). "Symmetric Respect and Memorate Knowledge: The Structure and Ecology of Individualistic Culture." *Southwest Journal of Anthropology* 22:389–415.

Gelb, I.J. (1952). *A Study of Writing.* Chicago: University of Chicago Press.

Gibson, James (1950). *The Perception of the Visual World.* Boston: Houghton Mifflin.

Gladwin, Thomas (1970). *East is a Big Bird.* Cambridge, Mass.: Harvard University Press.

Gleitman, L., H. Gleitman, and E. Shipley (1972). "The Emergence of the Child as Grammarian." *Cognition* 1:137–164.

Goldin-Meadow, Susan (1975). *The Representation of Semantic Relations in a Manual Language Created by Deaf Children of Hearing Parents.* Ph.D. dissertation, University of Pennsylvania.

Gombrich, E.H. (1960). *Art and Illusion.* Princeton: Princeton University Press.

Gombrich, E.H. (1972). "The Mask and the Face." In E.H. Gombrich, J. Hochberg, and M. Black, *Art, Perception, and Reality.* Baltimore: The Johns Hopkins Press, 1–46.

Gombrich, E.H. (1973). "Illusion and Art." In R.L. Gregory and E.H. Gombrich, eds., 193–243.

Goodenough, Ward H. (1968). "Componential Analysis." In Sills, ed., *International Encyclopedia of the Social Sciences,* vol. 3. New York: Macmillan.

Goodman, Nelson (1976). *Languages of Art.* Indianapolis: Hackett Publishers.

Goody, Jack (1968). "Introduction." In J. Goody, ed., *Literacy in Traditional Societies.* Cambridge: Cambridge University Press.

Goody, Jack and Ian Watt (1968). "The Consequences of Literacy." In J. Goody, ed., 27–68.

Grant, Campbell (1965). *The Rock Paintings of the Chumash.* Berkeley: University of California Press.

Grant, Campbell (1967). *Rock Art of the American Indian.* New York: Thomas Crowell.

Grant, R.V. (1945). "Chinook Jargon." *International Journal of American Linguistics* 11:225–233.

Greenberg, Joseph, ed. (1963). *Universals of Language.* Cambridge, Mass.: M.I.T. Press.

Greenberg, Joseph (1966). *Language Universals.* The Hague: Mouton.

Greenberg, Joseph (1968). *Anthropological Linguistics.* New York: Random House.

Greenfield, Patricia and Joshua Smith (1976). *The Structure of Communication in Early Language Development.* New York: Academic Press.

Gregory, R.L. (1966). *Eye and Brain.* New York: McGraw-Hill.

Gregory, R.L. (1973). "The Confounded Eye." In R.L. Gregory and E.H. Gombrich, eds., 49–95.

Gregory, R.L. and E.H. Gombrich, eds. (1973). *Illusion in Nature and Art.* New York: Charles Scribner's Sons.

Gregory, R.L. and J.G. Wallace (1963). "Recovery from Early Blindness: A Case Study." *Experimental Psychology Society Monographs,* No. 2, Cambridge.

Grimshaw, A. (1971). "Some Social Forces and Some Social Functions of Pidgin and Creole Languages." In D. Hymes, ed., 427–445.

Gudschinsky, Sarah (1968). "The Relationship of Language and Linguistics to Reading." *Kivung* 1:146–152.

Gudschinsky, Sarah (1976). *Literacy: The Growing Influence of Linguistics.* The Hague: Mouton.

Gustason, G., D. Pfetzing, and E. Zawolkow (1975). *Signing Exact English.* Rossmoor, Cal.: Modern Signs Press.

Haas, Mary (1940). *Tunica.* New York: J.J. Augustin.

Haas, Mary (1969). *The Prehistory of Languages.* The Hague: Mouton.

Hall, Robert (1944). "Chinese Pidgin English, Grammar and Texts." *Journal of the American Oriental Society* 64:95–113.

Hall, Robert (1955). *Hands Off Pidgin English.* Sydney: Pacific Publications.

Hall, Robert (1966). *Pidgin and Creole Languages.* Ithaca: Cornell University Press.

Hallet, Garth (1967). *Wittgenstein's Definition of Meaning as Use.* New York: Fordham University Press.

Halliday, M.A.K. (1970). "Language Structure and Language Function." In J. Lyons, ed., *New Horizens in Linguistics.* Baltimore: Penguin, 140–165.

Halliday, M.A.K. (1973). *Explorations in the Functions of Language.* London: Arnold.

Halliday, M.A.K. (1975). *Learning How to Mean.* London: Arnold.

Halliday, M.A.K. (1978). *Language as Social Semiotic.* Baltimore: University Park Press.

Hancock, I.F. (1971). "A Survey of the Pidgins and Creoles of the World." In D. Hymes, ed., 509–523.

Hanson, Norwood Russell (1958). *Patterns of Discovery.* Cambridge: Cambridge University Press.

Hanzeli, Victor Egon (1969). *Missionary Linguistics in New France.* The Hague: Mouton.

Harnad, Steven, ed. (1976). *Origins and Evolution of Language and Speech.* New York: The New York Academy of Sciences, vol. 280.

Harrington, John (1938; reprinted 1978). "The American Indian Sign Language." *Indians at Work*; reprinted in Umiker-Sebeok and Sebeok, eds., vol. 2:109–142.

Havelock, Eric (1973). "Prologue to Greek Literacy." In *Lectures in Memory of Louise Taft Semple,* Second Series. Norman: University of Oklahoma Press, 329–391.

Havelock, Eric (1976). *Origins of Western Literacy.* Toronto: The Ontario Institute for Studies in Education.

Havelock, Eric (1978). *The Greek Concept of Justice.* Cambridge, Mass.: Harvard University Press.

Hawkes, Jacquetta and Sir Leonard Woolley (1963). *Prehistory and the Beginnings of Civilization.* New York: Harper and Row.

Henry, Jules (1936). "The Linguistic Expression of Emotion." *American Anthropologist* 38:250–256.

Hermerén, Göran (1969). *Representation and Meaning in the Visual Arts.* Lund: Scandinavian University Books.

Herskovits, Melville (1953). *Franz Boas.* New York: Charles Scribner's Sons.

Hewes, Gordon (1974). "Gesture Language in Culture Contact." *Sign Language Studies* 4:1–34.

Hockett, Charles F. (1960). "The Origins of Speech." *Scientific American* (September) 203:89–96.

Hockett, Charles F. (1963). "The Problem of Universals in Language." In J. Greenberg, ed., 1–29.

Hockett, Charles, ed. (1970). *A Leonard Bloomfield Anthology.* Bloomington: Indiana University Press.

Hockett, Charles and Robert Ascher (1964). "The Human Revolution." *Current Anthropology* 5:135–168.

Holden, Donald (1979). "Why Profs Can't Write." *New York Times,* February 4, Op-Ed, p. E19.

Horne, Kibbey M. (1966). *Language Typology.* Washington, D.C.: Georgetown University Press.

Hubbard, Gardiner Green (1867). "The Education of Deaf Mutes: Shall It Be by Signs or Articulation?" Boston: A. Williams.

Humfreville, James Lee (1897). *Twenty Years Among Our Savage Tribes.* Hartford.

Huttenlocher, Janellen (1974). "The Origins of Language Comprehension." In R. Solso, ed., *Theories in Cognitive Psychology.* Hillsdale, N.J.: Lawrence Earlbaum Associates.

Hymes, Dell, ed. (1971). *Pidginization and Creolization of Languages.* Cambridge: Cambridge University Press.

Hymes, Dell (1972). "On Communicative Competence." In J.B. Pride and J. Homes, eds., *Sociolinguistics.* Baltimore: Penguin.

Hymes, Dell (1973), "Speech and Language: On the Origins and Foundations of Inequality in Speaking." *Daedalus* (Summer) 102:59–86.

Hymes, Dell (1974). *Foundations in Sociolinguistics.* Philadelphia: University of Pennsylvania Press.

Jackson, A.T. (1938). *Picture-Writing of Texas Indians.* Austin: University of Texas, Anthropological Papers, vol. II.

Jakobson, Roman (1960), "Closing Statement: Linguistics and Poetics." In T. Sebeok, ed., *Style in Language.* Cambridge, Mass.: M.I.T. Press, 350–377.

Jakobson, Roman (1962). "The Concept of the Sound Law and the Teleological Principle." In *Selected Writings,* vol. I. The Hague: Mouton, 1–2.

Jakobson, Roman (1971). "Linguistic Glosses to Goldstein's 'Sortbegriff.'" In *Selected Writings,* vol. II. The Hague: Mouton, 267–271.

Jankowsky, Kurt (1972). *The Neogrammarians.* The Hague: Mouton.

Jarka, Horst (1963). "The Language of Skiers." *American Speech* 38:202–208.

Jensen, Hans (1970). *Sign, Symbol, and Script.* Translated by George Unwin. New York: G.P. Putnam's Sons.

Jones, Richard (1932). "Science and Language in England of the Mid-Seventeenth Century." *Journal of English and Germanic Philology* 31:315–331.

Jones, Richard (1961). *Ancients and Moderns: A Study of the Rise of the Scientific Movement in Seventeenth-Century England.* St. Louis: Washington University Press.

Joos, Martin, ed. (1957). *Readings in Linguistics* I. Chicago: University of Chicago Press.

Kannapell, Barbara (1977). "The Deaf Person as a Teacher of American Sign Language: Unifying and Separatist Functions of American Sign Language." Paper presented at the First National Symposium on Sign Language Research and Teaching, Chicago, May 30–June 3.

Kanner, Leo (1943). "Autistic Disturbance of Affective Contact." *Nervous Child* 2:217–250.

Katz, Jerrold (1966). *The Philosophy of Language.* New York: Harper and Row.

Katz, Jerrold and Jerry Fodor (1963). "The Structure of a Semantic Theory." *Language* 39:170–210.

Kelley, David (1976). *Deciphering the Maya Script.* Austin: University of Texas Press.

Klima, Edward and Ursula Bellugi (1979). *The Signs of Language.* Cambridge, Mass.: Harvard University Press.

Knorozov, Yuri (1958). "The Problem of the Study of the Maya Hieroglyphic Writing." *American Antiquity* 23:284–291.

Konstantareas, M.M., J. Oxman, and C.D. Webster (1978). "Iconicity: Effects on the Acquisition of Sign Language by Autistic and Other Severely Dysfunctional Children." In P. Siple, ed., 213–237.

Kooij, Jan G. (1971). *Ambiguity in Natural Language.* Amsterdam: North-Holland Publishing.

Krauss, Robert (1968). "Language as a Symbolic Process in Communication." *American Scientist* 56:265–278.

Kroeber, Alfred (1958). "Sign Language Inquiry." *International Journal of American Linguistics* 24:1–19.

Kučera, Henry and Elizabeth Cowper (1976). "Functional Sentence Perspective Revisited." In L. Matejka, ed., *Sound, Sign, and Meaning.* Ann Arbor: Michigan Slavic Contributions, No. 6, Department of Slavic Languages and Literatures, University of Michigan, 191–230.

Kuno, Susumo (1972). "Functional Sentence Perspective." *Linguistic Inquiry* 3:269–320.

Kurath, Hans, ed. (1939–1943). *Linguistic Atlas of New England.* Providence: Brown University Press.

Kuschel, Rolf (1974). *A Lexicon of Signs from a Polynesian Outliner Island.* Copenhagen: Psykologisk Laboratorium, Københavns Universitet, Psykologisk Skriftserie nr. 8.

La Barre, Weston (1947). "The Cultural Basis of Emotions and Gestures." *Journal of Personality* 16:49–68.

Labov, William (1963, reprinted 1972b). "The Social Motivation of a Sound Change." *Word* 19:273–309; reprinted in Labov (1972b), 1–42.

Labov, William (1966). *The Social Stratification of English in New York City*. Washington, D.C.: Center for Applied Linguistics.

Labov, William (1971). "On the Adequacy of Natural Languages." Unpublished ms.

Labov, William (1972a). *Language in the Inner City*. Philadelphia: University of Pennsylvania Press.

Labov, William (1972b). *Sociolinguistic Patterns*. Philadelphia: University of Pennsylvania Press.

Labov, William (1973). "The Boundaries of Words and their Meanings." In C.-J. Bailey and R.W. Shuy, eds., 340–373.

Labov, William, Malcah Yaeger, and Richard Steiner (1972). *A Quantitative Study of Sound Change in Progress*. Philadelphia: U.S. Regional Survey.

Lakoff, George (1970a). "A Note on Ambiguity and Vagueness." *Linguistic Inquiry* 1:357–359.

Lakoff, George (1970b). *Irregularity in Syntax*. New York: Holt, Rinehart and Winston.

Lakoff, George (1972). "Hedges: A Study in Meaning Criteria and the Logic of Fuzzy Concepts." In *Papers from the Eighth Regional Meeting*, Chicago Linguistic Society.

Langacker, Ronald (1973). *Language and Its Structure*. New York: Harcourt Brace Jovanovich.

Lasch, Christopher (1978). *The Culture of Narcissism*. New York: Norton.

Laver, J. and S. Hutcheson, eds. (1972). *Communication in Face to Face Interaction*. Baltimore: Penguin.

Lee, Dorothy (1960). "Lineal and Nonlineal Codifications of Reality." In E. Carpenter and M. McLuhan, eds., 136–154.

Lehmann, Winfred P. (1973). *Historical Linguistics*. New York: Holt, Rinehart and Winston.

Lehrer, Adrienne (1970). "Indeterminacy in Semantic Description." *Glossa* 4:87–110.

Lenneberg, Eric (1962). "Understanding Language without Ability to Speak." *Journal of Abnormal and Social Psychology* 65:419–425.

Lenneberg, Eric (1967). *Biological Foundations of Language*. New York: John Wiley.

Leonard, L. (1972). "What Is Deviant Language?" *Journal of Speech and Hearing Disorders* 37:427–446.

Leopold, Werner (1947). *Speech Development of a Bilingual Child*, vol. 2. Evanston: Northwestern University Press.

Leopold, Werner (1949). *Speech Development of a Bilingual Child*, vol. 3. Evanston: Northwestern University Press.

Lévy-Bruhl, Lucien (1926). *How Natives Think*. Translated by L. Clare. London: George Allen and Unwin.

Lewis, I.M. (1968). "Literacy in Nomadic Society: The Somali Case." In J. Goody, ed., 265–276.

Lewis, David (1972). *We, The Navigators*. Honolulu: University Press of Hawaii.

Liddell, Scott (1978). "Nonmanual Signals and Relative Clauses in American Sign Language." In P. Siple, ed., 59–90.

Ljung, Magnus (1965, reprinted 1978). "Principles of a Stratificational Analysis of the Plains Indian Sign Language." *International Journal of American Linguistics* 31:119–127; reprinted in Umiker-Sebeok and Sebeok, eds., vol. 2:213–222.

Locke, Andrew, ed. (1978). *Action, Gesture, and Symbol.* London: Academic Press.

Lowie, Robert (1937). *The History of Ethnological Theory.* New York: Farrar and Rinehart.

Lunde,. Anders (1956). "The Sociology of the Deaf." Paper presented at the American Sociological Society Meeting, Detroit.

Lyons, Gene (1976). "The Higher Illiteracy." *Harper's* (September) 253: 33–40.

Lyons, John (1968). *Introduction to Theoretical Linguistics.* Cambridge: Cambridge University Press.

McCarthy, Frederick (1958). *Australian Aboriginal Rock Art.* Sydney: Trustees of the Australian Museum.

McCawley, James D. (1968). "The Role of Semantics in Grammar." In E. Bach and R. Harms, eds., 125–169.

McLuhan, Marshall (1960). "The Effect of the Printed Book on Language in the Sixteenth Century." In E. Carpenter and M. McLuhan, eds., 125–135.

Malinowski, Bronislaw (1923). "The Problem of Meaning in Primitive Languages." Supplement I to C.K. Ogden and I.A. Richards, *The Meaning of Meaning.* New York: Harcourt, Brace, 296–336.

Mallery, Garrick (1880a, reprinted 1978). *Introduction to the Study of Sign Language among the North American Indians as Illustrating the Gesture Speech of Mankind.* Washington, D.C.: U.S. Bureau of American Ethnology; reprinted in Umiker-Sebeok and Sebeok, eds., vol. 1:1–76.

Mallery, Garrick (1880b, reprinted 1978). *A Collection of Gesture-Signs and Signals of the North American Indians with Some Comparisons.* Washington, D.C.: Smithsonian Institution; reprinced in Umiker-Sebeok and Sebeok, eds., vol. 1:77–406.

Mallery, Garrick (1881, reprinted 1972a). *Sign Language among North American Indians.* Washington, D.C.: Bureau of American Ethnology; reprinted, The Hague: Mouton.

Mallery, Garrick (1893, reprinted 1972b). *Picture-Writing of the American Indians.* 2 vols. New York: Dover Publications.

Mandel, Mark (1977). "Iconicity of Signs and their Learnability by Non-Signers." Paper presented at the First National Symposium on Sign Language Research and Teaching, Chicago, May 30–June 3.

Marin, Peter (1975). "The New Narcissism." *Harper's* (October) 2:45–56.

Martinet, André (1952). "Function, Structure, and Sound Change." *Word* 8:1–32.

Martinet, André (1955). *Économie des changements phonétiques.* Berne: Francke.

Martinet, André (1958). "La Construction ergative et les structures élémentaires de l'énoncé." *Journal de psychologie normale et pathologique* 55: 377–392.

Martinet, André (1962). *A Functional View of Language.* Oxford: Clarendon Press.

Mathesius, Vilém (1964). "On Linguistic Characterology with Illustrations from Modern English." In J. Vachek, ed., *A Prague School Reader in Linguistics.* Bloomington: Indiana University Press.

Mayberry, Rachel (1978). "Manual Communication." In H. Davis and S.R. Silverman, eds., *Hearing and Deafness.* 4th ed. New York: Holt, Rinehart and Winston.

Mead, George Herbert (1934). *Mind, Self, and Society.* Chicago: University of Chicago Press.

Medeiros, Barbara (1979). "Iconicity and Learnability: Perception of Sign Language by Mentally Retarded and Normal Children." Honors Thesis, Department of Linguistics, Brown University.

Meggitt, M. (1968). "Uses of Literacy in New Guinea and Melanesia." In J. Goody, ed., 300–325.

Menyuk, Paula (1964). "Comparison of Grammar in Children with Functionally Deviant and Normal Speech." *Journal of Speech and Hearing Research* 7:109–121.

Miller, A. and E.E. Miller (1973). "Cognitive Development Training with Elevated Boards and Sign Language." *Journal of Autism and Childhood Schizophrenia* 3:65–85.

Miller, A.G., ed. (1975). *The Codex Nuttall.* New York: Dover Publications.

Miller, George and Noam Chomsky (1963). "Finitary Models of Language Users." In R.D. Luce, R.R. Bush, and E. Galanter, eds., *Handbook of Mathematical Psychology,* vol. 2. New York: John Wiley and Sons.

Mintz, S.W. (1971). "The Socio-Historical Background to Pidginization and Creolization." In D. Hymes, ed., 481–496.

Moore, G.E. (1959). *Philosophical Papers.* New York: Macmillan.

Moore, Timothy E., ed. (1973). *Cognitive Development and the Acquisition of Language.* New York: Academic Press.

Moores, Donald (1977). "Issues in the Utilization of Manual Communication." Keynote address, First National Symposium of Sign Language Research and Teaching, Chicago, May 30–June 3.

Moravcsik, Julius (1967). "Aristotle's Theory of Categories." In J. Moravcsik, ed., *Aristotle: A Collection of Critical Essays.* Garden City: Doubleday.

Mueller, Robert (1974). *Buzzwords.* New York: Van Nostrand Reinhold.

Narveson, Jan (1968). Review of Katz, *The Philosophy of Language.* In *Philosophy of Science* 35:195–197.

Nelson, Katherine (1973). "Some Evidence for the Cognitive Primacy of Categorization and Its Functional Basis." *Merrill-Palmer Quarterly of Behavior and Development* 19:21–39.

Nicholson, H. (1973). "Phoneticism in the Late Pre-Historic Central Mexican Writing System." In E. Benson, ed., 1–46.

Nida, Eugene (1954). *Customs and Cultures.* New York: Harper and Row.

Nida, Eugene (1959). "Principles of Translation as Exemplified by Bible Translation." In R. Brower, ed., *On Translation.* Cambridge, Mass.: Harvard University Press, 11–31.

Nida, E. and H. Fehderau (1970). "Indigenous Pidgins and Koinés." *International Journal of American Linguistics* 36:146–155.

Oxman, J., M.M. Konstantareas, and C.D. Webster (1976). "The Possible Function of Sign Language in Facilitating Verbal Communication in Severely Dysfunctional Non-Verbal Children." Clarke Institute of Psychiatry, Child and Adolescent Service, Substudy 76–10.

BIBLIOGRAPHY

BIBLIOGRAPHY

Pagden, A.R. (1975). *The Maya: Diego de Landa's Account of the Affairs of Yucatán*. Chicago: J. Philip O'Hara.

Pankhurst, E. Sylvia (1927). *Delphos: The Future of International Language*. London: Kegan Paul.

Patterson, Francine (1978). "Conversations with a Gorilla." *National Geographic* 154:438–465.

Paul, Hermann (1880). *Prinzipien der Sprachgeschichte*. Halle: Max Niemeyer.

Pike, Kenneth (1967). *Language in Relation to a Unified Theory of the Structure of Human Behavior*. The Hague: Mouton.

Pitkin, Hanna (1967). *The Concept of Representation*. Berkeley: University of California Press.

Pitkin, Hanna (1969). *Representation*. New York: Atherton.

Politzer, Robert L. (1974). "Developmental Sentence Scoring as a Method of Measuring Second Language Acquisition." *Modern Language Journal* 58:245–250.

Premack, Ann and David Premack (1972). "Teaching Language to an Ape." *Scientific American* 227 (October):92–99.

Proskouriakoff, Tatiana (1960). "Historic Implications of a Pattern of Dates at Piedras Negras, Guatemala." *American Antiquity* 25:454–475.

Proskouriakoff, Tatiana (1973). "The Hand-Grasping-Fish and Associated Glyphs on Classic Maya Monuments." In E. Benson, ed., 165–178.

Putnam, Hilary (1967). "The Innateness Hypothesis and Explanatory Models in Linguistics." *Synthese* 17:12–22.

Quine, W.V.O. (1978). "A Postscript on Metaphor." *Critical Inquiry* 5: 161–162.

Reighard, John (1971). "Some Observations on Syntactic Change in Verbs." In *Papers from the Seventh Regional Meeting*, Chicago Linguistic Society, 511–518.

Reinecke, John (1938, reprinted 1964). "Trade Jargons and Creole Dialects as Marginal Languages." *Social Forces* 17:107–118; reprinted in D. Hymes, ed., *Language in Culture and Society*. New York: Harper and Row, 534–546.

Reinecke, John (1969). *Language and Dialect in Hawaii*. Honolulu: University Press of Hawaii.

Riekehof, Lottie (1978). *The Joy of Signing*. Springfield, Mo.: Gospel Publishers.

Riesman, David (1960). "The Oral and Written Traditions." In E. Carpenter and M. McLuhan, eds., 109–116.

Rivers, W.H.R. (1901). "Introduction and Vision." In A.C. Haddon, ed., *Reports of the Cambridge Anthropological Expedition to the Torres Straits*, vol. II., pt. 1. Cambridge: Cambridge University Press.

Rivers, W.H.R. (1905). "Observations on the Senses of the Todas." *British Journal of Psychology* 1:321–396.

Robinson, Arthur and Barbara Petchenik (1976). *The Nature of Maps*. Chicago: University of Chicago.

Rock, Maxine A. (1979). "Keyboard Symbols Enable Retarded Children to 'Speak.'" *Smithsonian* 10:90–96.

Rosch, Eleanor (1973). "On the Internal Structure of Perceptual and Semantic Categories." In T.E. Moore, ed., 111–144.

Rosch, Eleanor, C.B. Mervis, W. Gray, D. Johnson, and P. Boyes-Braem

(1976). "Basic Objects in Natural Categories." *Cognitive Psychology* 8: 382–439.

Rosenberg, Jay (1974). *Linguistic Representation*. Dordrecht: D. Reidel Publishing.

Ross, A.S.C. (1962). "On the Historical Study of Pidgins." In *Symposium on Multilingualism*, 243–249.

Ross, W.D. (1923). *Aristotle*. London: Methuen.

Rowley, C. (1966). *The New Guinea Villager*. New York: Frederick A. Praeger.

Rumbaugh, Duane M., ed. (1977). *Language Learning by a Chimpanzee: The Lana Project*. New York: Academic Press.

Sachs, Jacqueline and L. Truswell (1976). "Comprehension of Two-Word Instructions by Children in the One-Word Stage." *Stanford Papers and Reports on Child Language Development* 12:212–220.

Samarin, W.J. (1962). "Lingua Francas, with Special Reference to Africa." In F.A. Rice, ed., *Study of the Role of Second Language*, 54–64; revised and expanded in J. Fishman, ed. (1968), 660–672.

Samuels, M.L. (1972). *Linguistic Evolution*. Cambridge: Cambridge University Press.

Sankoff, Gillian (1973). "Above and Beyond Variable Rules." In C.-J. Bailey and R. Shuy, eds., 44–61.

Sapir, Edward (1921). *Language*. New York: Harcourt, Brace and World.

Sapir, Edward (1949). "The Psychological Reality of Phonemes." In D.G. Mandelbaum, ed., *Selected Writings in Language, Culture, and Personality*. Berkeley: University of California Press.

Saussure, Ferdinand de (1959). *Course in General Linguistics*. New York: Philosophical Library.

Sayer, E.S. (1944). *Pidgin English*. Toronto.

Schank, Roger (1972). "Conceptual Dependency: A Theory of Natural Language Understanding." *Cognitive Psychology* 3:552–631.

Scheflen, A.E. (1972). "The Significance of Posture in Communication Systems." In J. Laver and S. Hutcheson, eds., 225–246.

Schele, Linda (1979). *Notebook for the Maya Hieroglyphic Writing Workshop at Texas,* March 24–25. Institute of Latin American Studies, University of Texas at Austin.

Schlesinger, H. and K. Meadow (1972). *Sound and Sign*. Berkeley: University of California Press.

Schofield, R.S. (1968). "The Measurement of Literacy in Pre-Industrial England." In J. Goody, ed., 311–325.

Searle, John (1972, reprinted 1974), "Chomsky's Revolution in Linguistics." *New York Review of Books* June 29; reprinted in G. Harman, ed., *On Noam Chomsky*. Garden City: Anchor Press, 2–33.

Sebeok, Thomas A., ed. (1968). *Animal Communication: Techniques of Study and Results of Research*. Bloomington: Indiana University Press.

Sebeok, Thomas A., ed. (1977). *How Animals Communicate*. Bloomington: Indiana University Press.

Sebeok, Thomas A. and Jean Umiker-Sebeok, eds. (1976). *Speech Surrogates*. 2 vols. The Hague: Mouton.

Segall, Marshall H., Donald T. Campbell, and Melville Herskovits (1966). *Influence of Culture on Visual Perception*. Indianapolis: Bobbs-Merrill.

Sheehy, Gail (1973). "Can Couples Survive?" *New York*, February 19, 32–37.

Sheils, Merrill (1975). "Why Johnny Can't Write." *Newsweek*, December 8, 86:58–65.

Shenton, Herbert N., Edward Sapir, and Otto Jespersen (1931). *International Communication: A Symposium on the Language Problem*. London: Kegan Paul.

Shuy, Roger (1964). "Tireworker Terms." *American Speech* 39:268–277.

Silverstein, Michael (1972). "Chinook Jargon: Language Contact and the Problem of Multi-Level Generative Systems." *Language* 48:378–406; 596–625.

Simon, John (1979). "The Waning of O'Neill." *Esquire*, January 30:77–80.

Siple, Patricia, ed. (1978). *Understanding Language through Sign Language Research*. New York: Academic Press.

Smith, Gerald A. and Wilson G. Turner (1975). *Indian Rock Art of Southern California*. Redlands: San Bernardino County Museum Association.

Smith, Mary Elizabeth (1973). *Picture Writing from Ancient Southern Mexico*. Norman: University of Oklahoma Press.

Snow, Catherine and Charles A. Ferguson, eds. (1977). *Talking to Children*. Cambridge: Cambridge University Press.

Sprat, Thomas (1667, reprinted 1958). *The History of the Royal Society*; reprinted by J.I. Cope and W. Jones, eds., St. Louis: Washington University Studies.

Stefánsson, V. (1910). "The Eskimo Trade Jargon of Herschel Island." *American Anthropologist* 11:217–232.

Steiner, George (1972). "After the Book?" *Visible Language* 6:197–210.

Stewart, Donald (1976). "The Unteachable Subject." *Change* 8:48–51, 63.

Stich, Stephen, ed. (1975). *Innate Ideas*. Berkeley: University of California Press.

Stokoe, William (1969). "Sign Language Diglossia." *Studies in Linguistics* 21:27–41.

Stokoe, William (1972). *Semiotics and Human Sign Languages*. The Hague: Mouton.

Stokoe, William (1974). "Classification and Description of Sign Languages." In T. Sebeok, ed., *Current Trends in Linguistics*, vol. 12.1. The Hague: Mouton, 345–371.

Stokoe, William (1978). *Sign Language Structure*. Silver Spring, Md.: Linstok Press.

Stokoe, William, D. Casterline, and C. Croneberg, eds. (1965). *Dictionary of American Sign Language on Linguistic Principles*. Washington, D.C.: Gallaudet College Press.

Swift, Jonathan. *Gulliver's Travels and Selected Writings*. New York: Random House, 1934.

Symposium on Multilingualism (1962). Brazzaville: CSA/CCTA Publication No. 87. London: Commission de cooperation technique en Afrique.

Taylor, Allan (1975). "Nonverbal Communication Systems in Native North America." *Semiotica* 13:329–374.

Terrace, Herbert (1979). *Nim: A Chimpanzee Who Learned Sign Language*. New York: Knopf.

Terrace, Herbert and Thomas Bever (1976). "What Might be Learned from Studying Language in a Chimpanzee." In S. Harnad, ed., 579–588.

Terrace, Herbert, Laura Pettito, and Thomas Bever (1976). "Project Nim: Progress Report II." Unpublished manuscript, Columbia University.

Thomas Aquinas. *Opera Omnia*. New York: Musurgia Publishers, 1950, Tomus XVII, Opuscula Theologica et Philosophica, Volumen Secundum.

Thompson, Eric (1959). "Systems of Hieroglyphic Writing in Middle America and Methods of Deciphering Them." *American Antiquity* 24:349–364.

Thompson, Eric (1972). *A Commentary on the Codex Dresden*. Philadelphia: American Philosophical Society.

Todd, Loreto (1974). *Pidgins and Creoles*. London: Routledge and Kegan Paul.

Toulmin, Stephen (1953). *The Philosophy of Science*. London: Hutchinson's University Library.

Trager, George (1974). "Writing and Writing Systems." In T. Sebeok, ed., *Current Trends in Linguistics*, vol. 12.1. The Hague: Mouton, 373–496.

Tsuzaki, S. (1971). "Coexistent Systems in Language Variation." In D. Hymes, ed., 327–340.

Umiker-Sebeok, Jean and Thomas A. Sebeok, eds. (1978). *Aboriginal Sign Languages*. 2 vols. The Hague: Mouton.

UNESCO (1973). *Practical Guide to Functional Literacy*. Paris.

Vachek, Josef (1966). *The Linguistic School of Prague*. Bloomington: Indiana University Press.

Velten, H.V. (1943). "The Growth of Phonemic and Lexical Patterns in Infant Language." *Language* 19:281–292.

Venturi, Lionello (1954). *Piero della Francesca*. Translated by James Emmons. Geneva: Editions d'Art Albert Skira.

Verner, Karl (1875, translated 1967). "An Exception to the First Sound Shift." In W. Lehmann, ed. and translator, *A Reader in Nineteenth Century Historical Indo-European Linguistics*. Bloomington: Indiana University Press, 132–163.

Voeglin, C.F. and F.M. Voeglin (1964). "Ibero-Caucasian and Pidgin-Creole." *Anthropological Linguistics* 6, no. 8.

von Frisch, Karl (1953). *The Dancing Bees*. Translated by Dora Ilse. New York: Harcourt, Brace.

von Glasersfeld, Ernst (1977). "The Yerkish Language and Its Automatic Parser." In D. Rumbaugh, ed., 91–130.

Voorhoeve, J. (1962). "Creole Languages and Communication." In *Symposium on Multilingualism*, 233–242.

Vossler, Karl (1932). *The Spirit of Language in Civilization*. Translated by Oscar Oeser. London: Kegan Paul.

Wartofsky, Marx (1968). *Conceptual Foundations of Scientific Thought*. New York: Macmillan.

Waterman, John (1963). *Perspectives in Linguistics*. Chicago: University of Chicago Press.

Watson, Oscar M. (1970). *Proxemic Behavior*. The Hague: Mouton.

Weaver, M. (1972). *The Aztecs, Maya, and their Predecessors*. New York: Seminar Press.

Webb, Walter P. (1931, reprinted 1978). *The Great Plains*. Boston: Ginn; reprinted in Umiker-Sebeok and Sebeok, eds., vol. 2:91–107.

Webster, C.D., H. McPherson, L. Sloman, M.A. Evans, and E. Kuchar (1973). "Communicating with an Autistic Boy with Gestures." *Journal of Autism and Childhood Schizophrenia* 3:337–346.

Weinreich, Uriel (1966). "Explorations in Semantic Theory." In T. Sebeok, ed., *Current Trends in Linguistics*, vol. 3. The Hague: Mouton, 395–478.

Wescott, Roger (1971). "Linguistic Iconism." *Language* 47:416–428.

West, La Mont (1960). *The Sign Language*. 2 vols. Ph. D. dissertation, Indiana University.

White, Leslie (1963). *The Ethnography and Ethnology of Franz Boas*. Austin: Texas Memorial Museum.

Wilbur, Ronnie (1976). "The Linguistics of Manual Language and Manual Systems." In L. Lloyd, ed., *Communication Assessment and Intervention Strategies*. Baltimore: University Park Press, 423–500.

Wilkins, John (1640). *Discourse Concerning a New Planet*. In *The Mathematical and Philosophical Works of the Right Reverend John Wilkins*. London: Printed for J. Nicholson, 1708.

Wilkins, John (1668, reprinted 1968). *An Essay towards a Real Character and a Philosophical Language*. London: reprinted by Scholar Press, Menston, England.

Willcox, Alexander (1963). *The Rock Art of South Africa*. Johannesberg: Nelson.

Wilson, P.S. (1974). "Sign Language as a Means of Communication for the Mentally Retarded." Paper presented at the Annual Meeting of the Eastern Psychological Association, Philadelphia.

Winkler, Capt. (1901). "On Sea Charts formerly used in the Marshall Islands, with Notices on the Navigation of these Islanders in General." *Annual Report of the Smithsonian Institution*, 1899, Washington, 487–509.

Winship, George Parker (1896). "The Coronado Expedition 1540–1542." *Annual Report of the Bureau of Ethnology* 14, Washington, 329–637.

Wittgenstein, Ludwig (1953). *Philosophical Investigations*. Oxford: Basil Blackwell.

Wittgenstein, Ludwig (1958). *The Blue and Brown Books*. Oxford: Basil Blackwell.

Wolfers, E. (1971). "A Report on Neo-Melanesian." In D. Hymes, ed., 411–425.

World Federation of the Deaf (1975). *Gestuno: International Sign Language of the Deaf*. Carlisle: British Deaf Association.

Wrolstad, Merald (1976). "A Manifesto for Visible Language." *Visible Language* 10:5–40.

Notes

I. INTRODUCTION

1. "How to Murder English," *The Illustrated Weekly of India*, 17 March 1974, p.7. The selection is reprinted from the London *Spectator*.

2. Excellent discussions of Wittgenstein's position can be found in Hallet (1967) and C.M. Brown (1974).

3. See Bhattacharya (1978) for a discussion of the paradox that language users must share a linguistic system of signs in order to be understood, while at the same time *not* fully share a system in order to have new things to say.

4. On the other hand, cf. A.W. Williamson (1881), "Is the Dakota related to the Indo-European languages?" Minnesota Academy of Natural Sciences, *Bulletin* 2:110–142.

5. For a detailed discussion of French missionaries' linguistic work in seventeenth- and eighteenth-century America, see Hanzeli (1969).

6. Within the Indo-European tradition, reconstruction was based on written materials as a matter of course. Americanists including Bloomfield (see Hockett, 1970 and Haas, 1969) have addressed the question of whether reconstruction is possible without written records.

7. This trend continues even today. The first written textbook for Cajun French was produced only in 1977 (*New York Times*, 25 June 1977), although Cajun French has been spoken in the American South for several centuries.

8. See Gelb (1952:206–207) and Basso and Anderson (1973) for some minor exceptions.

II. LANGUAGE AND REPRESENTATION

1. "The essential and characteristic human activity is representation—that is, the production and manipulation of representations" (Rosenberg, 1974:1).

2. For discussions of the question of representation in science, see Wartofsky (1968), including his lengthy bibliographical notes (pp. 489–491). The best theoretical treatment of cartography is Robinson and Petchenik (1976). Good references on artistic representation are the works of Arnheim (e.g., 1967, 1969) and Gombrich (e.g., 1960, 1972), although also see Hermerén (1969). Useful works on political representation are Pitkin (1967) and (1969).

3. See Wartofsky (1968:508–510) for an extensive bibliography concerning the question of what theories and models might be.

4. Toulmin uses the example of the sun casting a shadow behind a wall to illustrate the dependence of models ("diagram") on theory:

> [In our example] the diagram provides . . . something in the nature of a picture of the optical state-of-affairs; a picture with the help of which we can infer things about the shadows and other optical phenomena to be observed under the circumstances specified. But to understand how the explanation works, it is not enough to point to the phenomena on the one hand and the physicist's diagram on the other. For the physicist uses other terms, having at first sight nothing to do either with shadows or with diagrams, which nevertheless constitute in some ways the heart of the explanation. He talks, for instance, of light 'travelling', of rays of light 'getting past the wall' or 'being intercepted by it', and declares that this interception of light by the wall is what—fundamentally—explains the existence of the shadow. [1953:35]

5. See Wartofsky (1968:112) and Toulmin (1953:13) for discussions of how science alters ordinary language.

6. Chukovsky (1965:11) cites the unsuccessful attempt of a Russian child to replace *penknife* with *pencilknife,* a change whose logic was motivated by the realization that pocketknives are now used on pencil points rather than on quill pens.

7. Benveniste has argued that "Saussure was always thinking of the representation of the *real object* (although he spoke of the "idea")" (1971:47)—though such a claim is difficult to support on either textual or theoretical grounds, given Saussure's structuralist presuppositions (see Bhattacharya, 1979).

8. For discussions of early infant perception, see Gibson (1950), Fantz (1961), and Bower (1977).

9. For an excellent discussion of the innatist debate, see Stich (1975).

10. See Winkler (1901), Akerblom (1968), and de Brum (1962) for a more complete discussion of Marshallese stick charting.

11. See Lewis (1972:184–187).

12. This analogy is adapted from Gladwin (1970:183).

13. As far as we can determine, the phonological representations that Wilkins used have the following equivalents:

Wilkins's Symbol	Phonological Value	Modern English Example
œ	/ɔ/	law
a	/a/	lot
e	/ɛ/	bet
	/e/	bait
i	/ɪ/	bit
	/i/	beet
o	/o/	bone
४	/ʊ/	put
	/u/	soon
y	/ʌ/	but

We should be aware, though, that because the vowel system of seventeenth-century English was undergoing radical change, we cannot be certain of these values.

14. See Emery (1948) for an excellent description of Wilkins's scheme.

15. There are other problems stemming from the assumption that an immutable and monolithic language would ever be practical. Such a language scheme overlooks the fact that all known natural human languages are continually subject to change. Even if our theories of science, our natural environment, and systems of belief remain largely untouched, from all evidence, human languages are continually subject to changes in phonology, lexicon, morphology, and, to a lesser extent, syntax. Such changes may be introduced by children learning language or by fortuitous variation and may be adopted as part of the standard language if functional and/or structural pressures warrant it.

Consider as well the question of whether the same universal language could ever fill all of the functions envisioned for it. Philosophical languages of the seventeenth and eighteenth centuries were primarily designed as aids to clear thinking, but were also intended to serve as international means of communication. Nineteenth- and twentieth-century auxiliary international languages were also assumed to be more accurate mirrors of reality than natural languages. As Jonathan Cohen points out, the two goals are incompatible: naming, description, classification, generalization, reasoning, explanation, and prediction are the tasks of a scientific language but not of an ordinary language, in which the range of meanings needed is very different. Scientific theory is, Cohen argues, best served by a language

> which carries over the least possible irrelevant associations from non-scientific discourse. But an international auxiliary is most easily learnt if its radicals are already familiar and these are therefore best drawn from words already in international currency. [1954:62]

Moreover, it is not clear that a "scientific language" appropriate for one domain of inquiry is necessarily appropriate for another:

> while an unspecialised language must be capable of application to all fields of human experience, it is yet to be shown that the ideal of a systematic terminology can usefully operate not only at the level of each individual science but also at the level of science as a whole. [ibid.]

In fact, Ostwald (in Couturat et al. 1910:55) acknowledges the impossibility of combining a practicable international auxiliary language with an adequate scientific terminology.

Chapter 3 and especially chapter 4 will deal with the question of how an understanding of a language's functioning may shape our conception of what a language is.

16. Because most of our references are to Katz (1966), which contains an elaboration of the Katz-Fodor semantic model proposed in 1963, I refer to Katz as the exponent of the Katz-Fodor position.

17. This passage is quoted from chapter II, "Of the Nature of Genus and Species" (vol. 2, p.614), in Owen's edition of the *Organon*.

III. WHAT IS A LANGUAGE?

1. In most instances, nonhuman primates have been taught individual signs from American Sign Language which have been concatenated using English syntax (American Sign Language actually has a syntax of its own). The differences between English and American Sign Language are discussed in chapter 7.

2. See Mead (1934) for a discussion of how individual monologues develop from social communication.

3. Crystal does not, however, assume that all communication which is auditory or vocal is necessarily linguistic. Sounds not produced by the vocal apparatus (e.g., finger-snapping) may be communicative but nonlinguistic (Crystal, 1971:241). The same applies to heavy breathing and voice quality (ibid., pp.241–243).

4. As Neo-Melanesian begins to acquire more native speakers and to be used in a broader range of contexts, however, it may well enter into the historical analytic-synthetic cycle described by Reighard (1971).

5. Two exceptions are Bhattacharya (1979) and, in a less developed way, Quine (1978).

6. In the case of Sumerian, it has been argued (e.g., Jensen, 1970:83–84) that the reduction in the number of word signs from sixteen hundred to eighteen hundred in Uruk IV (c. 3700 B.C.) to eight hundred by 3000 B.C. reflects increased phoneticization.

7. In Sumerian, for example, we find "the reduction of thirty-one various signs for 'sheep' in the early Uruk period to one single form in later times" (Gelb, 1952:115).

8. Verner, believing all sound laws to be exceptionless, maintained that for any apparent irregularity in sound change there must be a rule. Our task is to discover this rule (Verner, 1875, reprinted in Lehmann, 1967:138).

9. See, for example, Sapir (1949). Consider, however, the hypothesis that literacy heightens an individual's notions of grammaticality (see Chapter 6).

10. Unfortunately, such assumptions have been common in linguistic literature. For example, it is generally believed that young children understand more language than they can produce. Although some experimental evidence has been gathered which supports this hypothesis more narrowly (e.g., Fraser, Bellugi, and Brown, 1963; Huttenlocher, 1974), the hypothesis has not proven correct for all levels of grammar or for all types of children (see Sachs and Truswell, 1976).

Similar overextensions of findings about comprehension and production have been made concerning children who are purported to understand language without being able to speak. In an isolated case study of an eight-year-old anarthric boy, Lenneberg (1962) reported that the child was able to respond correctly to yes/no questions (by nodding or shaking his head) and to carry out commands ("Take the block and put it on the bottle"). Without corroborating evidence, the import of these findings has been blown out of proportion—so much so that linguists write that people who cannot speak can, nevertheless, understand language "perfectly" (Langacker, 1973:14).

11. I am grateful to Nikhil Bhattacharya for developing this example.

12. As in the case of speech, sign language can be transmitted electronically, but the sign language used is derived from face-to-face encounters.

IV. FUNCTIONAL PERSPECTIVES ON LANGUAGE

1. Notable exceptions are the work of Halliday (1975), Bates (1976), and Greenfield (Greenfield and Smith, 1976).

2. See Cravens (1978) for an extensive discussion of the debate in the United States over the past century on the relative importance of heredity and environment.

3. E.g., Chomsky (1968, 1975, 1979). In his recent work, Chomsky draws

the analogy between linguistic development and the development of a human limb:

> It is a curious fact about the intellectual history of the past few centuries that physical and mental development have been approached in quite different ways. No one would take seriously a proposal that the human organism learns through experience to have arms rather than wings, or that the basic structure of particular organs results from accidental experience. Rather, it is taken for granted that the physical structure of the organism is genetically determined, though of course variation along such dimensions as size, rate of development, and so forth will depend in part on external factors. From embryo to mature organism, a certain pattern of development is predetermined, with certain stages, such as onset of puberty or the termination of growth, delayed by many years. [1975:9]

4. Ranging, for example, from Paul (1880) to Bloomfield (1933) to Samuels (1972) or Anttila (1972).

5. A good example here is the case of postvocalic /r/ (*car, four*) in New York City. Historically, the postvocalic /r/ has gone from being a nonprestigious feature to becoming a prestigious one (see Labov, 1966).

6. I should mention that functional explanation in phonology *is* possible in the restricted sense of lending social value to an arbitrarily selected phonological feature (see figure 4.1). Arbitrarily selected features are, however, not the sort that we are concerned with.

7. See J. Lyons (1968:350–371) for a clear explanation of the differences between nominative-accusative languages and ergative languages. The basic difference is that while nominative-accusative languages assign the same grammatical case (nominative) to all surface subjects, regardless of their semantic role ("He opened the door"; "He fell"), ergative languages give a special case marking to subjects which have the semantic function of agent ("He opened the door").

8. See Snow and Ferguson (1977) for extensive discussion of how adults speak to children.

9. For a classical discussion of reduplication in early child language see Leopold (1947).

10. See Hymes (1973) for a refutation of Chomsky's position.

V. SPOKEN LANGUAGE

1. For the most complete discussion of speech surrogates now available, see Sebeok and Umiker-Sebeok, 1976.

2. Should one wish to maintain that the productivity of whistling (for example) is dubious, we can still eliminate nonspeech vocalizations from the domain of language by placing physiological restrictions on the way in which the vocal apparatus is used to produce speech.

3. I am grateful to Nikhil and Lalita Bhattacharya for this example.

4. See Horne (1966) for an excellent survey of the literature on typological classification of languages.

5. See Greenberg (1963) for an initial statement of how one identifies language universals and Greenberg (1966) for a more detailed analysis.

6. The journal *American Speech* is a rich source of information here, providing data on the language of tireworkers (Shuy, 1964), of skiers (Jarka, 1963), or of traffic policemen (Dempsey, 1962).

7. My thanks to Angus Rockett and Peter Oppenheimer, for providing much of the information that appears in this section. In ordinary English, "Wipe the bugs off your plates" means "Watch out for police coming from behind."

8. Linguists (e.g., Nida and Fehderau, 1970:147) have sometimes pointed out the inconsistent use of terms like *pidgin, trade jargon, creole, koiné,* and *lingua franca* and the lack of formal characterizations of each of these language types (although see Samarin [1962] for one attempt at definition). The situation is particularly confusing in an area like Hawaii, where the same term, *pidgin,* has been applied to a whole linguistic spectrum ranging from knowledge of a few English words to near total mastery of the language (see Reinecke, 1969:144; Tsuzaki, 1971:326).

9. Bateson, for example, states that "[Neo-Melanesian Pidgin] is a systematic fitting of English vocabulary to Melanesian grammar and syntax" (1943:138).

10. See Hall (1966:xii); although, as an increasing number of linguists are recognizing, the presence of a few native speakers does not automatically transform a pidgin into a creole (see Todd [1974] and the work of Sankoff).

11. Voeglin and Voeglin write:

A remarkable feature of all modern European-based pidgin/creoles of the C-type is the location of their speakers: all are spoken on or near seaboards. [1964:43–44]

Samarin claims that

when located on a map, another significant fact appears, every [pidgin] is located adjacent to a marine expanse. The history of these pidgins is therefore somehow to be connected with oceanic travel. [1962:667]

12. The importance of these variables has been raised at several points in the past. Reinecke has noted that

the master-and-dependent relationship . . . does not obtain very strongly in trade situations. Between trading peoples there must be a modicum of mutual respect and freedom of action. [1938; reprinted 1964:537]

Reinecke has also posed the general question of whether

the vocabulary of pidgins [by which he seems to mean what we are calling trade jargons] (as contrasted with creole languages) [by which he means what we are calling pidgins] reflects to any considerable extent the circumstances under which they arise and the activities for which they function. [1969:16]

He nevertheless points out that "no study has yet been made inquiring into such a connection between milieu and expression" (ibid.).

Grimshaw, in trying to determine how creolization occurs, mentions as a relevant variable

the pattern of conflict relations, first between the dominant group of prestige language speakers and the subordinated population . . . [along with] . . . the industrial and commercial contexts within which contacts have occurred, viz.

trading or agriculture, farm or plantation, and so on. This variable also includes the social organization of work—indenture, slavery, contract, free. [1971:432]

Similarly, Voorhoeve (1962), Mintz (1971), Alleyne (1971), and others have commented on the importance of studying the kind of social relationship between the two (or more) populations in contact in order to understand—or predict—the kind of language that will emerge.

What still remains is to ask whether the *grammatical* characteristics of each interface language are determined by the relevant modes of activity and the relative social and political footing of each group. Reinecke has predicted that, while the vocabulary of trade jargons and pidgins may differ, "it is unlikely that the morphology and syntax of [trade jargons] and [pidgins] will differ much" (1969:20). This discussion will examine an alternative prediction.

13. Wolfers provides an example of the difficulty that the Department of District Administration in New Guinea has had in translating *majority rule* into Neo-Melanesian:

'Bihainim tingting bilong planti moa pipal', its final compromise, means no more than 'supporting the opinion of many people', and is inadequate for the task. The concept can be explained through lengthy circumlocution and demonstration, but the problem of finding an accurate, short means of translation still remains. [1971:416]

14. Material objects in the experience of the two groups may differ as well, although this difference is not critical when taken by itself.

15. Louis Leakey has found evidence of elementary forms of exchange over one million years old.

16. A topical example is the imposed labor system in New Guinea. As Rowley explains:

Cash can be made essential by government fiat. An example was the German system of head-tax, maintained until the second world war by the Mandate administration. The tax had to be paid by fit adult male villagers in cash; and cash could be obtained by selling coconuts or copra, or by going to work. [1966:99]

17. In some areas (e.g., New Guinea), the society had little hierarchical structure before it was introduced by the Europeans. Therefore,

when [the native] enters the Pidgin World, [he] must take on patterns which are foreign to him,—and he must act out the role of inferiority vis-à-vis the white man, and if he becomes a boss-boy or a member of the native constabulary he must act out the role of superiority vis-à-vis the other natives. [Bateson, 1943:140]

Nonmodernized societies may also have difficulty adjusting to Western notions of time. Referring to the common allegation that Hawaiians are lazy, Daws points out that

it was said that they had no stamina, that they were prodigal spenders of time, investing everything in projects that promised them dividends of excitement without any thought for the future. As a matter of fact the Hawaiians did not share the white man's view of time. Even after they were taught to count and how to use a western calendar they preferred to call the days, weeks, and the months of the year by the old native names. They liked to celebrate western holidays—the more the better—but they did not see the point of reckoning the year in four financial periods with a settling day at the end of each quarter. [1968:179]

18. Obviously, trading between equals can take place under a variety of social and linguistic circumstances, ranging from silent barter, to weekly markets to which traders bring their entire families, to villagers living side by side, who do not need to wait until market day to see each other. The interface language that may emerge in each of these situations will reflect the amount of contact between groups, the age of the people involved, and the range of topics talked about that do not directly relate to trade.

19. And therefore (except in the case of house servants or slavery), "native" women have no need to learn or use pidgin. Wolfers, speaking of Neo-Melanesian, observes that even now,

few women at all, anywhere in the Territory, speak anything other than their own *tokples* or local language—probably a symbol of their own generally lower social status traditionally, and now educationally. The women have never needed to learn pidgin as have men, for there is also very little employment available for them outside their villages except as teachers, nurses, etc. [1971:418]

20. In the case of subordinate groups, few of the people have had the opportunity to learn the dominant language. Speaking of the immigrant labor force in Hawaii, Reinecke writes that

the economic and social possibilities of most immigrants do not include positions where the learning of 'good' English is obligatory or even very helpful, or possible. . . . The essential reason for learning only the creole dialect is neither laziness nor dullness or mind but the distinct connection between the work one does and one's opportunity to learn English. [1969:101]

He also states that among the native Hawaiian population, education in English was originally restricted to the upper classes (ibid., p.33). Members of the dominant group generally did not bother learning the language of the subordinate group since the dominant group was in a position to make that group learn their (dominant) language (ibid., p.34).

21. If more than two groups are involved in trade, more than two so-called trade languages (i.e., jargons) may emerge.

22. Empirically, however, trade jargons seem to lack inflections (see Silverstein [1972:609] on Chinook Jargon).

23. Although according to R.V. Grant, Chinook Jargon does use a large number of compound expressions to translate a single English verb:

Yaka klatawa kopa lapee kopa chuck kopa boat
[he goes on foot in water to boat]
"He wades to the boat"   [1945:231]

We need to determine whether such expressions are widely accepted by all speakers of Chinook Jargon, and if so, whether there are many expressions of this type. We predict that there will be, in comparison with pidgin, a fairly small number of these expressions.

24. Horatio Hale's *An International Idiom* notes that

> the Indians in general—contrary to what seems to be a common opinion—are very sparing of their gesticulations. No languages, probably, require less assistance from this source than theirs. . . . We frequently had occasion to observe the sudden change produced when a party of natives, who had been conversing in their own tongue, were joined by a foreigner, with whom it was necessary to speak in the Jargon. The countenances which had before been grave, stolid, and inexpressive, were instantly lighted up with animation; the low monotonous tone became lively and modulated; every feature was active; the heads, arms, and the whole body were in motion, and every look and gesture became instinct with meaning. One who know [*sic*] merely the subject of discourse might often have comprehended, from this source alone, the general purport of the conversation. [1890:18–19; quoted by Silverstein, 1972:381]

Silverstein also observes that the extralinguistic context itself makes syntactic redundancy unnecessary:

> from the specificity of conditions under which jargons are employed, we can expect the extralinguistic context to be highly redundant (in the technical sense); hence the verbal code can avoid redundancy by seizing on this freedom from lexical specification. In other words, it can increase the 'information' of each unit. [ibid.]

Stefánsson makes a similar observation with respect to Eskimo Trade Jargon:

> In a system of speech comprising only a limited number of uninflected words, much depends on circumstances and context as to the interpretation of any set of them. A sentence perfectly intelligible and definite when used in the course of conversation between men who are face to face may become of uncertain meaning, of many meanings, or of no meaning at all, if divorced from its accompanying gestures and set down isolated in writing or print. [1909:221]

25. As in the case of trade jargons, there may be more than two groups—and two languages—involved. Cole (1953:3), for example, notes that Fanagalo (which may qualify as a pidgin by our definition) is used by Bantu laborers from forty or more different language backgrounds. Similarly, Neo-Melanesian Pidgin is used by speakers of a vast number of indigenous languages.

26. One of the reasons pidgins have been regarded as inferior is their comparatively small vocabularies. Cole (1953:7), for example, questions whether a language like Fanagalo, with a vocabulary of under two thousand words, can express anything more than straightforward ideas.

27. Although in some places (e.g., Hawaii), education in the dominant language did become available to everyone.

28. As recently as 1944, Sayer suggested to travelers visiting areas where pidgin is used to "give the native time to ponder and think—his brain works slower than yours" (1944:25). There are numerous instances in the literature (e.g., Hall, 1955:46; Epstein, 1968:322fn) in which "native" populations

have received ill treatment for addressing the dominant population in the dominant language rather than in pidgin.

29. Hall (1955:19) describes an incident in which a native laborer's misunderstanding of the word *bihain* (which means "later" in Neo-Melanesian but "behind" in standard English) earned him a clout on the head from a European who felt his orders were being disobeyed.

30. For example, in looking through texts of Hawaiian Pidgin English (in Carr, 1972 and Reinecke, 1969) and Chinese Pidgin English (Hall, 1944), I found almost no evidence of circumlocution. We will need to find out whether lack of circumlocution is an idiosyncratic feature of these particular texts or is really characteristic of the language.

31. Possible exceptions are Kituba and Police Motu, although it would be interesting to know how the expansion of Western trade and empire influenced the formation of these languages.

VI. WRITTEN LANGUAGE

1. For a comparative analysis of rock painting around the world, see C. Grant (1965:107–127).

2. For example, the so-called "x-ray" style, in which figures are outlined and then their musculature and some of the viscera are shown as well, is seen in both Europe and India. According to Brooks and Wakankar, the Indian examples "probably developed locally (1976:87).

3. The Codex Nuttall, which had been owned by an Englishman named Lord Zouche, was first brought to the attention of scholars by Zelia Nuttall. For this reason, the codex is alternatively known as the Codex Zouche, the Codex Nuttall, or the Codex Zouche-Nuttall.

4. For more details on the manuscript, see A.G. Miller (1975).

5. This comparison draws heavily upon M.E. Smith's (1973) discussion of the Bayeux Tapestry and Mixtec manuscripts.

6. Misunderstandings of written Chinese are prevalent, even in the scholarly literature. Writers as diverse as Gelb (1952:203) and Goody and Watt (1968:36) have assumed Chinese to be an impractical written language for the general population to use, given the large number of logograms and ideograms. Gelb has even gone so far as to imply that a language such as Chinese represents an early evolutionary stage in the development of writing.

7. Some authors, such as Havelock, argue that transcription is the ultimate aim of writing:

> Strictly speaking, written orthography should behave solely as the servant of the spoken tongue, reporting its sounds as accurately and swiftly as possible. It need not and should not have a nature of its own. [Havelock, 1976:15]

8. To the best of our knowledge (cf. Chadwick, 1958), Linear B was written with a syllabary. That is, a sign represented a phonological syllable. It seems ironic that while this phonetic script was used only for a highly restricted set of purposes, recent research (e.g., Benson, 1975) has suggested the ancient Inca quipus, whose status as writing has long been questioned, may have served a much vaster range of linguistic functions than did (written) Linear B.

9. *Webster's Seventh Collegiate Dictionary.* Pronouncing Vocabulary of Common English Given Names.

10. See Weaver (1972:99–109) for an explanation of the Mesoamerican calendar.

11. According to Nicholson,

> no two *tlacuiloque* probably conveyed their messages in precisely identical ways. Their penchant for varying place and name signs, employing different graphemes and grapheme combinations to produce the same results, is abundantly evidenced in the extant sources. Some scribes may well have inclined to greater phonetic use of graphemes to reduce ambiguity or just as a matter of preference, others to confining their use to a bare minimum. Perhaps the expected "readership" might have been a factor. When it was believed that sufficient understanding could be conveyed without phonetic employment of certain graphemes, some scribes might have preferred to omit them as unnecessary—particularly in the histories where a more or less formalized verbal narrative seems to have regularly accompanied use of the pictorial account, whose mnemonic function in this case was obviously fundamental. [1973:35]

VII. SIGN LANGUAGE

1. Another question, although one which we cannot go into here, is whether what we are calling nonlinguistic gestures do indeed have their own identifiable vocabulary and syntax, thus meriting at least the metaphoric label *language* (see the beginning of chapter 5). Crystal, while admitting that "it is too early to say," hypothesizes that "a formal grammar of kinesic effort cannot be written" (Crystal and Craig, 1978:155).

2. See Battison and Jordon (1976) for an empirical study of intelligibility in cross-linguistic signing.

3. Within the last few years, a number of studies have been done on the nonmanual components of sign language. See especially Baker and Padden (1978) and Liddell (1978).

4. The following analysis draws heavily on Wilbur (1976) and Bornstein (1973).

5. See Wilbur (1976) for a more detailed discussion of the morphology of the various signing systems.

6. A popular text for parents is Bornstein et al. 1975.

7. The history of signing and oralism in the United States reads like a comedy of errors. Thomas Gallaudet, who introduced formal sign language into this country in 1816, had actually gone to England to learn oralist techniques for instructing the deaf. For a complex set of reasons, Gallaudet was refused the opportunity to study with the leading oralist experts of the day. While in England, Gallaudet met the Abbé Sicard, student of the Abbé l 'Épée, the champion of French Sign Language. Sicard invited Gallaudet to study signing in France, with the result that signing, not oralism made its way to the United States. Hubbard (1867) describes the historical incident in some detail. For fifty years, the only programs for the deaf in America taught signing. It was not until the late 1860s that the first oralist schools were opened in opposition to the pedagogical use of sign (see Bell, 1894).

8. Of course, there *are* many teachers who do know and use signing systems closer to ASL. Facility with ASL is especially high among counselors and therapists who work individually with deaf students.

9. There are some others as well, such as that the Plains Indians learned the language from the Spanish in Mexico. This, as Taylor points out, is hardly likely,

since the earliest Spanish penetration of the Plains area, that of Coronado in 1541–42, encountered Indians who were using signs [Winship, 1896:504, 527; Taylor, 1975:330]

10. Diglossia has also been identified among users of American Sign Language (see Stokoe, 1969).

11. Although compare Dorothy Lee's (1960) article on "Lineal and Nonlineal Codifications of Reality." She argues that the Trobriand Islanders have a nonlineal encoding of their experience. The issue, of course, is what implications such as nonlineal encoding has for syntactic ordering within the sentence.

12. Interestingly, West suggests that the iconic properties of Plains Sign Language help "throw considerable light upon the ease of learning and communication characteristic of the sign language" (1960, vol. 1:89).

13. It also seems that gestural communication precedes speech among hearing children in oral households (see Locke, 1978; Bates et al. 1979).

14. The data were collected and analyzed by Barbara Medeiros as part of her Honors Thesis in Psycholinguistics at Brown University.

15. See Rock (1979) for more information on the project.

Author Index

Subject Index

299

Speech, Writing, and Sign

A Functional View of Linguistic Representation

By Naomi S. Baron

Linguistics has traditionally dealt with questions about structure—what are the parts of a language and how are they assembled? Naomi Baron adopts a new approach by asking what a human language is used for and how it achieves its goals. She carefully examines *what* is communicated, *why* it is important, and *how* the exchange is accomplished.

In the process of this basic redefinition, she fashions a lucid, systematic introduction to the study of linguistics. Her revolutionary approach, however, broadens the domain of linguistic inquiry from spoken language to linguistic representation in general. Baron demonstrates that problems of representation that arise in the area of speech have immediate parallels in written and gestural communication.

The initial chapters of this volume discuss language as a source and solution to the problems of human communication, the various aspects of representation, the definition of human language, and a methodology for the functional analysis of language. The three chapters that follow fully explore this functional perspective for spoken, written, and signed languages. Included are critiques of existing works in these fields, as well as new evidence to demonstrate the effect of social context on linguistic structure. The author enlivens these discussions with a vast range of examples from CB language, diphthongs on Martha's Vineyard, American Indian pictography, proper names, Cistercian Sign Language, and many other fascinating illustrations of language in use.

Speech, Writing, and Sign is profusely illustrated with drawings, photographs, and reproductions of artistic examples. Written to